THE BUSINESS OF COMPUTERIZED EMBROIDERY

THE BUSINESS OF COMPUTERIZED EMBROIDERY

First Edition

Barbara J. Behm

MELCO INDUSTRIES INC.
Westminster, Colorado

ISBN 0-9625496-0-6

Library of Congress Catalog Card Number: 90-91463

Printed in the United States of America

DEDICATION

This book is dedicated to the founders of Melco Industries Inc., William R. Childs, chairman of the board, and Randall (Chipper) Melton, president. Their intelligence, creativity and dedication revolutionized the embroidery industry. Their entrepreneurial spirit enabled thousands more to become entrepreneurs. Together, they built a business that provided many job opportunities for those of us who are *not* entrepreneurs. The most rewarding one was mine!

SPECIAL THANKS . . .

To Larry L. Pearson, vice president of Melco Industries Inc., who gave the approval for the writing of this book. His confidence and trust in me enabled this project to be done in the quiet of my home—at all hours of the day and night. Larry provided me with the equipment I requested, allowed me to work unrestricted, and yet, he was there to lend support when needed. *There* is a manager!

To Karen Fox, advertising director of Melco Industries Inc., for editing the text and overseeing the photography; and to another friend (who wishes to remain anonymous) who co-edited *The Business of Computerized Embroidery*. They transformed it into what I meant to say. They are true professionals.

To Doug Hunley, senior copywriter/designer of Melco Industries Inc., for designing the cover, creating the illustrations and handling the photo layouts. He is a most talented artist.

To Marc Allison, senior writer of Melco Industries Inc., for his assistance with exhibits.

To everyone who generously gave their time, samples, forms, knowledge and experience. It is through such sharing of information that the embroidery industry grows stronger and better every year. May you all fulfill your goals.

To my husband, David, for his support, encouragement, patience and love.

To my son, Steve, and my daughter, Susie, for their understanding and unknowing motivation.

Sincerely,

Barbara J. Behm

TABLE OF CONTENTS

LIST OF EXHIBITS

FOREWORD

The Business of Computerized Embroidery was written for everyone who is or hopes to be involved in the business of computerized embroidery. Owners and operators of embroidery equipment, those who sell embroidered products or services, suppliers of related materials—all could benefit from the knowledge and experience contained herein.

Many people in the embroidery industry and the business world were interviewed or observed to find out how they do what they do. Much trial and error time can be saved by learning from those who willingly share what they have learned. In the words of Admiral Hyman G. Rickover, "All of us must become better informed. It is necessary for us to learn from others' mistakes. You will not live long enough to make them all yourself."

As with most any business, there is no right or wrong way to proceed, but gaining as much knowledge as possible upon entering a new venture can certainly provide the means to get where one wants to be faster and easier. Those who are already in the business of embroidery will be the first to say they still have a lot to learn. Hopefully, this will provide the means for their advancement as well.

In order to have value for all embroiderers, this book is not intended to be product specific. It is not an operator's manual for machines, but rather a business handbook for embroiderers.

Barbara J. Behm
Author of "The Business of Computerized Embroidery" and
Melco's Director of Public Relations.
Photo by The Mystique of Light, Westminster, Colorado.

William R. Childs
Chairman of the Board of Directors and
co-founder of Melco Industries Inc.
Photo by Vicki Kerr of Denver, Colorado.

Randall Melton
President and co-founder of Melco Industries Inc.
Photo by Vicki Kerr of Denver, Colorado.

Larry Pearson
Vice President of Sales and Marketing, Melco Industries Inc.
Photo by Vicki Kerr of Denver, Colorado.

Doug Hunley programming the Epicor system by Melco Industries Inc. Also shown: digitizing tablet, paper tape reader, two EM-1 single-needle and two EMC-6 six-needle embroidery peripheral machines.

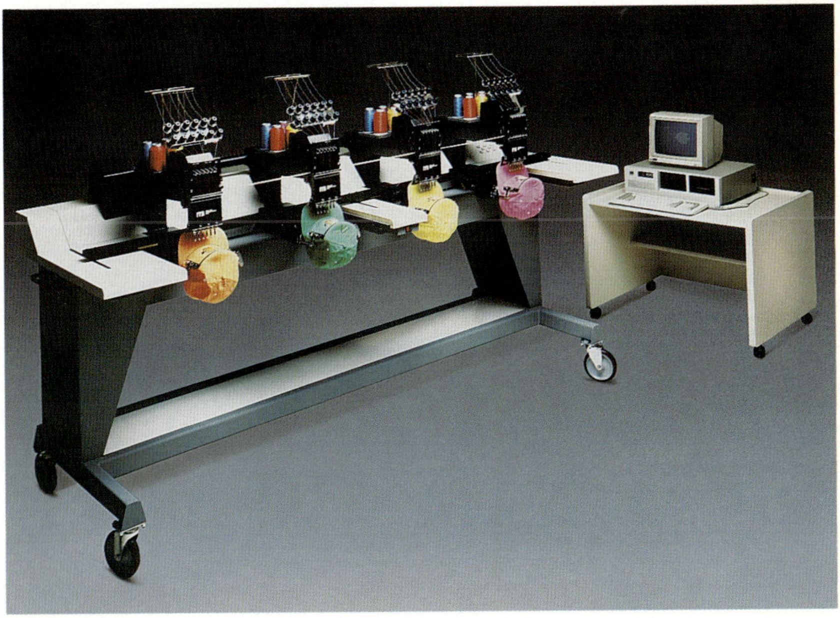

Epicor system and EMC-6-4 (four-head) peripheral embroidery machine with optional cap frames, by Melco.

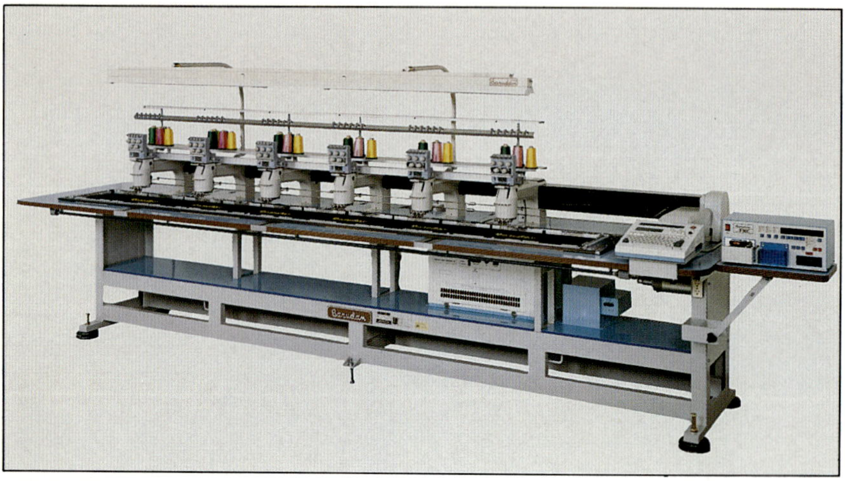

Barudan Profit 706 embroidery machine from Macpherson Monogram Inc.

Barudan's BEMRH embroidery machine, model MRH-UF-20 from Macpherson Inc.

Frame Press from Macpherson Inc.

TMLE coiling machine by Tajima.

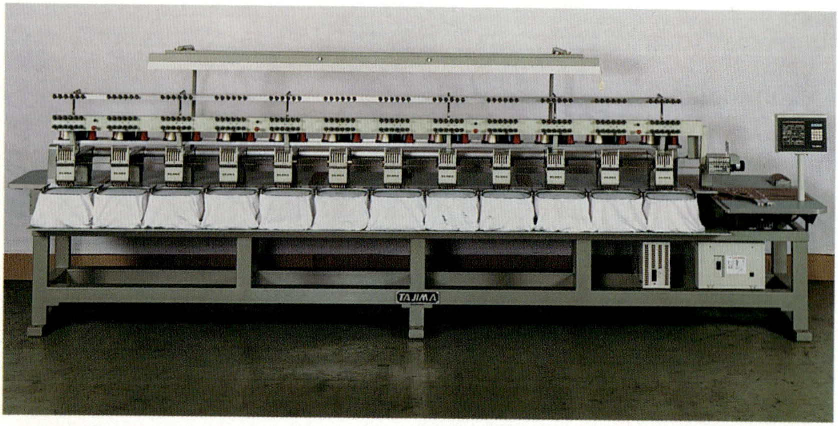

TME-HC612 embroidery machine with tubular frames for finished garments, by Tajima.

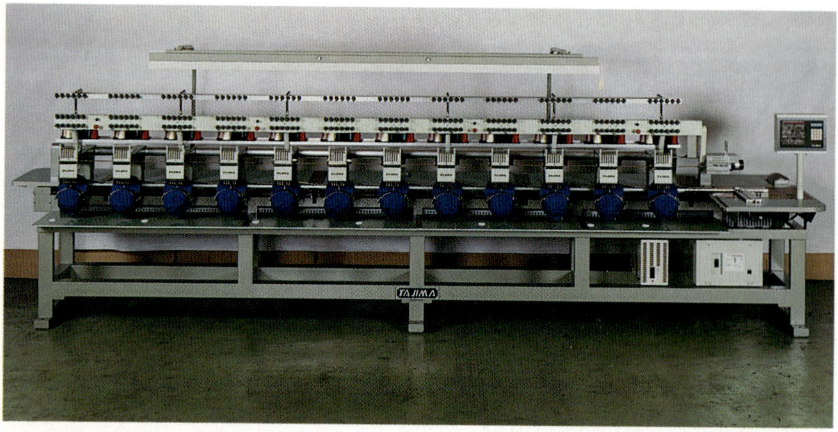

TMEF-HC612 embroidery machine with cap frames, by Tajima.

CHAPTER 1

TO BE OR NOT TO BE . . . AN ENTREPRENEUR

Congratulations! You're thinking of starting your own business and want to know more about it. It won't be an easy undertaking, but the advantages are numerous. You will gain a sense of independence and a sense of accomplishment. You will be your own boss and control your own destiny. That's a big positive—if you do well. Along with the positives, though, comes a tremendous load of responsibility. You will have an obligation to your creditors who want to be paid on time. Your customers will expect quality work and courteous service. Your employees, if any, will expect a timely paycheck, a safe and pleasant working atmosphere and a sense of pride in working for you and your business.

Therefore, it will be up to you to manage the business well. Management is the single most important factor that affects the success of any business. You may have a great product or service, an uncontested market potential, the best prices in town or the friendliest staff. However, if the business is not managed well, it will not survive, even with all those other attributes. So, in addition to learning the skills required for your particular business, and the time involved in producing the work, selling the goods or services, your primary role will be that of business manager.

Are you the right type to be in business for yourself? To determine that, answer the following questions, as honestly as you can:

1. Even if you're sometimes timid or shy, can you be assertive when necessary?
2. Can you make decisions without having to consult others?
3. Do you enjoy solving problems?
4. Do you like people, in general?
5. Can you communicate effectively?
6. Are you comfortable with not knowing how much money you will make from the business—next week, next month, next year?
7. Are you self-motivated and self-disciplined enough to work without a boss?
8. Do you have the time to devote to a business?
9. Do you have the support of those whose lives will be affected?

10. Do you have a strong desire to succeed?

A "yes" to most of these questions is reason enough to continue the research. A "no" to more than one or two should tell you you're not quite ready to go out on your own. Perhaps you need a partner, a person who has the characteristics you lack, who could complement your strengths and shore up your weak points.

Your next step should be to weigh the risks of entrepreneurship. The biggest risk is probably financial. The majority of start-up businesses fail to show a profit in the first three years. The majority of businesses that fold, do so in the first year. They do not plan to fail; *they fail to plan.* So, once you have an idea of the costs involved in operating your business, plan for operating capital to see you through until the business can support itself. This can be accomplished in many ways, such as starting the business on the side while you maintain a steady income from another job; securing a line of credit at a bank; acquiring grants that do not have to be repaid; finding venture capitalists to invest in your business; calling your rich uncle!

Consider if the type of business you are planning is a passing trend or fad. If you are planning for the long term, it is important to choose a business with a market, or demand, that will likely be around for years to come.

How difficult—or how costly—might it be to get out of the business should you need or want to do so? Does the equipment hold its value well? Is there a market for the business as an entity or for the used components?

Depending on your business structure, losses incurred in start-up years may be subject to tax write-offs. This means the government may share in your loss by foregoing part of the taxes owed on your other sources of income. In cases of excess losses beyond what you can deduct from your personal income, it may even be possible to obtain a tax refund from prior years or offset taxes owed in future years. Your tax accountant and attorney should advise you of these and other ways to minimize your risks, and this may be a determining factor in whether your business should be established as a corporation, partnership, sole proprietorship, or Subchapter S corporation.

Other risks to consider are the effects on you and your family, if you have one. Will having your own business require more work hours than you or your loved ones are willing to sacrifice? Will a business cause cultural shock in terms of reduced social life or other sacrifices? How physically demanding is the business, and will your health permit it? If you intend to maintain a current job, will it cause you problems at work in terms of productivity? Is there a conflict of interest?

Next, analyze the profit potential of the business. The key here is to ask the right questions of the right people. Talk to others in the business. Just learning whether they are profitable is not sufficient, however. Perhaps a lack of profitability is due to poor management or poor marketing or poor service on their part. Remember, you are researching the profit ***potential***. Ask about the costs of doing business, then compare their costs to others' and to other resources you can locate. Also, ask about their volume of business, pricing structures and perceptions of the problems in their particular niche.

If possible, talk to the end-users or customers of the businesses you are researching. A markedly common complaint can provide you with knowledge of how to enter the market more competitively. Such background knowledge can also make you aware of established problems that are not easily overcome. Talk to your own potential customers to see how receptive they are to your product or service. Find out what they would expect to pay and the volume they would expect to use.

Talk to vendors or suppliers. They may have some useful information and insight about the industry you are considering.

The U.S. Small Business Administration (SBA) can also give you other helpful ideas for researching the potential profitability of the business you are considering.

Much of the information you acquire through this exercise can be very beneficial in preparing a market analysis and business plan, so do take notes and keep copies of any and all printed matter you obtain.

And, while profitability should be the bottom-line result of your entrepreneurial enterprise, a most important goal in choosing a business is to pick one that you will enjoy. The more you like what you are doing, the more you will overcome obstacles in order to make it work. The more interesting you find your work, the more you will strive to learn about it. And the more pride you take in your work and your business, the more likely you will be to succeed.

Success is defined as attaining a desired outcome. If, by using the steps outlined in this chapter, you are able to decide if entrepreneurship is for you, then we have both climbed the initial rung of our ladder to success! Let's proceed by investigating the business of embroidery.

CHAPTER 2

IS EMBROIDERY FOR YOU?

Computerized embroidery has provided many people a wonderful, small business. It can be done full-time or part-time, at home or in a store or shop, as a retail or wholesale operation. It can be done with one person or with many employees as a larger operation. It can be a business in itself or an add-on service to another business. (The SBA defines a small business as one whose retail sales do not exceed $13.5 million; for wholesalers, less than 100 employees constitutes a small business.)

As an artistic medium, embroidery is so versatile that anything that can be imagined can be reproduced on an embroidery machine. As a form of embellishment, embroidery has a permanent place in the fashion industry, combined with other art forms or by itself. As a means of personalization, identification and advertising, embroidery is in high demand.

The first computerized embroidery machine was introduced in 1977. The industry is young, and since that time, the number of embroidery businesses has skyrocketed, machine technology has rapidly developed, and market demand for the service has exploded.

Some embroiderers, particularly in large cities, are feeling the pinch of competition and worry that market saturation may be fast approaching. Competitors become involved in price wars, vying for the same accounts. Yet, new markets and creative new ideas, as well as the revival of old ideas, keep the industry alive and well for those who are opportunistic enough to change directions when needed. Some communities are still virtually untapped markets for embroidery. Location and your area of specialty are very important factors to consider. I'll discuss more about this in Chapter 5 of this book.

It takes hard work and long hours to start and run a business, and embroidery is no exception. You must wear many hats. In addition to learning to operate the equipment, you need to know about various fabrics, needles and threads. You need to develop marketing skills such as sales, pricing, advertising and negotiating. You need a knowledge of basic bookkeeping and accounting. You'll do everything from inventory control to public relations to collections to janitorial work. You'll also become an expert at scheduling.

Yet, most people in this business will tell you that their work brings them a great deal of satisfaction. Being able to create something so attractive, elegant and personalized gives them pleasure and brings a sense of pride and satisfaction to their customers. Entrepreneurs like being their own boss and the feeling of having built their businesses themselves. All this, and getting paid for it too! Many embroiderers have formed lasting friendships with their fellow embroiderers by attending seminars, trade shows or training classes together. Some search the Yellow Pages when visiting another city and call upon embroiderers. Although there are those who fear competition, many are open to a friendly and helpful business relationship.

The rewards of this business are many and varied. So are people's reasons for entering the field of embroidery. There are homemakers, some with sewing or craft experience, or mothers who want a source of income without having to leave their children and work outside the home. There are retired people seeking a new adventure or needing supplemental income. There are those who simply have an independent spirit and want to prove to themselves they can make it on their own. Some just happened to see an embroidery machine in operation and said, "I want to do that!"

Others have related businesses that can be enhanced by embroidery. Still others, such as screenprinters and uniform companies, enter into embroidery to survive competitively. If ABC company is losing customers to XYZ because XYZ can add names to garments "johnny-on-the-spot," ABC must keep up with the market demand.

Regardless of your reasons for entering the wonderful world of embroidery, it is important to establish a goal. The goal becomes your personal measure of success. It must be realistic and attainable. If it's financial, your goal may be making the business self-sustaining in X number of months, or profitable within a certain time-frame. Perhaps your goal would better motivate you in terms of what the profit can buy, such as a trip, a bigger house, a nest egg for the children's education, a new car and so on. Another goal might be to become the biggest or the best embroidery shop in the area. It doesn't matter what the goal is, or whether it's long-term or short-term, so long as it is important to you to achieve it.

Once you've established a goal, write it down and refer to it ***every day***. This keeps you focused as you build your business. When you reach it, set another, but always work toward a goal.

To help you further in deciding if embroidery is for you, let's consider the basic needs of an embroidery business. Some of these will be discussed in more depth later; here is an overview:

Space — You will need a place for your embroidery system, which could range from a small, portable, tabletop model to a large multihead machine. As you shop for equipment, get the dimensions so you can plan space requirements.

You'll also need a work table on which to hoop garments and measure for proper placement. A cabinet and/or shelving for supplies and small tools is a necessity. A desk, phone, calculator and filing cabinet should also be in the plans. Such items as a small copy machine, personal computer or typewriter, sample display area, hooping jig and thread tree or wall-mounted pegboard are also nice to have. If you intend to inventory garments, plan shelf or floor space for this, including additional sample displays.

Utilities — Dedicated circuits are required for most embroidery machines. This means nothing else should be plugged into the same electrical line as the one used for the machines. The outlet must be grounded. Voltage stabilizers are recommended to keep the flow of current constant and free of power surges, which can cause interrupted work or loss of a program or design.

Air conditioning and heat may be required to maintain the temperature of the room between 65 and 80 degrees Fahrenheit. Humidity should be maintained at a level between 45% and 75%.

Bathroom facilities must be conveniently located. Clean hands are a must for handling garments.

Insurance — At a minimum, insurance against fire, theft and vandalism should be purchased. Other types of insurance you may wish to consider include a special policy for computers and stored data, and special coverage for garments, especially if expensive items, such as fur coats or designer garments, are in your care or possession.

Capital — Capital is defined as assets, resources and wealth. Operating capital will be needed to cover the expenses of the business until it can sustain itself with incoming revenue. After equipment is acquired, you will need funds for supplies, samples, rent, utilities, telephone, advertising, wages and so on. Needs will vary, depending upon your particular circumstances. Usually, six months' worth of expenses should be held in reserve. If you have savings or income from another source to cover such expenses, fine. If not, you will need a line of credit, a loan, grant or investment from other sources. Loan sources usually expect 20% to 25% of the total initial investment to be covered by you from cash resources.

Records — You will need to maintain a record of all sales, purchases, expenses, accounts receivable and accounts payable. A record of each job is also useful to refer to for repeat orders or similar jobs, and for maintaining a history of your customers' transactions. Other helpful records include a current inventory status, tracking of advertising results, correspondence files, a listing of suppliers and so on.

Legal Fees — Legal fees will be incurred. The amount will depend, of course, upon the complexity of the services and who handles them. A sole proprietorship (single owner of the business) requires less paperwork than a partnership. Incorporation requires more paperwork than a partnership. Talk to your tax accountant and your attorney to determine the best business structure for your particular situation. Most start-up businesses choose the S corporation because of the tax advantages in the event of a loss. That loss can be taken against personal income taxes. Later, when a profit is realized, the business can be changed to a C corporation, which pays taxes based on the sales and expenses of the business. Other legal fees could be incurred if, for example, you are buying an existing business and need a legal firm to draw up an agreement, or if you are purchasing used equipment and want to make sure it is not already encumbered with an outstanding loan, and thereby subject to repossession.

Equipment — The equipment needed will depend upon the type and volume of work you'll produce. There are various makes, models, sizes, features and price ranges. They range from single-needle, single-head, full-sized and portable machines, to machines with 5, 6, 7 or 9-needle heads in configurations of 1 to 30 heads.

Take into consideration the manufacturer, number of sewing heads and whether those heads must sew the same or different designs simultaneously, color change requirements, sewing field, computer features, in-house design needs, serviceability, space confinements and cost. See Chapter 4 for more about selecting your equipment.

Supplies — Required embroidery supplies include a variety of thread colors (there are several major brands of rayon, polyester and cotton threads especially made for high-speed computerized embroidery machines); bobbins, which are usually prewound and disposable; a variety of specialized needles; trimming scissors; backing materials; plastic topping material; and special hoops or frames of various sizes, shapes and depths. You will also need designs and lettering styles that are stored on circuit boards, cassettes, floppy or hard disks, or paper tape, depending upon your equipment. Many other helpful supplies are available for embroiderers. More about embroidery accessories is discussed in Chapter 10 of this book.

In terms of office supplies, you'll need order forms, invoices, stationery, business cards, record books, files, index cards or notebooks for customer information, pens, pencils, sharpeners, erasers, plenty of scratchpads, and telephone message pads. If you plan to ship, you'll need boxes, shipping labels and shipping log forms. If you have employees, you'll also need application forms, timesheets, and W-4 forms.

Employees — One person can usually operate up to two single-head or double-head machines. Beyond that, usually one person is needed per machine. If you're thinking of operating a one-person shop, remember all the different hats you'll be wearing. Plan for interruptions. As the business grows, plan to add employees to help you. Your needs can range from family members in their spare time, to a part-time person with flexible hours, to several shifts of many full-time employees. Some shops now are able to find people experienced on their type of equipment, particularly in large cities where there are more embroidery businesses. Other shops prefer people with no embroidery experience so that certain methods can be taught from the beginning, without having to undo bad habits learned elsewhere. Some businesses look for sewing or computer backgrounds, while others want experience in retail, ad specialty or other related businesses. However, most agree that regardless of experience, ideal employees are those who have common sense, commitment, honesty and loyalty. The rest can be taught.

Customers — Without customers, you have no business. From day one, they should be the central focus of your business. You should be working to acquire them and satisfy them—not just when you're getting started, but always. ***Almost everyone*** is a potential customer for your embroidery business! Think about it! Individuals want monograms on shirts, sweaters or blouses, and household linens—for themselves and for gifts. Businesses want their logos or names on employees' hats or uniforms. Sports enthusiasts, whether they participate or are just spectators, want to tout their team. Tourists are proud of where they've been, and hobbyists are proud of what they do. Children have a favorite object or character...the list can (and does) go on.

That's the most exciting part about considering embroidery as your business. There is virtually no end to the market that is either there or that can be created. And, it's here to stay. Embroidery has been around since Biblical times—only the methods and uses have changed. Today, it is more popular than ever before, and for those who manage their business well, it can be very profitable.

If you're ready to proceed, get some paper and a pencil.

CHAPTER 3

RESEARCH YOUR MARKET

Although some embroiderers try to do it all, most of the successful ones agree that it's best to find a niche, or area of specialty in the market. For instance, Exquisite Custom Design in Denver, Colorado, specializes in auto racing uniforms; National Embroidery in Orlando, Florida, specializes in caps for the major attractions in its area; Circle C Western of Xenia, Ohio, specializes in Western wear and designs for horse shows, rodeos, fairs and square dancing, to name a few. All of these shops may do other things as well, but having established themselves as specialists usually brings a larger portion of that market their way.

Finding your niche can be easy if you already have knowledge of or contacts in a given market. For example, if you're an avid golfer and are familiar with the golf courses and country clubs in your area, or if you know people who are involved with various golf tournaments, your niche would probably be anything and everything having to do with golf: golf club designs on apparel for the pro shops; country club logos on shirts, skirts, caps and sweaters; tournament logos; monograms on golf bags and club covers and so on.

Look over the following sample list of markets, then add some with which you may be familiar. Select several that appeal to you, and continue your research. A word of caution here: An understanding of copyrights and trademarks is needed before you plunge into selling or sewing. A subsequent chapter of this book will provide more information about this, but for now, remember that specific teams, company names, product names, pictures of products and logos of businesses and organizations must not be duplicated or sold without permission.

1. **Sports** — Think about teams as well as individuals, participants as well as spectators, professionals as well as amateurs.

   a. Baseball, softball
   b. Basketball
   c. Boating
   d. Bowling
   e. Boxing, wrestling
   f. Cheerleading
   g. Darts
   h. Fencing
   i. Fishing
   j. Football

k. Golf
l. Hot-air ballooning
m. Hockey
n. Hunting
o. Ice skating
p. Martial arts
q. Polo
r. Racquetball
s. Roller skating
t. Scuba diving
u. Skiing
v. Sky diving, flying
w. Soccer
x. Surfing
y. Tennis
z. Volleyball

2. **Tourism** — Analyze your surroundings to see what tourist attractions exist. Your local Chamber of Commerce would be a good source of brochures and other information about businesses and tourism in your area.

   a. Airports, train stations, bus depots
   b. Amusement parks
   c. Beaches
   d. Dude ranches
   e. Gift shops
   f. Local, state and national parks; memorials and attractions
   g. Marinas
   h. Museums and historical sites
   i. Resorts and resort hotels
   j. Ski resorts
   k. Summer camps
   l. Visitor centers

3. **Business & Industry** — Advertising of products and corporate logos is big business. In some cases the company itself will be your customer. In others, the employees will buy their own jackets, caps, sweaters and so forth with the logo and their name added. Also consider the after market potential, such as corporate sports teams, incentive/awards programs and unions. Pick some categories of businesses and leaf through your Yellow Pages to identify individual companies. Here are some examples:

   a. Large equipment manufacturers

   (1) Caterpillar
   (2) Crane
   (3) Ford
   (4) GMC

   b. Food and beverage

   (1) Anheuser-Busch
   (2) Best Products
   (3) Coca-Cola
   (4) Del Monte

(5) John Deere
(6) Kenworth
(7) Mack Trucks Inc.
(8) Peterbilt

(5) General Foods
(6) General Mills
(7) Heinz
(8) Procter & Gamble

4. **Service** — Although this is still a category of business, think of all the service-related industries and list specific ones in your community.

   a. Appliance repair
   b. Beauty, barber shops
   c. Carpet cleaners
   d. Caterers
   e. Clinics, hospitals
   f. Day care facilities
   g. Doctors, dentists
   h. Fitness centers
   i. Gas stations
   j. Heating and plumbing
   k. Hotels, motels
   l. Insurance companies
   m. Janitorial services
   n. Lawn care companies
   o. Moving companies
   p. Realtors
   q. Restaurants, bars
   r. Upholstery shops

5. **Entertainment**

   a. Major entertainment sponsors, promoters
   b. Casinos
   c. Comedy clubs
   d. Dinner theaters
   e. Movie theaters
   f. Musicians, bands, orchestras
   g. Nightclubs
   h. Opera companies
   i. Record, video stores
   j. TV, radio stations

6. **Hobbies, Clubs, Organizations** — These are good sources for direct sales and fundraising projects.

   a. Amateur radio (all ham radio operators have a different call sign)
   b. Animals (owners/breeders, 4-H clubs, animal shows)
   c. Autos (from Rolls-Royce clubs to antique car groups)
   d. Cards, games (bridge, chess)
   e. Crafts (sewing, knitting, model trains and planes, dolls, wall hangings)
   f. Gardening
   g. Gourmet cooking
   h. Military organizations (ROTC, Civil Air Patrol)
   i. Motorcycles
   j. Music and dance schools
   k. Photography

l. Professional groups (American Medical Association, American Management Association,Toastmasters, etc.)
m. Ritualistic orders (Masons, Knights of Columbus, Shrine, and all auxiliary organizations)
n. Boy Scouts of America, Girl Scouts of America
o. Service groups (Jaycees, Kiwanis, Lions, Elks, Rotary, Optimists)
p. 4-wheel drive groups

7. **Churches/Charity Organizations** — (Again, don't overlook their need for fundraising projects.)

8. **Political Campaigns**

9. **Wholesale Markets**

a. Ad specialty firms
b. Art galleries
c. Bath, linen shops
d. Children's, infants' shops
e. Christmas, novelty shops
f. Craft shops
g. Department stores
h. Dry cleaners
i. Furriers
j. Interior decorators
k. Men's stores
l. Pet shops
m. Screenprinters, T-shirt shops
n. Sporting goods, apparel shops
o. Trophy shops
p. Uniform companies
q. Women's apparel stores

10. **Mail-Order Catalogs**

11. **Garment Manufacturers** — Remember the alligator shirts? A trip to department stores and fashion stores can give you some ideas if you're considering the fashion market. This appears to be a growing market for embroidery and other types of embellishment.

12. **Other Embroiderers** — Here, the market is contracting work to and from other embroiderers. If you're a small shop, you can do overflow work for large shops. If you're a large shop, offer to do large volume orders for the smaller shops.

There really is no limit to the market for embroidery. I'm just priming your imagination.

Now, let's think about some of the garments and items that can be embroidered. Again, add to this list or make up your own, then cross-reference these with the markets you selected earlier for more research. What garments or other embroiderable goods can you sell to those markets?

Bed & Bath

Bath rugs
Bath sheets, wraps
Bedspreads
Blankets
Pillow cases
Sheets
Towels and towel sets

Linens

Dresser scarves
Napkins
Placemats
Tablecloths

Household

Aprons
Coasters
Dish towels
Hot pads, gloves, mitts
Small appliance covers
Pillows

Women's

Blouses
Dance costumes
Dresses
Fur coat linings
Leg warmers
Lingerie
Skirts

Children's

All clothing
Nursery, layette items
Soft toys
Wall hangings

Men's

Dress shirts
Sport shirts
Sweaters
Ties

Men & Women

Jackets, blazers
Jeans
Pajamas
Raincoats, rainhats
Robes, loungewear
Socks
Shorts
Sweaters
Western wear
Uniforms

Accessories

Belts
Eyeglass cases
Handkerchiefs
Head, wristbands
Make-up bags
Nametags
Purses
Scarves
Tote bags
Umbrellas
Wallets
Watchbands

Sportswear

Athletic bags
Back packs
Beach towels
Caps
Golf club covers
Golf bags
Jogging suits
Racquet covers
Ski wear
Sweats, warm-ups
Swimsuits, cover-ups
Visors
Windbreakers

Holiday Items

Crafts
Fabric greeting cards
Ornaments
Stockings
Tree skirts

Miscellaneous

Animal collars, blankets, sweaters
Award ribbons, banners
Birth, wedding announcements for framing
Bookmarks
Car mats, upholstery

Director's chairs
Musical instrument cases, covers
Soft luggage
Tarps
Tents
Wheel, car covers

Anything that a needle will penetrate can be embroidered, so again, this list is not complete. It's only a sampling to get your ideas flowing.

Along with identifying what and where your market is, you will need to decide how to serve that market. Basically, the choices are retail, wholesale, or contract embroidery, or a combination of these. Retail is selling to the end-user; wholesale is selling to a middleman who, in turn, sells to the end-user; and contract embroidery is selling the service for a specific job at an agreed price.

There is room for caution in trying to combine wholesale and retail. You could be in competition with your wholesalers by selling to the same retail customers or market. That would not make your wholesale customers filled with joy. However, combining contract work with a wholesale business is very common. There could be a problem in combining retail work with contract work. The most obvious scenario for a problem would be a retail store where the embroidery machine is visible to the public, yet a contractor includes a confidentiality clause in the agreement. Under those circumstances it would be rather difficult to hide the work being done for a contractor.

Another decision you'll have to make is whether to sell the garments, as well as the embroidery upon them. The benefits to selling garments are:

- You gain more profitability because you can mark up the garment as well as charge for the embroidery.
- It's a convenience for your customers.
- You gain control over quality.
- It increases sales through impulse buying.

The drawbacks to carrying garments are:

- It requires more space.
- It requires more capital.
- Inventories are difficult to plan and you may face out-of-stock conditions on some items and be overstocked on other items.

If you already sell garments, adding embroidery can give you a sales edge over your competitors. It's something you offer that they don't. It has an added advantage of reducing your returned goods because something personalized for one person cannot be sold to someone else, unless it is a generic or popular design.

If you want to sell garments, start collecting brochures and catalogs from major suppliers of the garments you're interested in. Find out such details as cost, minimum quantities and if those are per color or a combination of colors. Check available sizes, delivery time, payment terms, exclusive distribution arrangements, and so on. Also check the quality of those garments and the consistency of the quality by contacting others who use that particular garment. Are the garments washable, or must they be dry-cleaned? This will affect marketability. Are they subject to much shrinkage (which can cause the embroidery to look puckered after laundering)? Look for flaws, such as shirt pockets or plackets not sewn straight, sizing that is larger or smaller than the standard, non-colorfastness, to name a few. Caps with seams where embroidery might otherwise be placed could also cause problems.

Attending a trade show is a good way to research garments. Also, check advertisements in magazines that apply to your chosen markets. Talk to other embroiderers—some will readily share their sources.

Once you have an idea of the direction you want to go, make a more specific, complete listing of potential customers in that market and items you could sell to them. (Refer to Exhibit 1 for a sample market analysis.) Talk to some of them. Write a short summary of any potential customers who have expressed interest in your planned product or service, including the reason for that interest, and volume expectations over a given time period. Of course, if you are able to acquire written letters of intent or firm contracts, include them in your written marketing analysis. This will be beneficial in preparing your marketing plan and business plan, and will greatly enhance your success in securing any needed funding.

In researching your market, you are not necessarily confined to your own area. Those with a specific or unique niche can have much success marketing regionally or even nationally. If, however, you're specializing in small business logos, then you will probably be more confined to your immediate area because of marketing and delivery time and costs.

If you currently sell embroidery, but subcontract it or send it out to be done for your customers, you already have an idea of volume and pricing. Don't stop with that. Research more of that market or additional markets to anticipate the volume growth resulting from bringing the embroidery into your own shop.

Try to ascertain the size of your market. U.S. Government Printing Office Bookstores are located in most major cities and you may be able to find statistical data on the area population and number of businesses in a given category. Look for socio-economic trends and population shifts in the area over the past several years. A major retirement community, for example, may not be a good place to market business logos, but it might be a great market for hobbies, clubs and some sports. On the other hand, retirement communities may have a larger proportion of hospitals, restaurants or beauty parlors than other communities—and all these businesses need embroidery.

To gain a handle on expected volume, look at the size of the businesses you are researching. If you're targeting small business logos, ascertain the number of employees, number of uniforms or other garments needed per employee, employee turn-over rates, and so on. If you're targeting a university bookstore, find out how many students are enrolled and what percentage of them purchase garments at the bookstore. Another way to research this market would be to survey the students via a simple questionnaire to determine their interest in your products/services. A questionnaire might also be useful for ad specialty companies so they can determine the interest level of their clientele.

Your equipment needs will be greatly influenced by your anticipated volume. The type of embroidery your customers will need—monogramming, lettering, small designs for logos on shirts or caps, large jacket back designs—is equally influential.

Another factor to consider is the seasonality of some businesses. If you're headed for a retail market, holidays, special occasions and traditional sale months can affect your volume. Seasonal sports may also affect your business volume.

Find out who your competitors are and develop a written profile on each one. Your profile should include:

- Company name and location
- Type of equipment (make, model, number of heads, number of machines)
- Lettering styles, stock designs, in-house design capability
- Type of work (retail, wholesale, contract embroidery)
- Markets served

- Quality of work (Does it look good?)
- Garments sold (type and brands, fiber content, prices)
- Price structure—(by stitch count, by garment, by number of letters per name, and so on)
- Turn-around time
- Extra services such as pick-up and delivery
- Are they busy?
- Do they advertise?
- Are they friendly?
- Are they profitable?

List strengths and weaknesses in your profiles, as well. Refer to Exhibit 2 for a sample.

You may find other embroiderers who will not really be competition for you. If you are considering a kiosk in a mall to handle retail lettering and monogramming, don't worry about the large multi-head shop three blocks away. It cannot afford to shut down 11 heads to do a one-of-a-kind monogram on one sewing head. If that larger shop is running a profitable business, it will be doing volume runs. Or suppose no one in your area has finished-cap capability and that happens to be a large segment of the market you seek. You have no competition—at least for now.

Start making notes about how you can capture a segment of the market not being served, and how you can better serve the existing market.

Keep approaching various markets on these bases until you find the area or areas that look and feel right. It should *look* right when analyzed on paper, and it should *feel* right when you imagine yourself doing that particular work for that particular clientele. Excitement upon finding your niche is what you're after!

You will have to refer to this section again after you have looked into equipment, space and other fixed-cost items. Only after you have a handle on your costs can you determine whether you can compete with price. Only after you know which equipment you want and how much you can afford can you determine if you will be competitive on turn-around time. However, researching your market in this manner should bring you closer to finding your niche.

Exhibit 1

SAMPLE MARKET ANALYSIS FOR POTENTIAL CUSTOMERS

BUSINESS	LOCATION	JOB	GARMENTS	QUANTITY	TIME-FRAME	COMMENTS
RESTAURANTS						
Alexanders	Lakeshore Mall	Employee names	They supply uniforms	18	Replace 3/yr.	Replaces plastic nametags
Bell Cafeterias	Southeast Mall, Englewood	Logo	We supply caps	65 5	Initial order Every 2 months for turnovers	Needs pickup
Lucy's	Downtown	Custom monogram	They supply table linens	240	Initial order	Possible uniform order
REALTORS						
Century 21	26 offices	Logo	They supply uniforms	125	Initial order	10% annual turnover
TRAVEL AGENCIES						
Judy's World Travel	North Main Street	Large custom design	We supply jackets	6	Fall	Special Hawaii promotion
WEIGHT CONTROL						
Diet Center	Fifth & Vine	Names & titles	They supply uniforms	15	Initial Order	Possible national account
Nutri-system	14th & Main	Names & titles	They supply uniforms	12	Initial Order	
Weight Watchers	125 E. Green	Logo & names	They supply uniforms	36	Initial Order	Possibly 30 offices in 8 states

Exhibit 2

SAMPLE COMPETITIVE PROFILE

ABC Embroidery
15 Main Street
Anytown, USA
222-1111

Owner: Tom Gray; three years in embroidery business.

Details:

Wholesale & contract embroidery for medium-sized businesses and organizational logos

Sells poplin and curduroy caps; Hanes® nylon jackets.

One shift, one operator. Owner markets the business. Quality is excellent.

Advertises in Yellow Pages under embroidery heading

Turn-around time: Up to four weeks

Equipment: Barudan six-head, cap option, five needles, Traditional Script, Two Color Athletic Block, Broadway, Sports Figures

Pricing: Keystone garments; charges $0.60 per 1,000 stitches for embroidery, plus cost of tape. Discounts for six dozen or more to $0.45.

Observations: Offers no extra services such as pick-up and delivery. Shop is busy year-round. Operator is competent. Owner is friendly and knowledgeable. No plans for expansion.

Strengths: Quality of work, knowledge of their business.

Weaknesses: Turn-around time, lack of versatility in what garments and services could be offered. Owner markets to same clients—not interested in growing. Plans to retire in two years.

Comments: Heavy repeat business indicates customer satisfaction. Do not compete for his business until closer to his retirement. Many markets left untouched by ABC Embroidery. Contact owner for overflow work to help improve his turn-around time.

Optional Scenario: While many markets remain untouched, a portion of ABC's market could be gained by offering in-house design work and improving turn-around time. More variety in garments could gain additional business from this existing market.

CHAPTER 4

SELECTING YOUR EQUIPMENT

How do you select equipment? Approach it on the bases of production needs; machine features; design availability; support, such as serviceability and training; and cost and space limitations. Another important factor is the manufacturer and/or distributor. As in all major purchases, it's best to choose a company that is reputable and progressive. An equipment company's ability to keep pace with your needs as you grow is particularly important in any computerized business, because technology advances so rapidly within the industry. For this reason, specific machine features will not be discussed in-depth in this book. (Such information could become outdated before publication!) Discuss specific machine features with company sales representatives. Gather sales literature—brochures and price lists—and then arrange to see demonstrations of the models that interest you. This can be done at trade shows or by visiting the closest sales office of the brands you want to see.

The manufacturers in the following list are all reputable and progressive companies. Their sales forces, as a group, are highly knowledgeable about their products and skilled at helping fill your needs.

At this point, some clarification of terms is needed, because as you talk to various people within the embroidery industry, you could become quite confused. Some people refer to one- through four-head units as monogramming machines, and six or more heads as embroidery machines. This is incorrect and needs to be changed by those using such definitions! Monogramming is a form of personalization involving using initials. A monogram can consist of one, two or all three initials, and can be with or without a border. Monograms can be created in many ways besides embroidery: glass can be monogrammed by cutting or etching; metal can be monogrammed by engraving; paper can be monogrammed by embossing and so on. What you want is an ***embroidery*** machine, regardless of whether you plan to do monogramming, lettering or designs.

Manufacturers

There are many manufacturers of computerized embroidery equipment throughout the world. Following are their names and addresses, and some basic product information:

Happy Industrial Corp. 9-5, Taito 2-chome Taito-ku, Tokyo, Japan 03-834-0711	Model HM702 EM3 Series	2-heads 8-,10-,12-,15-, 16-,20-,24-heads
Macpherson Inc. 3517 W. Wendover Ave. Greensboro, NC 27407	Barudan BESR Series Prosperity Plus Profit 700 Series Barudan Golf Bag	12-,15-,17-,20-, 21-,24-,26-heads 1-head 2-,4-,6-heads 2-,4-,6-heads
Meistergram Inc. 3517 W. Wendover Ave. Greensboro, NC 27407	M800 800XLM	1-head (zig-zag stitch) 1-head (zig-zag stitch)
Melco Industries Inc. 1575 W. 124th Ave. Westminster, CO 80234	Epicor Stellar	1-,4-heads, add-on system (up to 16 peripherals) 1-head (portable)
Pantograms Mfg. Co. Inc. 6814 S. MacDill Ave. Tampa, FL 33611	Toyota AD 500/510 Toyota AD 800	1-head (portable) 1-head
Pfaff Industriemaschinen GmbH Koenigstr.154 D-6750 Kaiserslautern West Germany	KSM Series	5 to 28 heads

Company	Model	Heads
Tajima Industries Ltd. 620 Kinderkamack Road River Edge, NJ 07661	TMCE-S Series	Chain Stitch/ Chenille 4-,6-,8-,10-, 12-heads
	TMLE-100	Taping/Coiling 6-,8-,10-, 12-heads
	TMEF Series	4-,6-,8-,10-, 12-,15-,18-, 20-,24-,30-heads
	TME Series	6-,8-,10-,12-heads
	TMEF-H & TME-H Series	6-,8-,10-,12-heads
	TME-C & TME-SC Series	12-heads
	TMM Series	6-heads
	TMEF-P Series (Sequins)	4-,8-,10-,12-, 15-,18-,20-, 24- heads
Ultramatic Embroidery Machine Co. 60 United Drive P.O. Box 518 North Haven, CT 06473-0518	6-needle	1-,2-,4-,6-,8-, 12-heads
	1-needle	1-,2-,4-,6-,8-, 12-heads
	Junior	1-head (portable)
ZSK USA Ltd. P.O. Box 6068 42 Franklin St. Laconia, NH 03246	169 Series	6-,8-heads
	170,171	4-,6-,8-,12-heads
	173,175	6-,8-,12-heads
	220,224	20-,24-heads
	KSA 300	6-,8 heads (Chain Stitch/Chenille)
	172,174	6-,8-,10-,12-heads
	201	1-head
	2-700	2-heads

Eighty percent (80%) of the computerized embroidery machines sold throughout the world are Macpherson (representing Barudan and Meistergram machines), Melco or Tajima machines (in alphabetical order). Therefore, discussion will be focused on these three and the companies who represent them. However, in the United

States, according to 1989 figures, 39.2% of the computerized embroidery machines in operation were Melco's, 31.2% were Meistergram's, 14.1% Barudan's.

Barudan is a Japanese firm. Their machines are sold and serviced worldwide by Macpherson Inc. The United States headquarters is in Greensboro, North Carolina.

Barudan currently has a Profit series of machines available in 2-, 4-, and 6-head models. The Profit machines have all multi-needle heads and come with cylinder arms. The Prosperity Plus is a single-head, multi-needle machine and is sold by both Barudan and Meistergram. Multi-heads also are available in BESR models with up to 26 heads. In addition, Barudan has a golf bag machine with a variety of frames suitable for embroidering shoe pockets, ball pockets, gloves and head covers for golf clubs.

Macpherson also markets Meistergram machines. This brand differs from the others substantially because it uses a zig-zag stitch, instead of a satin stitch. The zig-zag machine produces horizontal, back-and-forth stitching only. This allows much greater speeds during operation. However, satin stitch machines produce multi-directional stitching, which affords more versatility in design.

ZIG-ZAG
STITCH

SATIN STITCH

Melco's products are sold and serviced by its own sales representatives, sales agents and worldwide distributors. Earlier models of Melco embroidery machines include the Star, Starlet and Superstar series. The current system is the Epicor. It consists of a central computer from which commands and data are conveyed to peripherals. From one to 16 peripherals can be added to a single Epicor computer. Embroidery peripherals include the EM-1 (single needle), the EMC-6 (6 needles) and the EMC-4-6 (4 heads, 6 needles). This means that if you need an odd number of sewing heads, you can buy only what you need—no more and no less. It also means that your equipment can grow as your business grows. Another advantage to this concept is that multiple embroidery peripherals can do different or like jobs simultaneously.

The MC-1 peripheral connects some other models, such as Superstar, Tajima and Barudan machines to the Epicor computer. Programming of all the machines is then facilitated at one work station and the need for multiple copies of paper tapes and disks is eliminated.

Other peripherals can be added to the Epicor, including digitizers for creating custom work and laser engraving peripherals (LE1).

A portable table-top model, Stellar 1, is also available through Melco.

Tajima is a Japanese company, with Nomura America Corp. in New York, as its national headquarters. In the United States and Canada, the machines are sold and serviced by distributors, most of which are also Melco sales representatives or distributors. In addition, there are worldwide distributors.

Tajima manufactures multi-head equipment with a minimum of six and a maximum of 30 heads. Various models of embroidery and other specialized equipment are available, including chenille and sequin machines, and various other decorative-type production equipment. Tajima machines use Melco electronics. Melco machines, except for the Stellar, use Tajima sewing heads and related parts. Therefore, the Melco and Tajima machines are very compatible in many ways.

The most popular models of Tajima machines are the TMM 6-head, which has the integrated keyboard unit for use with lettering and designs stored on circuit boards, and the TMEF series, which is a bridge unit enabling loading and unloading of the frames from the back or the front. Another advantage to this series is the user's ability to shut down certain sewing heads to accommodate large garments such as jacket backs. The TME series, on the other hand, can only be loaded from the front, and all heads will operate at once. The TMEF-H and TME-H are more economical units with fewer features.

Number of Heads/Number of Machines

The phrase *production needs* refers to the number of sewing heads and the number of machines you should have. Review your marketing analysis and consider how many like pieces you want to embroider at the same time on a regular basis. Like pieces means the same design sewn at the same size, same density. They need not be identical because many could involve different colors, different fabrics, different backings, and so forth. Be sure you judge the number of like pieces you'll be doing on the basis of an average. You can always negotiate a longer turn-around time on a now-and-then large volume order, or subcontract it out to someone with more production capability. Likewise, if you're planning for mostly large runs, one-of-a-kind or small jobs can be subcontracted out to a small shop. Such networking among embroiderers is becoming more popular.

Plan for some increase in volume of work after you are open for business. How much of an increase depends upon your market potential, your marketing efforts, competition, quality and service.

If your work will be primarily monogramming, most will be one-of-a-kind combinations of initials, even though the overall volume of work may be heavy. For any business with mostly one-of-a-kind needs, single-heads make the most sense, because multi-heads cannot do different jobs simultaneously. With multi-head equipment, the only way you can vary the work per run is to use different garments or fabric, and different colors or types of thread. (Threads should be of the same weight, however.)

Some sales representatives have pet theories they use in recommending numbers of heads. For example, Earnie Allen of C. H. Holderby in Seattle, Washington, suggests 2 heads for 6 of a kind, 4 heads for 12 of a kind, and 12 heads for 150 of a kind. Jay Bumm of Macpherson in Greensboro, North Carolina, uses this formula: A single-head for 1 dozen pieces, a 2-head for 2 dozen pieces, a 4-head for 3 to 5 dozen pieces, and a 6-head for 5 to 10 dozen pieces.

The number of machines required should be evaluated on the basis of work volume, cost, space and operators needed. Carl J. Moritz, III of The Moritz Embroidery Works Inc., Mt. Pocono, Pennsylvania, prefers three 4-heads or two 6-heads to a 12-head machine. He believes the operators can manage them better, thereby increasing production. They can keep up with hooping, loading and unloading, programming and re-threading; and they seem more comfortable with the 4- and 6-head machines.

Carl also accurately states that there are situations where a 12-head machine with one operator would be more efficient, depending on the number of stitches and size of order. A job for 1,000 pieces with 10,000 stitches in the design would be better handled on a 12-head or 24-head machine. However, 8 to 12 small-run jobs with 3,000 to 7,000 stitches can be done more efficiently on two 4-head or 6-head machines with one operator per machine. So, the type of work, as well as the volume expected, should weigh heavily in your decision on how many of what type machines you need.

Don't be misled by the quoted sewing speed of machines. Regardless of the top sewing speed possible, the average sewing speed for good quality work done on a satin-stitch machine is 500 to 550 stitches per minute. When figured in terms of actual output over an eight-hour shift, the average goes down to 250 to 450 stitches per minute, even though the sewing speed may remain fairly constant. The difference is due to down time— the time when the machine is not stitching. Some down time is unavoidable because of loading and unloading hoops, changing needles, changing threads, lubricating and cleaning the machine, and programming the next job.

The more duties the operator must perform, the less output there is from the machine. For example, if the person operating the machine must also answer the phone, handle walk-in customers, trim and fold garments, order supplies, open the mail and so on, you can understand how production time will be reduced. Conceivably, it could become a matter of the normal 250 to 450 stitches per minute becoming 250 to 450 stitches per hour with such interruptions. Therefore, when planning your equipment needs based upon output of the machine, approach it realistically.

In situations where an operator is dedicated only to minding the machine, the chart that follows will be useful in determining the time it will take to sew designs of different stitch counts at various speeds. For jobs over 10,000 stitches, add output times together to arrive at needed combinations; for example, for a 15,000-stitch job sewn at a speed of 350, add the time for 10,000 stitches to the time for 5,000 stitches (28.58 + 14.29 minutes). The total time of a 15,000-stitch job will be 43.27 minutes.

The chart is figured on a ***per run*** basis. To find the time needed per order, divide the number of pieces on the order by the number of sewing heads. Fractions must be counted as another full run. Then, multiply the number of runs by the number of minutes per run. For example, figure the time involved in sewing a 6,000-stitch design on 142 garments, with a 4-head machine, at an average of 450 stitches per minute:

142 ÷ 4 = 36 runs x 13.33 minutes per run = 479.88 minutes, or 8 hours. The same job on a 12-head would take 2 hours and 40 minutes. On a single-head, it would take 32 hours, or 4 days.

Stitch Count	Sewing Speed (Stitches Per Minute)					
	250	350	450	550	650	750
	Sewing Time In Minutes					
1,000	4.00	2.86	2.22	1.82	1.54	1.33
2,000	8.00	5.71	4.44	3.54	3.08	2.67
3,000	12.00	8.57	6.67	5.45	4.62	4.00
4,000	16.00	11.43	8.89	7.27	6.15	5.33
5,000	20.00	14.29	11.11	9.09	7.69	6.67
6,000	24.00	17.24	13.33	10.90	9.23	8.00
7,000	28.00	20.00	15.56	12.73	10.77	9.33
8,000	32.00	22.86	17.78	14.55	12.30	10.67
9,000	36.00	25.71	20.00	16.36	13.85	12.00
10,000	40.00	28.58	22.22	18.18	15.38	13.33

If you're considering buying multiple machines to handle volume work, think about adding shifts instead of or in addition to more machines. It is usually more profitable to run more shifts per machine than to add more machines per shift. The drawback is that someone needs to manage each shift. That usually means either long hours for someone or possible communication problems between shift managers. These problems can be overcome, but it's something to think about.

Some people prefer a mix of equipment. For example, a single-head might be used for small orders or for redo's, should a defective piece come off of the production machine. If you're also considering doing in-store promotions for your retail customers, or traveling to fairs, rodeos, conventions or trade shows, a portable machine would be ideal for adding names on-the-spot to garments that have previously been embroidered with designs.

Some people who have multiple machines like to mix brands so they have the greatest flexibility and assortment in lettering styles, designs and so on. Usually, this proves more costly because lettering styles, hoops and spare parts are generally not interchangeable between brands of equipment. You'd have to buy some for each machine. Frequent servicing from more than one source could also add to the costs.

Number of Needles

Although any number of colors can be sewn with a single-needle machine, it does take even an experienced operator between 20 and 40 seconds to change threads. This takes precious time away from other duties that could be done while the machine is stitching a multi-color job. Automatic color change is definitely a time-saving feature worth having. The number of needles per head will vary among manufacturers. Some have a standard number of needles on color-change machines, with an option for additional needles per head.

Even when single-color jobs are the norm, threading the most popular colors used on a multi-needle machine will save you time. Or, if the same thread colors are used, but on different fabrics, a multi-needle head will help you save time if you keep different needle types and sizes in the machine. Needle #1 might be a sharp point, needle #2 a ball point and so on.

Some machines feature a take-up lever that only permits the needle doing the sewing to move, thus enabling the operator to thread the other needles while the machine is stitching. This can be a further timesaver when stitching designs that have more color changes than your machine has needles.

Sewing Field

The sewing field of the machine must be adequate for the garments you will be embroidering. The small, portable machines on the market have a smaller sewing area. They may be adequate for some jobs, but *not* for full jacket-back designs or lengthy names or large lettering. There are also some models of multi-heads that have limited space between the heads. This may prevent 12 jacket backs from being run simultaneously on a 12-head machine, for example. Some models allow every other head to be shut down so that 6 large items can be done at a time on a 12-head machine.

Sewing areas may be further limited by the available hoop sizes for a particular machine. When discussing this with your sales representative, be sure you ascertain the actual, usable sewing field.

Other Features

A cylinder arm machine will help you embroider non-flat articles more easily. Special cap frames are available for cylinder arm machines. A better quality of embroidery on caps can be produced when caps are stitched in their natural, curved shape. Other special hoops for cylinder arms will help you embroider shirt pockets, sleeves, pants, socks and gloves.

Other helpful features you may wish to investigate include computer memory capability, programmability, scaling and density control (number of stitches per inch). Scaling of a design up or down in size beyond about 10% requires the ability to also change the density. Otherwise, the embroidery will have too many or too few stitches to maintain its original quality prior to scaling. Arcing, which is the ability to sew letters in a circular clockwise or counterclockwise direction, is only possible with a satin stitch machine. The zig-zag machine's version of this is arching, which is accomplished by raising or lowering a letter's position in relation to the previous letter.

Formats, Media, Storage

Computerized embroidery machines read different formats, or languages. Stellar and Meistergram formats are not interchangeable with other brands, but the rest of the leading models are. However, most of the other formats can be converted to Stellar format, depending upon how the design was created.

Design storage media range from electronic circuit boards to hard disk, floppy disk and paper tape. Designs stored on paper tape and floppy disk can be read by most machines—regardless of brand—that are equipped with paper tape readers or floppy disk drives. The current standard is 3-1/2" floppy disks, but 5-1/4" disk drives still exist, so be sure to check the size a machine or disk drive needs before you buy it. The 3-1/2" disks are generally more durable.

Lettering styles, monogram styles and designs stored on electronic circuit boards are interchangeable between some Melco and Tajima models, but could not be used in a Barudan or other brand of machine. Barudan's circuit boards can only be used in Barudan machines. In some models of Tajima machines, the addition of a special keyboard unit may be required to enable it to use Melco circuit boards.

Alphabet and monogramming styles are usually stored on either circuit boards or hard disk. (Stellar 1's alphabets and monograms are on floppy disks.) Because the circuit boards and hard disks are not interchangeable, manufacturers control the lettering styles available for their equipment. A wide variety of styles is available and some may be included with the purchase of a machine. When you're comparing costs, be sure to find out what lettering styles are included.

Stock designs and custom designs are typically stored on floppy disk or paper tape. Because most of the leading brands are able to read these in any of the major formats, you will have no trouble finding and using designs for your machine.

Optional Equipment

Disk drives and paper tape readers may be included with your machine. Others may be sold as options. Be sure you find out what is included in the machine's price, and what else is available as an option.

Cap frames and cap drivers, for example, are usually considered options on cylinder arm machines.

Automatic thread trimmers are available mostly on larger, multi-head equipment because of their expense. Trimmers with durability are thought to be cost-prohibitive on machines with fewer than six heads.

Bobbin sensors (devices that alert the operator when the bobbin thread is getting low) are offered with some multi-head equipment and are standard in the Stellar machine.

Some machines also come with a monitor (a screen that allows you to see a design before sewing), while others offer a monitor as an option. Even those that include monitors may have an upgraded version as an option.

There are also embroidery machine computers and design system computers that are compatible with some standard business application software programs, such as accounting, payroll information and inventory control. A frequently asked question is whether the embroidery software alone can be purchased for those who have existing personal computers. The manufacturers have answered this with a resounding no. Because they are in a niche market, the proprietary information contained in their software is, understandably, wise protection from their being absorbed by conglomerate corporations against their will.

Upgraded software features or added memory capability may be offered as an option. Find out what is available for the models you are considering.

Embroidery Design Equipment

Digitizers are popular for those who want the ability to create their own designs. They are available in many sizes, and with varying features and prices. Digitizing equipment is sold as an optional item or as a stand-alone system by some manufacturers. Melco offers it both ways. Its stand-alone system is the EDS (Embroidery Design System), which features built-in editing capabilities. Gunold + Stickma of America, Marietta, Georgia, offers Punchmaster, a stand-alone design system, which also has editing features. Data-Stitch Inc. of Fort Worth, Texas, offers two systems: The Stitchitizer, probably the most inexpensive design and editing system available, and the Data Stitch Senior, which is IBM compatible. Wilcom (USA) Inc. of Chicago, Illinois, is another manufacturer of design equipment.

The term punching is often used to describe the digitizing process by which design patterns are created. Before the electronic age of embroidery, individual holes were manually punched into cards or tape. When the process was computerized, digitizing became the method. Tapes were still punched, but by an automatic tape punching device. Today, designs are commonly created without paper tape, and even when stored on paper tape, the designer does not physically punch them. Thus, the term punching is becoming outmoded, but many still use it to describe the designing process.

There are significant advantages to having your own design system:

1. It can be more cost-efficient to produce designs in-house rather than sending them to a design center. It depends upon the amount of custom work needed. Several designs per week are the minimum needed to justify the cost of having your own system.
2. Turn-around time for producing the design is usually shortened. Design centers typically quote anywhere from five business days to four weeks to produce a design at their standard fees. The actual time can be even longer if revisions are necessary.
3. The ability to create a custom logo without the expense of paying a design center can be a most effective marketing tool.
4. You can maintain control over how the design is created; e.g., size or size ranges, beginning and ending points, color change sequence, type of stitch used, length and direction of stitches, detailing and so on. The quality of the design is very important to the quality of the embroidery.

Adding a design ***editing*** system also has numerous advantages to designers and embroiderers. True editing enables a designer or embroiderer to change designs by adding, deleting or moving stitches or segments; and by changing the size or any specification of the design. This can be beneficial if the design was not created correctly, or if the design is going to be used in a different way and it needs adjustments, or if a portion of a design is needed to create a wholly separate design.

As you are researching editing features, be sure to get enough specifics about what editing functions are offered. There seems to be a broad use of the term editing. For example, one product on the market advertises editing capability. Yet, the product is only capable of backing out the last mark or command entered. True editing would enable changing marks or commands throughout the design.

When comparing brands of any embroidery equipment, ask specific enough questions about the price, functions and features to be sure you are comparing apples to apples. Find out what is included for the price quoted. If terms are used that seem to be catch-all phrases, such as in the editing example cited, ask for more details and definitions, or ask for a full demonstration of such features.

Support

Warranties on parts and labor are standard in the industry for new machines, and for used machines purchased from some manufacturers. Compare warranties when comparing equipment because the coverage varies from 90 days to one year, depending upon the make and model. Also compare the availability, price and duration of extended warranty agreements.

Should a field service call be necessary, a technician's travel expenses are usually not covered by the warranty. Read your warranty carefully so you thoroughly understand what is and is not covered.

Fortunately, the trend in recent years has been toward more telephone diagnosis of problems. Both Melco's and Barudan's service departments report successful telephone diagnosis in the majority of their calls where problems exist. When parts need to be replaced, instructions are sent or given by phone to the machine operator or whoever will be installing the parts. This makes proximity to service centers less important when selecting which equipment to purchase. However, this factor should not be totally disregarded because the need for a field service call may arise.

Operator's manuals and/or training are usually included with machine purchases. The quality and thoroughness of training is, unfortunately, quite varied. This becomes more critical as technology becomes more sophisticated. Training may consist of an installation technician setting up your equipment, testing it to be sure it is in working condition and showing you basically which buttons to push. More thorough training may involve a classroom session at the manufacturer's or distributor's facility or an independent training school. There you will probably learn more about techniques and in-depth use of your machine's features and functions.

Consultants in the industry are also available to help train, as well as to suggest efficient operating policies and procedures for your business.

Some manufacturers publish newsletters featuring helpful hints, new products, new ideas, policy changes and so on. Trade magazines are also available. *Impressions Magazine* of Dallas, Texas, is mainly for the screenprinting industry, but it also has a section devoted to embroidery. *Stitches Magazine* of Littleton, Colorado, is written exclusively for embroiderers. *Stitches Magazine* also publishes an annual computerized embroidery machine guide, which would be helpful to review as you plan your equipment needs.

Many seminars for embroiderers and designers are also given throughout the year by manufacturers, magazine publishers and trade show sponsors. Most have proven very beneficial to those who attend.

As the industry matures, more support becomes available. However, at this writing there is no well-functioning organization of embroiderers. Trade associations have tried and failed. The reason for failure? Too busy with embroidery work!

Cost

The least expensive models of machinery are the portables. From there, the prices go up to practically whatever you want to spend. Computerized embroidery equipment isn't cheap, but it is affordable if:

1. You do your homework in terms of market research and planning, so you can get financing approved easily.
2. You market your products and/or services well.
3. You price your goods reasonably, yet profitably.
4. You satisfy your customers with good quality and service.
5. You manage the business well.

Only you and your financial advisors or lenders know how much you can afford for equipment. As to how to spend it, make a list of your needs in order of their priority. Add your "wants" to the list, too. Add in all the costs, and then make any necessary adjustments. Once your decision is made, live with it, but don't lose sight of any priorities or "wants" you couldn't afford. Make them your goal; work toward being able to afford them.

Sales representatives can help you assign priorities to your list. They are not interested in overselling their customers because they rely upon heavy repeat business. To oversell or mislead a customer is self-defeating. Take advantage of their knowledge and experience in helping others get started.

Cliff Nixon of Melco South recommends, "When in doubt, err on the side of flexibility. Your market may change from what you think it will be shortly after you open your business. A full-sized sewing field with automatic color change, cap capability, and either design equipment or the ability to add it easily are the right priorities for a small start-up business."

Steve Nunn, Sales Manager of Melco, recommends, "If you go into a machine with four or more heads, have commitments or have the ability to get to that level of production quickly. It's better to have two heads busy than four heads with two of them shut down most of the time."

Don't buy on the basis of price alone. Buy on the basis of ***value***. Price can only be a legitimate factor when two identical products or services are compared. When there are differences in products or services, then there is justifiable reason for a difference in price. Usually, the difference is in the quality, the features, the service and the support.

Consider this quote from the writings of John Ruskin: "It is unwise to pay too much . . . But it's worse to pay too little. When you pay too much, you lose a little money . . . and that is all. When you pay too little, you sometimes lose everything . . . because the thing you bought was incapable of doing what it was bought to do. The common law of business balance prohibits paying a little and getting a lot . . . it can't be done. If you deal with the lowest bidder, it is well to add something for the risk you run. And if you do that, you will have enough to pay for something better."

If the machine's price is not a package deal, you will need to add in the cost of alphabets, hoops, threads, backing and other needed accessories. Also, ask for a recommended list of spare parts.

Used Equipment

If you're considering buying a used machine from someone other than the manufacturer or distributor, find out everything you can first. Get the make, model and serial number. Call the manufacturer to see when the machine was made, if it is still being manufactured, if parts are available for it, and if possible, the service history of the machine. Try to arrange for an authorized technician to examine it. The condition and care of the machine are important in determing a fair price, and later in the successful operation of your business. Be sure to have the technician check that the machine's software is the correct version for the machine and any options added. Also, get proof that the machine is not encumbered by a lease or loan. Your attorney may need to help you with this. An attorney can also help draft a bill of sale and the terms of the sale.

As a rule of thumb for pricing, find out the retail price at the time the machine was originally purchased. Reduce it by 10% just for rolling it out the door, and 10% per year thereafter. If it is a discontinued model or in poor condition, offer an even lower price, or forget it and find a more current model or one in better condition.

Generally speaking, it's safer to buy a used machine from the manufacturer's sales representative or distributor. Usually, they will bring the machine to good working condition and put a 30-day warranty on it. However, good used machines are also available from individuals who go out of business or need a bigger machine or one with more features. Check the trade magazines for ads, then, once again, do your homework.

Space

Measure the height, length and width of the equipment you're considering. Be sure to allow space for service access to the internal workings of the machine, if the machine is too big to move easily. Also be sure your machine will fit through the door. It may sound like a nightmare, but there have been cases where walls have had to be removed so that big machines could be installed! Review Chapter 2 for other space needs.

CHAPTER 5

SITE SELECTION

At Home

The issue of embroiderers working out of their homes has been a highly controversial one in the past. One reason was the Industrial Homework Ban, which resulted from a number of hearings held in the 1940s by the Department of Labor when the Fair Labor Standards and the Fair Wage and Hour Law were first passed. All industries were reviewed, but there were seven industries where homework caused particular problems in the enforcement of minimum wage and overtime provisions. Bans were established against homework in those seven industries, one of which was the embroidery industry. However, during the Reagan administration, the embroidery industry's homework ban was lifted. This became effective Jan. 9, 1989. Now embroiderers can have their machines in their homes, operate their business from their homes, and even employ people in their homes. Local ordinances prevail, however, and many prohibit employees other than family members from working in the home. If your local ordinances do permit you to hire non-family employees, then you must first obtain a certificate to do so. Write to:

Administrator of the Wage and Hour Division
U.S. Department of Labor
200 Constitution Ave., N.W.
Washington, D.C. 20210
Room S-3516

Certification to employ in your home people other than family members must be renewed every two years. There is no fee for such certification.

If you are considering starting your business out of your home, **first check with your city, county and state governments to learn their restrictions**. They may vary, but some of the more common ones are:

1. No employees—The business must be operated by members of the household.

2. No garages or other buildings—The business must be located in the living quarters of the home.
3. Restricted floorspace—The business may not use more than 20% of the total floor space of the home.
4. Licensing—A license must be obtained to operate the business and for collecting sales taxes.
5. Signage—Signs will be restricted in number and size, and the business must have no other outward appearances of a business.
6. Machines—No machines with motors larger than two horsepower are permitted. (Computerized embroidery machines are well within this limit.)

The penalties for non-compliance with such regulations may include hefty fines and/or jail sentences! Usually, though, if you are cited for non-compliance, you'll be allowed a grace period to bring the business into compliance, or the choice of moving or closing the business.

Working at home has numerous advantages and conveniences. For example, you can deduct a portion of your house and utilities payments for tax purposes. Housecleaning and trash pick-up services may also qualify for proportional deductions. If not, at least include those portions in your business expenses. See your tax accountant for guidelines.

You will also avoid traffic and weather-related problems in getting to and from work. If you offer pick-up and delivery service, you still will have to travel, but at least you can schedule it during non-rush-hour periods.

When you work at home, it is not so inconvenient to schedule personal deliveries, repairs on appliances and so on. Some people are also able to run a business with their small children at home, avoiding day care expenses while bringing in additional income. Small children should not be permitted near the machines, however. Safety hazards are abundant, including pins on the floor, fingers getting into machines and electrical shock from outlets, to name three.

Ruth Guenther started her business, Letter Perfect, in her home in Racine, Wisconsin, when her first child was two months old. She selected one machine over another, partially because of the difference in noise levels. She wanted one that would not disturb a sleeping baby. The business is part-time only. Ruth puts her family first, embroidering "on the run" as time permits. On the average, the machine is operating three to four hours per day, but not continuously.

When the Guenthers' second child arrived, so did Ruth's second embroidery machine! Her production doubled, even though now after seven years and a third child, the business is still part-time, with production still at three to four hours per day. Overflow production is sent out to a larger embroidery shop so that ***customers*** are maintained rather than sent elsewhere.

"I have the best of both worlds," exclaims Ruth. "I can be a mother to my children and still own a business that has proven moderately profitable, even on a part-time basis. I have a very supportive husband who is tolerant of interrupted meals when customers come, and of the house not always being clean. I also have friends who know that when they drop in for an unexpected visit, they may be put to work trimming threads. I enjoy what I do, and I am determined to make it work."

It's possible to keep late night or early morning hours when you work at home. For instance, Ruth spends an early morning hour writing programs for the day's work. If you have customers calling or visiting, however, standard business hours are also a must.

A typical problem encountered by those who work at home is getting friends and family used to the work discipline. There may be a tendency for others to assume that you have nothing but free time to devote to them and their plans. You will have to be assertive, yet tactful, and let them know when you are busy and when you can schedule time for this errand or that bridge game and so on.

A separate phone line is advisable. If your personal and business phone numbers are the same, callers will become easily confused. Answering with a plain hello on a business phone, and answering with your business name on a personal line can cause hang-ups.

It's best if you start your home business on good terms with your neighbors, too. If customers are bringing work to you, the extra traffic and parking on your street may annoy them. Address such concerns up front to avoid hassles later.

Another obvious advantage to working at home is saving rent or lease money on a building or store space. This is great for cash flow, but it can be a costly mistake if you do not charge your business something for rent. Because expenses should be considered in determining the pricing of your products and services, you will actually be underpricing if rent is not a factor. Underpricing only serves to reduce the value of embroidery in the marketplace, and it will be difficult for your customers to adjust to price increases when you grow enough to move out of your home and have to start paying rent or lease payments. Therefore, include it from the beginning in your business plan.

Wholesale Location

In most communities, if you are selling and embroidering garments, you'll need to seek a location with a commercial zone (C-1) rating. However, if you are heavily involved in the manufacturing of garments as well, you may need to locate in an industrial zone.

The wholesale shop should be near major transportation arteries for easy accessibility by your customers. Appropriate signage will help make it easy to find. Parking is an important consideration and, if large shipments are involved, a ramp and loading dock will help tremendously. The key is to make it easy for your customers to do business with you.

Of course, from your marketing analysis, you should have a good idea of where your competitors are located. This should be considered in selecting your site. If you have a good idea of who your major customers will be, locating your business convenient to theirs could also be an advantage.

Other factors to consider are available utilities such as sewer, water, power and gas. Is there adequate police and fire protection? What other businesses are in the neighborhood and how will they affect your business?

What is the spirit of the community? Do the business people in the area cross paths frequently or stick to themselves? Is there an active Chamber of Commerce? Are the people involved in community affairs? Is the neighborhood clean and in good repair? These concerns may *seem* irrelevant, but apathy could be a symptom of a dying area.

Cost is an important factor. Not only should you be concerned with the cost per square foot, but also any hidden costs. If rennovation is required (painting; adding, moving or removing walls; electrical or plumbing changes and so on), who pays? Are any utilities included in the rent or lease amount? What does the building insurance cover? Are there any business association expenses involved? Who maintains the grounds? How long is the lease? How much are the taxes? Commercial Realtors should be able to help you select a choice location, keeping in mind all your priorities and needs.

Retail Store

A successful retail setting requires a location that will attract the clientele who will buy the goods you sell. A truly unique store that is already well known or that can advertise heavily will attract the clientele—regardless of its location—so long as it has the basics of accessibility, parking, safety and so on.

Most retail stores count on impulsive buying for a major portion of sales. Therefore, a shopping district with the highest volume of passersby will make the best site. To research those locations that appeal to you, visit at different times of the day and week, track the flow of shoppers, particularly those who buy, as evidenced by the packages they are carrying. Study the type of clientele; for example, men vs. women, age group and dress preferences. This will help you determine if the goods you plan to sell are appropriate for the type of customers drawn to the area.

There are advantages to locating your store near similar type stores. For example, if you sell sweats or fleecewear, by locating near a T-shirt shop (one that does not offer embroidery), you will attract their customers as well as your own. Even if the T-shirt shop also carries fleecewear, yours is personalized with embroidery.

Locating in a mall opens up possibilities for many cooperative arrangements with department and other retail stores. Giving their store clerks an incentive for referral business or offering the other stores coupons for a discount on your personalization service may help sell more garments for them. Of course, the discount amount you give can be paid by the stores you are helping to promote. The more garments you carry that compete with their garments, however, the less likely they will be to work with you. So, if you're going to carry garments, you will either need to have a big enough inventory to compete and be self-sustaining, or be prepared to market outside the mall area for some contract work to supplement your business.

If you specialize in unique items, consider locating near related businesses. Locating near a bed and bath shop or a wallpaper shop or an upholstery shop provides opportunities for cooperative business—in addition to monogramming sheets and towels, placemats or other household linens, these could also be embroidered with the same motif as a wallpaper, or china pattern, or upholstery, to name just a few ideas.

On the other hand, locating near a similar business may saturate the market. One example would probably be gift shops. If there are already gift shops in a shopping area, there may not be sufficient customers to support another, even if the gift items are different. Chances are you would only share a smaller portion of the same market they have.

Here again, a Commercial Realtor can be of great benefit. Make a list of priorities to help you narrow down the site choices. Then, be prepared to be flexible because the ideal site may be either unaffordable or unavailable.

As with the wholesale location, other important factors to consider in choosing a retail site include parking, safety, the condition of the neighborhood, length and terms of the lease, hidden costs and so forth.

A retail store is more expensive than a wholesale operation. Rent averages four to five times as much. A retail store must have aesthetic appeal, as well. The more attractive and interesting you can make it, the better. Therefore, decorating, lighting and displays are needed. Ask about any restrictions the landlord may have in this regard.

Retail location is very dependent upon the goods and services you will offer, the competition on a scope broader than just embroidery, and the volume of shoppers in the area. Plan your market niche well before signing a lease.

CHAPTER 6

BUYING AN EXISTING BUSINESS OR FRANCHISE

Existing Business

Buying an existing business bypasses a lot of the headaches of starting up a new business, but it also requires thorough investigation. First, ask why the business is for sale. Are the owners suffering from poor health or at retirement age? Is the business failing? If the business is failing, is it because of management or marketing problems that you can correct? If so, you may be able to negotiate a bargain price. On the other hand, if the failure is due to poor equipment or sub-quality inventory of merchandise, correction of the problem may be more costly, even considering a bargain price for the business. Failure due to poor service or poor treatment of customers takes more time to correct and probably will require a name change for the business, which, in turn, means new logos, letterhead, ads and so forth.

Have an attorney check to make sure the equipment and property are free of liens, that copyrighted designs are transferable, and what, if any, unfulfilled contracts exist. You will also need an accountant to determine receivables, liabilities and tax liabilities, and to review the records for profitability, net worth and such. The growth rate of the business since its beginning should definitely be determined.

Examine such items as tax returns, sales receipts, freight costs, inventory records, payments for merchandise, payroll and Social Security records. Find out if invoices are discounted, if there are any pending damage claims or lawsuits. Does the building comply with codes? How's the location? Will key personnel leave if the business is sold? Will major customers continue to buy under new ownership?

The price of a business is usually based upon the fair market value of the assets, plus an amount set for the value of its capacity to bring in a profit. Once you have determined these factors, you must decide if you can afford it and how long it will take you to recover the costs. A payback time of five years or fewer is preferable.

The more knowledge you have about a particular business, the better you can negotiate with the seller. Be prepared for a difference in what the seller is asking and what you want to offer. Once you get beyond the financial facts, you must also consider the competition and emotions:

How badly does the seller want to sell?
How badly do you want to buy?
Are there others bidding?
Are there other similar businesses for sale?

Once there is an agreement, have an attorney write a contract. The contract should include:

- A listing and description of everything included in the sale;
- The price;
- The method and time frame for payment;
- A statement of any needed adjustments and how they will be handled. (One example is inventory. A clause should be added to prevent the seller from holding a "going-out-of-business sale" and depleting the inventory. Yet, what inventory can be sold will need to be accounted for at the time of closing);
- Assumption of contracts and liabilities;
- Seller's warranty against false information, inaccurate financial data and undisclosed liabilities;
- A non-compete agreement to prevent seller from starting a similar business in the same area; and
- Time, place and procedures of closing.

The buyer must give notice of the sale to creditors and customers. The notice to creditors should go out as soon as there is an agreement, but before the closing. This will enable any creditors holding heavy debt from the seller to file liens and so forth, which could affect your decision to close.

A notice of new ownership should be sent to the business' existing customers soon after the closing. The tone should be one of your enthusiasm for their continuing to do business with you.

Buying an existing business can have many great advantages: You stand to gain the location, the customers, the equipment, the vendors, the inventory and the employees. If the business has done well, all you have to do is manage it well. The rest of the start-up acquisition process is complete.

As an alternative to buying the business, John King, an attorney with Gorsuch, Kirgis, Campbell, Walker and Grover of Denver, Colorado, suggests consideration be given to buying the assets of the business only. By purchasing the equipment, the inventory and even the customer list, you avoid ownership of the liabilities of the business. This would mean a change in name, and therefore, you would not acquire the reputation or goodwill of the existing business.

Franchise

Investing in a franchise offers the advantages of large-company management and structure to a small business person. If the name is established as a well known enterprise with a good quality of product and service, little or no marketing effort is needed to build the business. This can save years of experience and considerable cost in advertising and promotional expense.

Franchisors may also offer such other benefits as help with site selection and negotiating a store lease, store layout and displays, garments or garment sources, pricing and forms. Training should also be included—business training as well as operation of the equipment. For the inexperienced business person, a franchise structure greatly enhances the chance of success.

The disadvantages of franchising may include exposure to only one brand of equipment; required standards of operation, thus limiting your ability to be the boss; shared profits with the franchisor; time spent preparing reports for the franchisor; a shared burden of possible mismanagement on the part of the franchisor; and limited management decisions.

To date, there have been very few embroidery shop franchisors. One offered embroidery as an add-on service to its T-shirt business. Others offered retail embroidery stores or kiosks in mall settings. These franchisors have sold out while many of their retail store competitors are thriving. New franchisors are starting up, but as yet, there have been none with successful longevity. (Hmm, a possible expansion idea for some of you who are experienced retail embroiderers!)

The newness to the industry seemed to be the downfall of those franchisors. Becky Cooley of Monograms Today in Lafayette, Louisiana, bought her business through a franchisor in the early days of its development (November 1987). The franchisor has since changed ownership and the program is now very different from when she first purchased, but as an inexperienced business person, Becky is still glad she chose the franchise method. The franchisor helped her select equipment, arrange leasing of both the equipment and the store space in the mall, and provided three days of training on the operation of the equipment, plus two days training in sales and pricing. The franchisor also provided garment sources, and a few basic forms, such as daily tally sheets, logo cards and gift certificates. Becky and her husband, Robert Cooley, paid a franchise fee for this assistance. They signed a six-year agreement to pay a flat-rate monthly fee to the franchisor. They realize now how limited this assistance was at the time, but still feel it was the correct way for them to start a business. Their sales have exceeded their monthly operating expenses from the start.

The Cooleys think the lack of experience on the part of the franchisors has enabled them to be more in control of their own business. For example, they designed their own sales order forms and inventory logs, established their own pricing structures, and continue to select their own garments.

Another embroidery franchise is the Waco, Texas-based Monograms Plus, an off-shoot of the T-Shirts Plus franchises. It enables those who do not want or cannot afford a large inventory to enter the retail business for less. The franchise fee is approximately 44% of the total start-up costs; a royalty percentage and advertising fee is added on to that. The franchisor selects the equipment (Meistergram), helps negotiate space at the mall for a kiosk or cart, provides training and assists in getting the business ready for opening. The businesses usually offer such items as T-shirts and sweatshirts, seasonal jackets, towel wraps, tote bags and knapsacks. They rely upon customers bringing in garments purchased elsewhere for 40% to 50% of their business.

When considering a franchise, again involve your attorney and accountant. The franchisor should provide a basic disclosure document that should be reviewed by your legal and financial advisors. Such a document should contain 20 categories of information, according to the J.K. Lasser Tax Institute in its book, How To Run A Small Business:

1. It must provide the name under which the franchise does business, its trademark and the name and address of the parent company.
2. The directors of the franchise and the franchise's chief executives for marketing, service, operations and training should be identified by name, and their business experience and previous employment during the last five years should be revealed.
3. The operators should state the length of time they have been selling the franchise. If the parent company has been selling

other franchises, the names of these franchises and the length of time they have been sold must also be revealed.

4. The franchise owner must reveal and describe the history and settlement of any court actions for felony convictions, embezzlement, restraint of trade, injunctions and civil actions that have been made against any of the franchise operations of any of the franchise owners.
5. The disclosure statement must reveal the bankruptcy history of any of the franchise directors, officers or executors, including reorganization due to insolvency.
6. The franchise business, the product line and probable market for the product must be fully described.
7. There must be a listing of the initial funds required to be paid to the franchise or its affiliates, such as downpayments, rents, inventory costs and other fees.
8. The periodic payments the investor must make to the franchise owners should be fully listed, such as leases and rentals. If some of these fees are expressed as percentages of the outlet's volume, estimates must be provided as to what the percentage fees may amount to.
9. The purchaser must be provided with a list of persons with whom the operation will be required to do business and the affiliation these people have with the franchise.
10. If the purchaser is required to do business with certain people, the disclosure statement must give a basis for calculating what revenue the franchise receives from these people (thus disclosing rebates and kickbacks).
11. The purchaser must be given a list of materials he is required to lease or purchase. If the materials must be purchased from a specific person (including the franchisor), the names and addresses must be provided.
12. Financing arrangements provided directly or indirectly by the franchise must be disclosed, including the names of lenders, amounts to be lent, percentages charged, collateral necessary, and the default provisions.
13. The franchisor must state any limits as to what products may be sold, whom they may be sold to, where they may be sold, and what sales territory is protected.
14. If personal participation in the franchise is required of the investor, a description must be provided of the duties he or she is expected to perform. This may indicate that silent investors are not wanted.

15. The disclosure statement must spell out the terms by which either the purchaser or the franchisor can terminate, cancel or renew the contract to run the franchise. It should also reveal any obligations that might exist after termination or expiration. Is the investor allowed to sell the operation? What are the rights of the purchaser's heirs? If the purchaser should leave the franchise, what would be the nature of any non-compete covenants?
16. The disclosure statement must include statistics as to the number of franchise operations, the number voluntarily terminated, the number terminated by the franchisor, the number for which renewal was refused, and the number of operations canceled by the franchise in the middle of the agreement. The franchisor must also provide the owners' names and addresses of the 10 franchised locations nearest to the one being purchased.
17. It must be stated whether the franchisor must approve the location of the site of the purchaser's operations. If so, the statement must specify the range of time between the signing of the franchise agreement and the site selection, and the usual length of time between the signing of the franchise agreement and the opening date for a purchaser's location.
18. The minimum amount of training required of a franchise operator must be indicated, as well as the type and cost of training offered by the company.
19. If a public figure is involved in the promotion of the franchise, the statement must reveal that person's investment in the franchise, his remuneration, and specifically the celebrity's obligations to the franchise.
20. The franchisor must provide the investor with a balance sheet and income statement for each of the last three years.

Evaluating this information and the willingness of the franchisor to provide it should help you decide if a franchise is for you.

CHAPTER 7

THE BUSINESS PLAN

Remember the cliché—businesses don't plan to fail; they fail to plan. Oh sure, we can name some who succeeded without a business plan, but that style of business leaves much to luck or chance. That is especially tenuous, considering the competition facing today's embroiderers. Good financial planning and management are two of the surest ways to avoid failure because you can spot problems before they get out of control and build upon strengths for greater profitability. You'll achieve the goals you have established.

The business plan will also be your best sales tool for raising needed capital. A bank or leasing company may require only certain parts of the total plan; however, your investors will expect a fully rounded plan.

A business plan is not just for start-up businesses. Existing embroidery shops can *and should* prepare more accurate plans, because there is a history of financial data, assuming appropriate records have been kept.

A one-year plan is a good place to start. It should be reviewed monthly and adjusted at least quarterly. Eventually, up to five years should be planned at a time if you would like the business to grow or even maintain present levels in a more competitive environment.

A complete business plan consists of three major components: (1) a dialogue about the business; (2) financial data; and (3) supporting documents.

Dialogue

The dialogue should consist of a written summary of the business, including a description, the market, the competition, the location, personnel and any unique concepts you bring to the industry such as protected designs, exclusive rights to sell a certain garment or special licensing arrangements. Describe any assumptions you have made about the industry and how your business will fit into the industry. What do you plan to accomplish, what changes will you make and what steps will you take to fulfill your plans? If you have an existing business and are adding something new or making any change in direction, describe those changes and what steps you will take to implement them.

Financial Data

First, list any and all sources and application of income. This could be from other jobs, savings, loans, leases, lines of credit and such.

Next, make a list of all existing capital equipment, such as the embroidery machines, furniture, office equipment to name a few.

Balance Sheet

If you have an existing embroidery business, prepare a balance sheet based on actual figures. If you are a start-up business, your balance sheet will be *pro forma*, or projected figures. (See Exhibit 3 for a sample balance sheet format.)

It is a good idea to prepare balance sheets at start-up, and monthly or quarterly for the first year, as well as at the end of each fiscal year thereafter. The balance sheet shows the bottom-line worth of a business and how that worth is distributed.

Net worth equals assets minus liabilities. Current assets include cash, receivables, inventory, securities and anything that can be converted to cash within one year. Fixed assets are long-term items such as land, equipment and furniture. They are recorded on the balance sheet at net cost less accumulated depreciation. Other assets may include copyrighted designs, royalties due and any notes receivable from officers or employees of the business.

There are also intangible assets such as the reputation and goodwill your business enjoys in the community.

The third category of assets is owner's equity. This includes capital investments and retained earnings.

Liabilities are the debts the business accrued. Current liabilities, owed but not paid, include accounts payable, notes payable to the bank or other loan sources, wages and benefits, current portions due on long-term debt, and all obligations due within one year. Long-term liabilities are mortgages, long-term bank loans, equipment loans or leases, and any debt with a maturity factor of longer than one year.

Statement Of Income

The statement of income (or profit and loss statement) is a record of the company's sales and expenses. Prepare it at the same intervals as the balance sheet. The categories in this statement are net sales (gross sales less returns and allowances), cost of goods sold (cost of inventory and labor), gross margin (gross profit on sales before operating expenses), selling and operating expenses (wages, payroll taxes, benefits, rent, utilities, maintenance, supplies, insurance, depreciation, travel and advertising), operating profit, other income, other expenses (such as interest), net profit before taxes, income taxes and net profit after tax. (See Exhibit 4.)

The formula used to derive the statement of income is net sales less cost of goods sold equals gross margin, less selling and operating expenses, equals operating profit, plus other income, less other expenses, equals net profit, less income taxes, equals net profit after tax. The flow chart that follows outlines this formula:

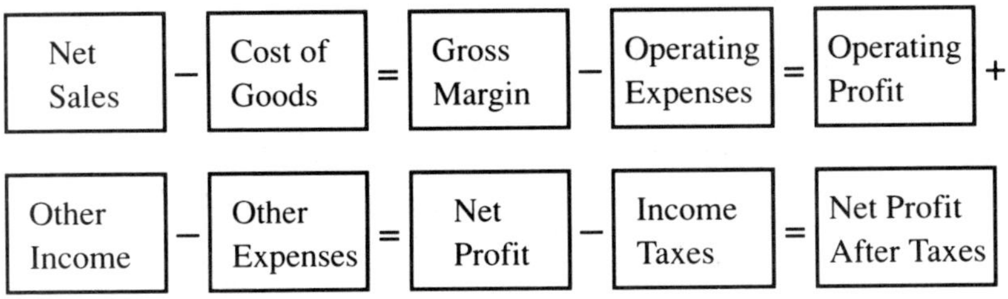

Cash Flow Statement

Sometimes called a *pro forma* income statement, the cash flow statement is a projection of business performance. (See Exhibit 5.) This process is a standard requirement on loan and lease applications.

An existing business can base projections on prior financial statements. You may then assume, for example, that sales will increase, say 10%. To determine the projected sales, multiply last year's net sales figure by 1.10. Look for trends in monthly sales volumes to determine slow and peak seasons, then adjust your projections accordingly. Or, if you are dissatisfied with the slow season and want more year-round business, a new marketing plan may be in order. Any new marketing efforts you employ should be reflected in the cash flow statement. You must also anticipate any changes in cost of goods sold or expenses, such as price increases in garments, wage increases for employees, additional equipment needed, changes in rent, increased advertising and so forth.

If you are just starting your business, your best guesstimate will have to do. However, the figures should not just be pulled out of thin air. You can develop educated estimates through good planning and by gathering cost information. Preparing a marketing plan will also help. These exercises will force you to think through what it will take to be successful, to see if your plans lead to a bottom-line profit, and to determine if the cash will be available every month to pay operating expenses.

A monthly comparison with actual performance will keep you alert as to how your business is doing. Only through this procedure can you accurately pinpoint problems and develop remedies. You may find that more effort is needed in collections, or perhaps the cost of goods sold is too high, or maybe variable expenses need to be controlled better. It may be that a price increase is in order. If your cash flow statement indicates a profit, yet your actual performance shows a loss, it will be easy to locate the line items that went over or under projections, and determine exactly why the loss occurred. This is better than sitting back wondering how such a thing could happen, and using trial and error to change things, hoping one of those changes will address the unknown problem!

The cash flow statement also serves as a budget. You will know when certain funds are due and can make sure they are available. You will have the advantage of scheduling purchases and payments. This has the added benefit of protecting your valuable credit rating, so that when additional funds are needed, you won't be caught without the necessary cash. Protecting your credit rating is vital to your ability to get more capital when you need it. It also protects you from being charged the highest interest rates reserved for those high-risk accounts labeled as "slow paying."

Break-Even Analysis

This study shows the level of financial activity needed to maintain a business at neither a profit nor a loss. It provides insight into the relationship between volume, costs and revenue.

There are several methods of analysis, depending upon whether you address sales in terms of dollars or units sold. A retail shop should calculate the break-even point in sales dollars. This assumes:

1. A change in sales volume will not affect the selling price per unit;
2. Fixed expenses will remain the same at similar volume levels; and
3. Variable expenses will increase or decrease in direct proportion to the sales volume.

Classify your expenses into two categories: variable and fixed. Convert the variable expenses to a percentage of sales (sales divided by variable expenses). Then apply the following formula:

S = F + V (Sales at break-even point)
F = Fixed expenses
V = Percentage of variable expenses to sales

For example:

Sales	=	\$250,000
Variable expenses	=	\$137,500 or 55%
Fixed expenses	=	\$100,000

S	=	F + V
S	=	\$100,000 + .55 S
S – .55 S	=	\$100,000
.45 S	=	\$100,000
S	=	\$222,222

Check your math:

Sales at break-even	\$222,222
Less variable expenses at 55%	122,222
Marginal income	\$100,000
Less fixed expenses	100,000
Profit/Loss	\$ 0

Suppose you want to determine the break-even point to obtain a certain level of net income, perhaps \$40,000. The formula then becomes:

$$
\begin{aligned}
S &= F + V + \text{Desired net income} \\
S &= \$100{,}000 + .55S + \$40{,}000 \\
S - .55\,S &= \$140{,}000 \\
.45\,S &= \$140{,}000 \\
S &= \$311{,}111
\end{aligned}
$$

Wholesale or contract embroidery shops might do better calculating the break-even point based upon units to be sold. This can be per job to help determine pricing or profitability. If you do a large volume of caps, for example, your unit measure can be caps. If you're doing various jobs, the number of stitches would be your units. A reason for calculating break-even point based on units is that the price is subject to change depending on volume, because it is customary to offer quantity discounts. Figuring break-even on units is easier to determine with variable pricing than on sales dollars. For this formula, you will need to calculate based on the different prices charged.

$$\text{Break-even sales} = \frac{\text{Fixed expenses}}{\text{Unit sales price} - \text{Unit variable expenses}}$$

(S = Units)

$$S = \frac{\$100{,}000}{\$20 - \$11} = \frac{\$100{,}000}{\$9}$$

$$S = 11{,}111 \text{ units}$$

Based on the above, you must sell 11,111 units at \$20 to break even.

To determine break-even point in units needed to sell to obtain a desired net income (\$40,000), the formula becomes:

$$S = \frac{\text{Fixed expenses} + \text{Net income}}{\text{Unit sales price} - \text{Unit variable expenses}}$$

$$S = \frac{\$100{,}000 + \$40{,}000}{\$20 - \$11} = \frac{\$140{,}000}{\$9}$$

$$S = 15{,}555 \text{ units}$$

Break-even analysis is a very helpful way to learn how to price your embroidery and embroidered goods. It is not enough to just keep the machines running, thinking that more work means more profit. If your work is not profitable, you must lower your costs or raise your prices.

Supporting Documents

The final section of your business plan should include such items as:

Personal resumes	Letters of intent
Job descriptions	Copies of leases
Personal financial statements	Contracts
Credit reports	Legal documents
Letters of reference	Marketing plans

Exhibit 3
Balance Sheet

Name of Company
Date

Cash	$2,342	Notes payable, bank (Maturities of one year or less)	$3,500
Accounts receivable	1,933		
Prepaid expenses	1,184	Accounts payable	820
Inventory	5,950	Accruals	600
Total current assets	$11,409	Total current liabilities	$4,920
Equipment and fixtures	30,725	Total liabilities	21,475
Total other assets	30,725	Net worth*	20,739
Owners equity	5,000		
Total equity assets	5,000		
Total assets	$47,134	Total liabilities and net worth	$47,134

*Assets – Liabilities = Net worth

Exhibit 4

STATEMENT OF INCOME (PROFIT AND LOSS STATEMENT)

	MONTH 1	MONTH 2	MONTH 3	MONTH 4	MONTH 5	MONTH 6	MONTH 7	MONTH 8	MONTH 9	MONTH 10	MONTH 11	MONTH 12
Total net sales												
Cost of sales												
GROSS PROFIT												
Controllable expenses												
Salaries												
Payroll taxes												
Security												
Advertising												
Automobile												
Dues and subscriptions												
Legal and accounting												
Office supplies												
Telephone												
Utilities												
Miscellaneous												
Total controllable expenses												
Fixed expenses												
Depreciation												
Insurance												
Rent												
Taxes and licenses												
Loan payments												
Total fixed expenses												
TOTAL EXPENSES												
Other income												
Other expenses												
NET PROFIT (LOSS)												
(Before taxes)												
Taxes												
NET PROFIT (LOSS)												

Exhibit 5

CASH FLOW STATEMENT

NAME OF BUSINESS

OWNER

YEAR	Pre-start-up Position Estimate	Pre-start-up Position Actual	Month 1 Estimate	Month 1 Actual	Month 2 Estimate	Month 2 Actual	Month 3 Estimate	Month 3 Actual
1. CASH ON HAND (Beginning of month)								
2. CASH RECEIPTS								
(a) Cash sales								
(b) Collections from credit accounts								
(c) Loan or other cash injection (Specify)								
3. TOTAL CASH RECEIPTS (2a+2b+2c=3)								
4. TOTAL CASH AVAILABLE (Before cash out) (1+3)								
5. CASH PAID OUT								
(a) Purchases (Merchandise)								
(b) Gross wages (Excludes withdrawals)								
(c) Payroll expenses (Taxes and so on)								
(d) Outside services								
(e) Supplies (Office and operating)								
(f) Repairs and maintenance								
(g) Advertising								
(h) Car, delivery, and travel								
(i) Accounting and legal								
(j) Rent								
(k) Telephone								
(l) Utilities								
(m) Miscellaneous								
(n) Taxes (Real estate and so forth)								
(o) Interest								
(p) Other expenses (Specify each)								
(q) Miscellaneous (Unspecified)								
(r) Subtotal								
(s) Loan principal payment								
(t) Capital purchases (Specify)								
(u) Other start-up costs								
(v) Reserve and/or escrow (Specify)								
(w) Owner's withdrawal								
6. TOTAL CASH PAID OUT (Total 5a through 5w)								
7. CASH POSITION (End of month) (4 minus 6)								
ESSENTIAL OPERATING DATA (Non-cash flow information)								
A. Sales volume (Dollars)								
B. Accounts receivable (End of month)								
C. Bad debt (End of month)								
D. Inventory on hand (End of month)								
E. Accounts payable (End of month)								
F. Depreciation								

CHAPTER 8

FINDING FUNDS

The most common way to finance a small business is with a combination of your own cash assets—savings and CDs—with the balance in the form of a bank loan. Even if you can afford to pay cash, it's smart to borrow. The cash can be used for other start-up costs and for monthly operating expenses until the business is self-supporting. If you do pay cash, you should consider it a loan to your business and pay it back monthly. This makes sense in terms of tax advantages, and also helps ensure that your pricing reflects the actual cost of the equipment.

If you have been in business before, you will usually have an advantage in getting a bank to loan you money because of your experience. If your business reputation is good, if your credit rating is good, and if your business has been profitable, you should have no problem. Be prepared to provide financial statements for the past two or three years, along with your projected financial statement and monthly cash flow projections for the new venture. If you are starting your first business, you will be expected to show a personal financial statement. (See Exhibit 6.)

However, many people have been turned down by banks because their loan officers were unfamiliar with computerized embroidery. Some bankers view the purchase of such equipment as highly speculative. In such cases, the most convincing approach is to present contracts and letters of intent as part of your proposal. If that is not possible, be prepared to show samples of embroidered work, competitive profile sheets (which help substantiate that such businesses do exist), your market analysis and your business plan. The more research and facts you present, the better your chances of gaining approval of your loan.

Lending institutions will also be examining your abilities as a business manager. The image you project will not only affect the loan application outcome, but also the interest rate you will be charged if your loan is approved. This is another reason to be prepared with all the financial facts. It will demonstrate your ability to assess a business situation, which is vitally important to your success.

If you are turned down for a bank loan, do not despair. Ask the bank for a written assessment and the reason for rejection. Then, address these problem areas and try elsewhere: other banks, savings and loan institutions, credit unions and so on.

It has been said that the time to borrow money is when you *have* money. There is a good deal of truth in that statement. Lending institutions are most concerned with a person's ability to repay a loan. Banks don't have any use for repossessed embroidery equipment. For this reason, they usually will require a mortgage on your house or other collateral to secure the loan. Other sources of income will also help. If you are starting the business in your spare time while retaining income from other employment, you can easily demonstrate minimal risk to the bank.

If you have one or more loan rejections from a bank, the Small Business Administration (SBA) may be able to help you. The SBA will guarantee 85% to 90% of your loan, if approved, depending upon the amount you are borrowing.

You may also be well advised to lease embroidery equipment, rather than include this in your bank loan. Many businesses find this a tax advantage (consult your tax accountant to determine how leasing would affect your particular situation), but there are many other advantages to leasing. Usually, less cash down is required. Banks usually loan no more than 75% to 80% of the amount needed, whereas a leasing company will go as high as 90%, depending upon your financial situation. This may sound like a small amount, but in terms of cash dollars, it could go a long way towards needed capital for monthly operating expenses. Likewise, leasing your equipment frees up your line of credit at the bank for operating expenses or start-up costs. Leasing companies will also finance training fees, extended warranty agreements and other add-ons, whereas a bank usually will not include these in their loan amounts.

Do not confuse equipment leasing with apartment-type leasing. Equipment leases are usually structured as lease purchases. They are long-term commitments, not monthly rentals to be cancelled at any time. The duration can be up to five years, with either a 10% or $1 buy-out fee at the end of the lease. As with a bank loan, the lease duration and equipment value determine the monthly payments, but with a lease the type of buy-out (10% or $1) will also affect the monthly payment amount. Because of the advantages of leasing, interest rates are usually higher than bank loans.

Your equipment sales representative should be able to recommend a leasing company to you. It is wise to use those recommended because they are usually already familiar with embroidery equipment. This will save the time of explaining and convincing someone unfamiliar with the industry that there really is a market for embroidery!

As an alternative to loans or leasing, or in combination with these methods, you may want to seek venture capitalists. Venture capital firms provide working funds for a business in exchange for an equity interest in the business. They become your partner or a shareholder. Whereas a bank or leasing company makes money from interest returns, venture capitalists are interested in the long-term growth and increased value of your business, in which they share ownership. They expect to sell their portion of the business at a later date for a profit. Such profits are taxable as capital gains, rather than ordinary income. Because of their long-term interest in your business, your management expertise becomes even more important; thus, the complete business plan outlined in Chapter 7 will probably be needed. Your accountant and attorney may be good sources for finding venture capitalists.

Private investors are another source of funding. Family members, friends and business acquaintances may be interested. If you don't know of anyone who would make a good investor, there is the Ad-Venture approach, in which brokers will find lenders for you. They will charge a fee, usually a percentage, right off the top. If you use this method, be sure to check into the background of those lenders found for you before signing any agreements, and have your attorney review the arrangements to be sure there are no violations of the law. One such company you may wish to write is Venture Capital Networks Inc., P.O. Box 882, Durham, New Hampshire 03824. This firm's business is to match venture capitalists with companies seeking investors.

The SBA may be a good source of other financial aid sources. Small Business Investment Companies (SBICs) are licensed by the SBA to supply equity capital to companies unable to raise funds from other sources.

Special funding is often available through the SBA for special circumstances. Minorities, women, handicapped people, and Vietnam veterans sometimes receive special consideration, not only in the form of loans, but also government grants that never have to be repaid. Such grants may also be available for those starting a business to do work for the government or to export goods.

Exporting embroidered goods seems unlikely at this writing, because embroidery can usually be done for less in most foreign countries. In fact, much embroidery is imported to this country.

However, if you can gain a contract for such work, the government may be a possible source of capital. This usually requires a lot of time and red tape to pull it all together, but it could prove worthwhile if you're patient. Of course, you can start your business and then apply for government work, seeking grant money for expansion if a contract is acquired. Funding from the SBA is not restricted to start-up costs.

Once you are in business, other types of loans may be useful or necessary. Those who are well established with the highest credit standing and who have a good history with their financial institution may be granted ***character loans***. These are of short-term duration and are unsecured—no collateral is needed.

A ***line of credit*** may be established on a revolving basis. The banker will establish a maximum amount of credit and certain conditions that apply to its usage. This type of financing is useful for occasional cash flow problems or seasonal slumps.

Term loans are either of short duration, from 30 days to a maximum of one year, or long duration, running more than 5 years, sometimes for as long as 10 or 15 years. Collateral, as well as excellent credit, is usually necessary. Payments may be negotiated for monthly, quarterly, semi-annual or annual installments, or a series of notes may be established to come due at specified times.

Collateral loans may also be short-term or long-term. Your inventory may be acceptable collateral for shorter durations, whereas longer term loans may need to be secured by real estate, stocks, bonds or life insurance.

Commercial credit or finance companies may loan money based on your accounts receivable. The lender may assume the accounts and be responsible for all collection responsibilities. However, as the borrower, you are still required to pay the loan in full should the accounts receivable not cover the full amount. This type of borrowing is rare in the embroidery business, because most are small businesses with relatively small accounts receivable.

Suppliers may grant trade credit. For example, you may purchase a large quantity of jackets, and make monthly payments or otherwise delay full payment. The supplier may go along with a slight extension at no charge, but over longer periods will probably charge you interest on the unpaid portion. You may also lose cash discounts that are often available for paying right away. Trade credit may prove wise in certain situations, but always be sure it is agreeable to the supplier. Blatant failure to pay on time without such an agreement will result in an unfavorable credit rating, a poor reputation in the industry, suppliers refusing to do business with you, or legal action. Proper cash flow planning can usually prevent such situations. When unforeseen circumstances make it necessary to delay paying a creditor, honesty and a sincere desire to meet your obligations will usually be met favorably by your suppliers.

Exhibit 6

PERSONAL FINANCIAL STATEMENT **CONFIDENTIAL**

TO: First National Bank, Westminster

The undersigned furnishes the following true Financial Statement as of ______________, 19____, to the above named Bank:

Name__________________________________ Number of Dependents ____________________________

Home Address___________________________ Home Phone___________Business Phone_____________

Business Address_________________________ Occupation_______________________________________

Purpose of Loan__________________________ Place of Employment______________________________

ASSETS				LIABILITIES			
Cash in First Nat'l Bank, Westminster				Notes Payable - Banks			
Cash in Others				To:			
(Give Name)				To:			
Stocks and Bonds (see schedule)				To:			
Investment in Own Business Book Value (% owned)				Notes Payable - Others To:			
Accounts and Notes Receivable				To:			
Accounts and Notes Receivable from relatives				To: Real Estate Mortgages Payable			
Real Estate Owned (see schedule)				To:			
Automobile(s)				To:			
Personal Property				To:			
Cash Value - Life Insurance				Accounts Payable			
Investments other than above (itemize)				Unpaid Taxes			
				Other Debts (itemize)			
				TOTAL LIABILITIES			
				NET WORTH (Total Assets minus Total Liabilities)			
TOTAL ASSETS				TOTAL LIABILITIES & NET WORTH			

Personal Information:

If this Financial Statement is being submitted to obtain secured credit or joint credit with a co-applicant, complete the following information:

Co-Applicant's Name_______________________ Employment_______________________________

APPLICANT SOURCE OF INCOME				CO-APPLICANT SOURCE OF INCOME			
Salary				Salary			
Commission and Bonus				Commission and Bonus			
Dividends and Interest				Dividends and Interest			
Real Estate Income (net)				Real Estate Income			
Other - You need not disclose income from alimony, child support or maintenance or the source of such income unless you choose to disclose it for repayment purposes.				Other - You need not disclose income from alimony, child support or maintenance or the source of such income unless you choose to disclose it for repayment purposes.			
TOTAL				TOTAL			
CONTINGENT LIABILITIES				**CO-APPLICANT CONTINGENT LIABILITIES**			
As endorser, co-maker or guarantor?				As endorser, co-maker or guarantor?			
Leases or contracts?				Leases or contracts?			
INSURANCE				**INSURANCE**			
Life Insurance in force				Life Insurance in force			
Health and Accident Insurance in force				Health and Accident Insurance in force			

OVER - COMPLETE ALL SCHEDULES AND SIGN ON REVERSE SIDE

GENERAL INFORMATION

Partner or officer in any other venture or other employment? ______________________

Do you have a will?__________ Approximate date?____________ Name of executor__________________

Are you a defendant in any legal action? If so explain ______________________

Are there any unsatisfied judgments?__________ Have you ever taken bankruptcy?__________________

Personal bank accounts carried at: ______________________ ______________________

Name - Checking Account No. Name - Checking Account No.

COMPLETE THE FOLLOWING SCHEDULE IN DETAIL

SCHEDULE OF STOCKS AND BONDS OWNED

No. of shares or Par Value of Bonds	Description	In Name Of	Market Value	Market Where Traded	Pledged

REAL ESTATE OWNED

Description and Location	Title in Name of	Date Acquired	Purchase Price	Market Value	Mortgage Amount	Mortgage Payment	Mortgage Maturity	Type (FHA etc)
Residence:								
Other:								

SCHEDULE OF NOTES PAYABLE

Creditor	Note in Name of	Balance	Monthly Payment	Collateral

CREDIT REFERENCE

Name	Date	High Credit	Basis

The foregoing Financial Statement has been furnished to the above named Bank by the undersigned for the purpose of inducing the Bank to advance credit, to make loans, to grant renewals or extensions of credit or loans to, or accept the obligations of the undersigned, alone or jointly with other persons, and is represented and warranted to be a true and accurate statement of the financial condition of the undersigned. The undersigned further represents and warrants that title to all of the assets listed herein is in the sole name of the undersigned unless otherwise noted. The undersigned agrees to notify the Bank immediately of any material change in the financial condition represented herein which may occur while the undersigned is indebted or obligated to the Bank, and, in the absence of such notification, the undersigned represents and warrants the continuing truth and accuracy of this statement for purposes of any future occasion on which the undersigned requests or is granted an additional credit loan or a renewal or extension of any debt or obligation of the undersigned to the Bank. The undersigned certifies that both sides hereof and the information inserted therein has been read and is true and correct. I authorize the Bank to obtain a Consumer Credit Report or/and contact the above references and to report the credit history of this account as allowed by law. The undersigned agrees that this application and any records generated in connection with credit granted to the undersigned are the property of the Bank.

______________________ ________ ______________________ ________

Applicant's Signature Date Co-Applicant's Signature Date

S.S. No.__________________ ________ S.S. No.__________________ ________

Birth Date Birth Date

Witness:______________________ Witness:______________________

CHAPTER 9

NEVER STOP LEARNING

There is an old saying, "The more you know, the more you know you *don't* know." Computerized embroidery is not as simple as the handwork Grandma used to do on pillow cases. There is a lot to learn—not only about managing your business, but also about the rapidly changing technology of the machines, fabrics, designs, hooping, threads, needles and much more.

Fortunately, today there are many sources available for learning. Those who used mechanical embroidery machines, and began businesses when computerized equipment was first introduced, as well as those who manufacture and sell the equipment, have pioneered the methods. They learned the hardest and most time consuming way: by trial and error. You can shorten the learning curve substantially by taking advantage of their expertise.

Manufacturer's Classes

When you first acquire a new or used piece of equipment, or when you hire an operator who is unfamiliar with your equipment, schedule training with the manufacturer if it is available. This is a far better option than relying on field service technicians; frankly, they are not known for their thoroughness in training. They are very adept at installing equipment and ensuring that it is in proper working condition, but service and repair are their fields—not the production of versatile, high quality embroidery.

The training available from a manufacturer will generally either be classroom-style or hands-on in nature. The classroom method of learning is more in-depth with regard to the features and operation of your machine and will include the basics of application techniques. Hands-on training, where the student actually uses the equipment, is the best method. This approach also has the advantage of getting you away from such interruptions as phone calls, customers, employees, children and so on. In the classroom setting, you can devote full attention to learning your equipment.

Even experienced embroiderers may benefit from a refresher course with a manufacturer. It's far too common for embroiderers to purchase equipment with sophisticated features designed to make embroidery better, easier, faster or more versatile, and then waste their investment by not learning how to use those features. Programming, digitizing and editing are areas where this frequently occurs. If you have these capabilities and are not using them to their fullest extent, do yourself a favor and enroll in a class!

Even after you've gone through basic training, you're still not ready for the business battle zone. Thoroughly read and comprehend your operator's manual and any other material provided by your manufacturer or distributor. If you have questions, feel free to call them. Most are very good about spending whatever time is needed to help you understand and master a procedure.

Experiment & Practice

The next step is to practice using your machine and working with different fabrics. There are charts and articles available to use as practice guidelines, (one such guide is included in this book), but there is no substitute for experience and gaining the feel of your machine and various fabrics first-hand. **Don't make the mistake of accepting orders for immediate delivery in your business' first few weeks!** Until you've had sufficient practice, there is a high risk of operator error in using the machine, improper techniques of hooping and setting tensions, incorrect spacing, or inappropriate sizing or placement. Keep in mind that your business depends on repeat orders from customers; their first impression of your work is critical.

A good way to begin using your embroidery machine is to run a complete sew-out of all of your lettering styles and designs. Sew them on felt. It is relatively inexpensive material, and its nature will hide minor imperfections. Watch these designs as they are stitched and take notes for future reference. Note such things as starting and stopping points, any heavy or light areas where density could be adjusted, and any adjustments needed for width, if you have the ability to make such adjustments. This will certainly acquaint you with the details of your styles and designs, but here's the bonus: these sew-outs can then be placed in plastic sheets, inserted in a notebook and used as an ideal sales portfolio. You can also frame them and arrange them on your shop walls in a decorative, selling display. Make them colorful and large enough to attract the attention of potential customers. Creating a sample sew-out is a good habit to form whenever you acquire a new design or lettering style.

Next, purchase remnants of various fabrics for further experimentation. Some should be knits, some should be woven goods. Select both loosely and tightly knit and woven materials. Choose fabrics of various weights, too, from heavy denim to sheer chiffon. Experiment with different fibers as well, from pure cotton, linen, rayon and so forth, to those that are blends. Choose some that are smooth and some with a nap like terry cloth and corduroy. Then, refer to your collected fabric charts and start practicing. Try the recommended backings, toppings and needles, according to the chart. Watch as they sew and again, make notes about any needed adjustments. If you see something that needs improvement, make only one change at a time so as to remove any guesswork about what adjustments correct the problem. Changing the backing, the needle size or type, and the tension all at once before the next run will leave you still wondering what actually made the difference. This exercise will prove time-consuming, but it's better to go through it all in the beginning than to have to experiment with every future job to attain consistent high quality.

Now you're ready for actual garments. Just this once, don't give that bag of used clothing to your favorite charity. Use it for practicing hooping, measuring, placement and color coordination. Then go through your closets and drawers, and embroider your own towels, shirts, sheets and so on. You need the practice *now*, and besides, once your business takes off you won't have time to do all of your personal items! If you still need the practice and aren't too busy, keep embroidering. Use generic designs on sample garments or on gifts for family, friends and prospective customers.

Publications

Get on the mailing list for your manufacturer's and/or distributor's newsletters and any other communications they may provide. Keep them informed of any changes in your name, address or phone so you won't miss any issues. These publications will help keep you informed about new products, policies, helpful hints, success stories and many other items of interest. Usually, your name is automatically placed on their mailing list when you make your first purchase, but if you bought used equipment from another source, you will have to make yourself known to your suppliers as a customer and request their publications.

As mentioned in Chapter 4, there are two industry magazines available for embroiderers: *Stitches Magazine*, which is devoted exclusively to embroidery, and *Impressions*, which is mainly for screenprinters, but also contains a section on embroidery. I recommend you subscribe to both to gain all the available information you can about your chosen field. In addition to the articles written by their own staff members, various experts contribute articles on a variety of subjects relevant to embroiderers. The magazines are also useful for finding suppliers of garments, embroidery supplies and designers, because many suppliers advertise in these publications. They are also good sources for ideas, trends and management tips. Here's how to reach these magazines:

STITCHES MAGAZINE
Wiesner Publishing
5951 S. Middlefield Road
Littleton, CO 80123

IMPRESSIONS
Gralla Publications
P.O. Box 801402
Dallas, TX 75380-9990

If you specialize in a certain segment, or plan to also sell garments, there may be other publications that would be helpful:

BOBBIN INTERNATIONAL INC. 1110 Shop Road P.O. Box 1986 Columbia, SC 29202	(For apparel manufacturers, with occasional articles on fashion and fabric trends.)
THE PRESS 5951 S. Middlefield Road Littleton, CO 80123	(Screenprinting and custom apparel retailing, with ideas on merchandising, wholesale and retail shops and trends.)
PRINTWEAR P.O. Box 1416 Broomfield, CO 80020	(Screenprinting.)
SCREEN PRINTING 407 Gilbert Ave. Cincinnati, OH 45273-9799	(Screenprinting only, but good for trends, creative ideas and designs.)

SPORTING GOODS BUSINESS*
P.O. Box 1935
Clinton, IA 52735-1935

SPORTING GOODS DEALER*
Sporting News Publishing Co.
1212 N. Lindbergh Blvd.
St. Louis, MO 63132

SPORTS TREND*
Shore Communications, Inc.
P.O. Box 1505
Riverton, NJ 08077

TEAM SPORTS BUSINESS
13402 N. Scottsdale Road.
B-185
Scottsdale, AZ 85254
(Team uniforms and equipment.)

*These three publications are sources of sports fashion trends and ideas. They are free to qualified wholesalers and retailers.

Seminars & Workshops

Many embroidery seminars are offered throughout the year in different regions of the United States. They are presented by various manufacturers and distributors, trade show sponsors and magazine publishers.

Relevant topics are addressed by many different speakers. Some events include the opportunity to see products demonstrated and to buy them at a discount. Other events offer open discussion among the attendees. It has been my experience through hosting the seminars sponsored by Melco Industries, and in speaking for others, that 99% of attendees enthusiastically endorse the events as well worth their time and money.

For example, Verl Chase, owner of C & C Monograms in Bellevue, Nebraska, attends a seminar program every year and is, without fail, the first to register! He says he always learns something new and he likes meeting other embroiderers.

Ruth Guenther of Letter Perfect in Racine, Wisconsin, is another workshop regular. She brings her entire family and combines seminars with a vacation.

It is gratifying to me to observe the open exchange of information that occurs among competitors at such seminars. Embroiderers are very willing to share experiences with those who ask, and as a group, they are open-minded to learning better ways and new ideas. Seminar participants often swap business cards to expand their resources for information, find subcontractors or continue newly formed friendships. Successful embroiderers are ideal role models for those who are just beginning or those who want to expand, and a seminar is a great place to meet such a role model.

The positive atmosphere of these events is invigorating, as everyone's passion for embroidery is renewed and the enthusiasm spreads. Take advantage of these opportunities.

Trade Shows

All major suppliers of equipment, accessories, gadgets and garments participate in numerous trade shows throughout the year to display their wares. These are great ways for embroiderers to keep up with new technology, collect fashion ideas, do comparison shopping and possibly even find a bargain. Many embroiderers attend, so again it's an opportunity to establish and renew valuable business contacts. Refer to the industry magazines or call your manufacturer or distributor to find out about trade show dates and locations.

Consultants

Over the past few years, some good embroidery consultants have emerged. These fee-paid professionals will visit your shop or host a class at their facilities to evaluate your problems and recommend solutions. They can help with training, organizing and arranging your shop; with attaining higher productivity and profitability; and with just about any problems or weak areas needing attention. The good ones are very quality conscious and understand the details of fine embroidery so well that they can quickly troubleshoot, saving you precious time, money and a lot of frustration. Here are the names of a few of them, and a description of their areas of expertise:

Frank Gawronski is the CEO of Embroidery Educational Services Int'l. in Columbus, Ohio. He is also an independent consultant. His specialties are training, production efficiency, troubleshooting and pricing. He gives special attention to helping embroiderers understand and use the full capabilities of their computerized equipment. Frank is knowledgeable on most all systems and has successfully helped small, medium-sized and large embroidery shops.

Walter Floriani, Jr. is the CEO of Floriani Embroidery Enterprises in Tehachapi, California. This company is multi-functional, being composed of a design center, a training center for artists and for those who digitize. Walter also performs consulting work, specializing in production efficiency and designing for production. A firm believer in profitable production, Walter teaches the importance of understanding what is involved in producing top quality designs that run smoothly on the machines. Therefore, his emphasis is on the marriage of operators and designers that helps a shop achieve efficient, top quality work.

Barbara Chmara owns and operates Barbara's Embroidery in Tucson, Arizona. She is also a consultant, specializing in sales and marketing strategies, production efficiency, plant layouts, training for both operators and middle management and customer service. Barbara experiments extensively with fabrics and threads, emphasizing application techniques for top quality work.

Deborah Jones of Data-Stitch Inc. in Fort Worth, Texas, has more than 20 years of experience in embroidery. She does consulting, specializing in start-up businesses, efficiency and specialized applications. Deborah can also develop a customized curriculum for training future employees.

Lance and Cindy Sabo own and operate The National Embroidery Co. in Gilbert, Arizona. Lance also performs consulting work, mainly at his facility, but also at the customer's site if needed. Because his area of specialty is start-up companies, both in terms of embroidery and design, Lance prefers to charge lower daily rates, encouraging his clients to spend two or more weeks in his shop with on-the-job training and observation. He believes this gives the newcomer a better idea of what to expect in terms of time and commitment.

Many embroiderers who have attended seminars and hired consultants will freely testify to their value. Says Ed Geller of Logos & Such in Morristown, New Jersey: "I learned more in two days at a seminar than I learned in six months of on-the-job experience."

Here's another example: An executive of a large U.S. garment manufacturer was running a profitable company, but its embroidery production department was consistently operating at a loss. Production rates were low on all of the firm's numerous 12-head machines. An embroidery consultant determined that the work would go faster if only six heads were operated at a time, with the other six ready to go as soon as the first six were finished. This was due to the shortness (two minutes or fewer) of the runs. The operators could achieve uninterrupted, consecutive runs with six heads, but not with 12. The time for hooping, loading and unloading 12 heads at once actually caused more down time. Based on the consultant's advice, this company's production department became profitable immediately.

Both seminars and consultants can prove costly when you total up airfare, hotel and meals, and the fees. But, when you consider the cost of not doing things right the first time, these services and events could save you money. The trial-and-error method of learning is expensive and time-consuming, but if you think education costs, try ignorance!

Business Management

If you are weak in the areas of business management, there are many sources of help. The Small Business Administration offers a Service Corp Of Retired Executives (SCORE). This group is composed of volunteers who possess a broad range of business expertise and a great willingness to help small businesses. They work closely with SBA to help provide information and advice.

Business colleges and universities offer courses on most areas of business. Employment councils offer personnel and supervisory classes. There are also organizations, such as The American Management Association, that publish magazines and books, and offer seminars, workshops, conferences and at-home study programs.

Do not overlook your library and favorite bookstore either. Browse through the business section for standard references as well as best sellers on sales, marketing, personnel and accounting. Biographies and autobiographies of successful businesspeople are also educational and inspirational.

In short, the information is available. The key is to use it!

CHAPTER 10

ACCESSORIES

Hoops

Embroidery hoops—also called frames—are usually not interchangeable among different brands of computerized embroidery machines. Therefore, you should purchase these from your manufacturer's sales representative. You can choose from various shapes and sizes.

Hoops are made of either plastic, wood, or metal, or a combination. Plastic and metal hoops cause less snags on garments, but wooden hoops have the advantage of screws that are more adjustable, particularly if a screwdriver can be used to tighten them. Metal hoops are usually spring-loaded for quicker insertion of the inner hoop, but these can prove too tight for some garments and leave creases or bruises in the fabric.

Some embroiderers wrap their plastic or wooden hoops with adhesive tape to prevent snags and to create a tighter hold on the garment. Preventing snags might be better accomplished by filing or sanding any rough spots on the hoop. Twill tape is preferable to adhesive tape for holding slippery garments more tightly in the hoop because it leaves no sticky residue. Twill tape is available at most fabric stores.

There are also double-height hoops available for some machines. These are excellent for extra thick garments, such as heavy blankets, jackets with heavy lining, plush towels and so on. The added height of the hoop prevents the garment from suddenly popping out. It is most frustrating to have a garment pop out of a hoop during sewing, because it is extremely difficult to re-hoop and get the exact same placement. Of course, double-height hoops can also be used on most thinner fabrics as well, avoiding the need for duplicate hoop sizes in both heights.

Of the various shapes available, circular hoops are best because they provide the most even tension around the fabric. Ovals are second best, followed by square and rectangular hoops. To increase the tension in oval, square or rectangular hoops, try inserting a small piece of heavy paper or thin cardboard between the inner and outer portions of the hoop in the corners or outermost points.

You will need a variety of sizes, depending upon the range of garments you plan to embroider. For the best quality work, use the smallest hoop that will accommodate the lettering or design being sewn. There are hoops small enough for just a monogram on a shirt cuff or pocket, large enough to handle a jacket back, and many sizes in between for sweaters, towels and all the other garments you may embroider.

Hoop sizes usually refer to the measurement of the inner hoop. For circular hoops, the size refers to the diameter; for ovals and rectangles, the measurements are usually height and width, consecutively.

Some machines also accommodate special patch hoops. These enable multiple patches to be embroidered in a single hooping process. They are available in standard patch sizes.

Barudan and Tajima multihead machines feature a holding frame that enables a single long piece of fabric to span the full sewing field of the combined heads. This is useful for extra long lettering jobs because each sewing head can embroider a different word to create banners, flags and so on. Of course, only one head would be sewing at a time, but the project could be done in only one hooping operation. This one-time method of framing is most common for patches, with all heads stitching at once. A width of material spanning the length of the frame is embroidered before it is cut into individual patches.

Machines with cylinder arms also accommodate special cap frames, which are designed to stitch a constructed cap in its natural curved shape. There are various sizes of cap frames to fit caps with different crown heights, including visors. Without this type of apparatus, embroiderers who do a lot of caps usually opt for a panel program—embroidering cap panels prior to construction. Constructed caps can also be embroidered flat using regular hoops, but they are difficult to hoop and anything more than a single letter or very small design will appear distorted because of the curved shape of the cap.

How many hoops should you have? Once you have determined the sizes and shapes you will need, start with at least two per sewing head. Then, add to your supply as needed. The greater your volume of short runs, the more hoops you will need. This is because hooping one set of garments while the first set is running will keep your machine operating with less downtime. On short runs, it is a good idea to have several sets pre-hooped so that the operator is not kept waiting to reload for the next run.

Another reason to have extra hoops is they do wear out, become warped or damaged. You don't want to get behind in production while waiting for your supplier to ship replacement hoops. For this reason, it is also wise to keep extra hoop screws on hand. As with anything, the more care you give your hoops, the longer they will last. Knowing the proper way to hoop (see the chapter on applications), and avoiding hitting the hoop with the needle or needle bar will preserve them from wear and tear.

Hooping Devices

A hooping device is any apparatus that enables you to hoop more quickly and easily. Hooping a garment while the outer hoop is fixed in the machine's hoopholding device is not recommended. It puts excessive stress on the machine and wastes production time. A hooping device can be as simple as a hoopholding bar like the one in your machine, installed on your work table or wall. This simply prevents the hoop from moving as you sandwich the garment between the hoops. Some devices are more elaborate, featuring measuring and placement aids. Others are made to accommodate certain types of garments—shirt fronts, jacket backs and so on. Still others automatically insert the inner hoop into the outer hoop.

Shop around for the type of device that best fits your needs. Unlike hoops, hooping devices for various makes of machines are available from different suppliers.

In general, hooping devices are well worth the investment because they enable you to hoop more quickly, easily and effectively. This is very important because proper hooping is essential to top quality embroidery.

Lettering, Monogramming & Design Styles

Discussion here will be limited to those lettering, monogramming and design styles stored on circuit boards, disks, Style Paks® or cassettes—those that you plan to use the most.

Both Melco and Barudan offer a variety of lettering and monogramming styles and popular stock designs. They are not interchangeable directly between brands of machines.

Melco circuit boards can also run on a Tajima machine, but most Tajima models will require the addition of a multihead keyboard unit (MKU) from Melco. The TMM model requires no additional keyboard to utilize the alphabet boards. Melco hard disk designs can run on a Tajima machine if the machine is connected to an Epicor computer by an MC-1.

Lettering is grouped into block and script styles. Some blocks are plain, while others have serifs, or stems off the letters. There are also plain and fancy scripts. You will find some are available in upper and lower case letters; others have upper case only. Most have numerals and some punctuation marks.

ABC	ABC	*ABC*
Plain Block	Serifs	Script

Alphabet styles should not only be selected on the basis of their look, but also for their function. They will differ in range of recommended sewing heights, width of letters, number of colors and degree of slant. On most machines, these variables can be adjusted from the keyboard, but there are limitations to how much adjusting you can make without causing distortion. Therefore, it is usually wiser to purchase a specific alphabet style to fit your needs.

If you are just starting, I recommend you select two blocks and two scripts, one plain and one fancy of each. If you will be doing monogramming, select one or two styles made for monogramming. While you can monogram with most any lettering style, those styles made for monogramming only will usually have the center letter of a 3-letter monogram proportionately larger than the other two letters. As a rule, monogramming styles also offer one or more borders.

Also choose design boards or disks that apply to your market or niche, such as sports symbols or children's designs, to name two examples. Periodically add to your styles to increase your versatility and marketability. Your manufacturer may offer a discount plan for the purchase of additional styles.

Custom alphabets are also available from your manufacturer at a premium price. It can be a great marketing tool to have exclusive rights on a particular style of lettering, but be sure the volume of work will justify the expense. If you have your own design and editing equipment, you can generate your own custom work, or you can alter a standard style or combine the features of various styles for use solely on your equipment. Some editing systems have these capabilities built in or available as optional software. This is the answer to the prayers of those who have never seen a decent "J" on a fancy script. It's a lifesaver for those who have been embarrassed by script "o's" that look like "a's" when sewing the abbreviation for Brothers. Think about that one!

It is very important to select alphabet styles to suit your market needs. Although your personal preference—and that of your customers—plays a major role, there are other factors to consider. The style should be appropriate for the garment and its function. If you'll be working with knits or fabrics with a nap, the letters must be a little wider to compensate for the stitches' tendency to sink into the fabric, becoming indiscernible. Some styles have a definite masculine or feminine look, while others are neutral. There are formal styles and casual styles. Again, personal taste will differ, and there are no strict rules of etiquette, but until you develop your own sense of uses and functions, here are my personal preferences for the use and function of the styles available for the Melco machines:

Styles for Melco Machines

Athletic Block—Upper case only. Used for lettering or initials on sports apparel and accessories.

Block—Upper case only. Plain, simple style for general use.

Border Block—Two colors, upper case only. Features column stitch, rather than fill stitch, for inside color. Used to create a shadow effect when colors are subtly different, or a bold, eye-catching effect when contrasting colors are used.

Floral Block—Upper case only. Multi-colored. An attractive style for initials on linens and ladies' apparel and accessories.

Full Block—Upper and lower case with serifs. Very popular for general lettering uses; also used for men's monograms when initials are desired at the same height.

German Block—Upper and lower case. Plain style used for men's wear and all-purpose lettering. Slightly narrow, this style is particularly good in small sizes.

Greek Block—Contains the Greek letters and symbols for sororities and fraternities. Symbols can also be used for the fields of science and math.

J.R. Block—Upper case only. Wide lettering ideal for initials on men's and Western wear.

Knit Block—Upper case only. Wide letters with plain styling. Ideal on knits and garments with nap.

Melco Block—Upper and lower case. Plain style (same as Open Block), specifically designed for small lettering needs.

Military Block—Upper case only. Official lettering style for U.S. government and military uses.

Open Block—Upper and lower case. Plain style for general lettering needs.

Roman Block—Upper and lower case. Thin letters with serifs, slightly slanted. Versatile for many markets, but especially good for advertising and adding a touch of elegance to a garment.

Slant Block—Upper and lower case. Rounded edges give it a unique look. Letters always sew on a slant. Good for monograms on accessories and linens.

Tapered Block—Upper case only. Each letter's individual taper gives a unique look to monograms on men's wear and linens.

Bean Stitch—Upper and lower case. A simple running stitch forms this script used for identification purposes on hats, emblems, uniforms and so forth.

Brush Script—Upper and lower case. Wide letters, slightly slanted, give this style an active look suitable for advertising or names on jackets and hats.

Custom Script—Available in upper case only or both upper and lower. Semi-fancy upper case letters, but not so fancy as to be feminine. Very popular for names.

Diane Script—Upper and lower case. Very fancy, elegant upper-case letters with traditional lower case. Ideal for ladies' apparel and monograms on linens.

Freehand Script—Upper and lower case. Upper-case letters are scroll-like in style, while lower case letters have a slight slant. Popular for names.

Juliette Script —Upper and lower case. Upper case is similar in style to upper case of Freehand Script. Lower case is a more basic connecting script without the slant.

Legende Script—Upper and lower case. Originally designed for the Arabian horse market, this style is very attractive for linens and novelty items.

Melco Script—Upper and lower case. Upper case is a block style on a slant; lower case is a slanted connecting script. Specifically designed for small lettering.

Roman Script—Upper and lower case. Upper case is a simple block style with serifs, slightly slanted; lower case is a very readable connecting script. Suitable for all-purpose lettering.

Script—Upper and lower case. The most standard of the scripts, this one has universal appeal.

Astra—Upper and lower case. Very unique, non-connecting letters. Used for men's wear, linens and novelty items.

Athletic Flair—Upper and lower case with variable sized flair as an option. Ideal for sports, schools and advertising.

Chain Stitch—Upper and lower case. Hand-embroidered look for use on linens, advertising and team sport shirts.

Curl—Upper and lower case. Partly scrolled upper case with non-connecting script lower case. Multi-purpose style used for monograms on linens, men's and ladies' apparel and names.

Fishtail 2—Upper case only. Unique letters with optional dot under each letter. Suitable for men's monograms, baby and novelty items.

Melanie—Upper and lower case. Upper case is very fancy, suitable for monograms on ladies' apparel (looks nice on fur coat linings), linens. When combined with lower case, very suitable for names where a fancier look is desired.

Olde English—Upper and lower case. Classic style for linens and men's monograms. Also appropriate for novelty gifts and Christmas items.

Oriental Script—Upper and lower case. Suitable for names and monograms whenever a touch of the Orient is desired. Especially nice on linens and loungewear.

Ribbon—Upper case only. Often overlooked as a single-initial monogram for linens and accessories.

Casual Flair—Monogramming only. Lower case with a flair, this is appropriate for women's casual wear.

End Scroll—Monogramming only. Feminine style with choice of borders for women's wear and linens.

3-Letter Point—Monogramming only. More masculine look, but also suitable for linens.

Tackle Twill—Pre-fabricated letters with embroidered edge. Especially popular for large lettering needs.

There are other styles available through Melco and Accessory Resource Corp. (ARC), including some specifically designed for the European market. There are also many designs available on circuit boards and disks, such as sports symbols and figures, mascots, nautical and water-related designs, holiday and religious symbols and so on.

Styles for Barudan Machines

Michelle Marino of Macpherson, offers her recommendations for the Barudan alphabet styles:

Balloon—Upper case only. Bold block for multi-purpose use. Also good for children's market.

Century Bold—Upper and lower case. Available in two size ranges: one for small letters and another for up to three inches. This is a block style with serifs suitable for most any lettering needs.

Children's Block—Upper and lower case. Styled after a child's printing, this is a fun one for the little ones.

Extended Block—Upper case only. Extra-wide letters with serifs. Popular for monograms on brief cases.

Flash—Upper and lower case. Bold block for making a statement. Also good for children's clothing and accessories.

Gold Rush—Upper case only. Block style with serifs features optional one- or two-color use. Good for sports apparel.

Harrington—Upper and lower case. Uniquely styled block used for children's wear.

Mock Meistergram 8—Upper and lower case. Quick sewing, simple block used for uniforms and simple men's monograms.

Olde English—Formal, classic style for monograms on linens and men's wear. Also suitable for some advertising needs.

Open Block—Upper case only. This outline block can be used plain or with applique. Useful for sportswear and, with applique, for children's wear.

Stymie Serif—Upper and lower case. All-purpose block with serifs.

Zapf—Upper and lower case. A unique block for business logos and advertising.

Athletic Swoosh—Upper and lower case. Sporty script style with optional flair. Ideal for sports, schools and businesses.

Brush—Upper and lower case. Popular for sportswear and advertising. Shows action.

Casey Cursive—Upper and lower case. Suitable for men's and women's apparel, names and business uses.

Casual Script—Upper and lower case. Features small, medium and large extenders for excellent arcing results. Use for sportswear and advertising markets.

Commercial Script—Upper and lower case. Classic thick and thin lines in each letter with scrolling capitals gives this style a feminine look. Good for monogramming.

Diana Script—Upper and lower case. Fancy capital letters gives this a feminine look. Use on linens, womens' wear, names and such.

Elegant—Upper and lower case. Multi-purpose style, especially good for logos and sports. When used for initials, it has a custom monogram look.

Kaufman Script—Upper and lower case. Unique, "funky" look good for monogramming.

Pearl Script—Upper and lower case. Good for arcing. Contemporary look for linens, household items and sports apparel.

Traditional Script—Upper and lower case. Ideal for names and for sportswear.

3-Letter Diamond—Monogramming only; optional border. Monogram forms the shape of a diamond. Good for men's and womens' wear and linens.

Circle Script—Single-letter monogramming only; optional border. Ideal for women's wear, accessories and linens.

Monogram Script—Monogramming only. Use one, two or three letters with optional, reversible border. Suitable for mens and womens' monograms and linens.

Macpherson offers other styles of lettering and many choices of Style Pak® designs, such as sports symbols, childrens' designs and florals, to describe a few.

Threads

Computerized embroidery machines require threads specifically made for high-speed electronic machines. Never use other types of industrial thread or household thread.

Thread denier, or weight, is identified by different numbering systems, depending upon the thread manufacturer. This equivalency chart will make it easy to decipher sizes:

Fine or thin thread	0000	#50 weight
Medium thread	000	#40 weight
Heavy or coarse thread	00	#30 weight

#40 weight is the most commonly used and is suitable for most all fabrics and designs. However, there are good reasons and appropriate times to use the others. #50 weight will give a cleaner, crisper, finished look to extremely small lettering or fine detailing in designs. There are occasions when designers refuse to digitize, or worse, when they *unsuccessfully* digitize lettering or designs so small that the artwork is finer than the thread. In some cases, using a #50 weight thread could solve the problem.

#30 weight thread is overlooked for production efficiency. In designs that have light density (where stitches do not cover the fabric as well as desired), #30 weight will provide the extra coverage. In designs where coverage is not a problem, and if your machine is capable of reducing density, you can lighten the density by 25 percent and use #30 weight thread to achieve the same coverage as stitching at normal density with #40 weight. However, the best results will occur with this thread weight when designs are created specifically for it. This tactic reduces stitch count and makes the sewing go faster because of the design's decreased number of stitches—without having to adjust density. #30 weight thread is also particularly good when using a fill stitch; you can get maximum coverage with fewer stitches. Some say large designs created for #30 weight thread can be reduced to a smaller size than normally recommended by substituting with #40 weight thread.

The most commonly used types of embroidery thread are rayon, polyester, cotton, neon and metallic. Rayon has been the most popular because of its high sheen, which is the preferred look in embroidery today. Polyester was tried in embroidery previously and was overwhelmingly rejected because of its low sheen and high stretchability. However, new technologies have overcome these problems. Today's polyester embroidery thread has the same (in some cases more) sheen and stretchability as rayon. Here are some advantages and disadvantages of the various types of threads:

Rayon—High sheen. Available in more colors. Easily breaks by hand for trimming while sewing. Washable, dry cleanable, mostly colorfast.

Polyester—Available in high sheens. Fewer thread breaks when sewing. Too strong to break by hand. Washable, dry cleanable, very colorfast, less expensive and withstands bleach.

Cotton—Low sheen. Breaks by hand. Washable, dry cleanable, colorfast. Requires extra care in the cleaning of embroidery machines because of its tendency to produce lint. Many prefer it on towels, shirts and other low lustre fabrics.

Neon—High sheen (glowing). Available in rayon or polyester, washable, dry cleanable, colorfast.

Metallic—Depending upon brand, color selection may be limited. Dry cleanable. Sometimes tricky to sew, again depending upon brand. Very attractive look for embroidery.

Bruce Anton of Robison-Anton Textile Co. says that as a guideline the more lightfast, the less washfast threads are. Also, certain colors are more lightfast than others, but there is no rhyme or reason to it.

When you change from one type, weight or brand of thread to another, the amount of tension needed on the upper tensioning mechanism of your machine will change. It may also affect the bottom, or bobbin, thread tension. For example, polyester and neon will require more upper tension than rayon. Metallic requires less tension than rayon. Different threads may require different needle sizes, as well. Refer to the following section on needles for more information about this.

Threads for computerized embroidery machines must be left twist. All the major manufacturers of threads for these machines comply with that. Threads are wound on a variety of containers —tubes, spools, king-spools and cones. These distinguish the amount of thread on the container, which in turn, will vary among manufacturers. Also, the base container seems to affect the ease with which the thread unwinds during use. King-spools seem to work best for preventing excess thread from falling off the container during use. They hold 5,000 to 5,500 meters of thread and are cylindrical in shape with a base at the bottom. Tubes (also known as spools) are the smallest containers, usually holding 1,000 meters of thread and are cylindrical in shape. Cones are larger, holding 5,000 to 5,500 meters and are cone-shaped.

If you're just starting a business for multi-purpose embroidery, I recommend you purchase larger quantities of the basic colors (white, black, navy, gold, red, tan, brown, gray) and smaller quantities of other colors you think necessary. Then, when you can identify the most popular colors for your customers and uses, order those in larger quantities.

Because of various dyeing processes, thread is susceptible to the effects of extended air exposure. "Dye rot" can occur, making the thread brittle and weak, and thereby causing excessive thread breaks. Therefore, inventoried thread should be kept wrapped and stored in airtight containers or in cabinets with doors. The shelf life of thread is generally about five years, but what you don't know is how long the manufacturer and the distributor have had it on *their* shelves. Don't keep thread longer than two to three years. When you finish with a particular thread, adhere the end properly. Do not use tape; its adhesive will damage the thread. Do not leave it loose either, because the cone will unravel if it falls or is stored on its side. Either use the slot at the end of the container, if it has one, or tie a slip knot.

Sometimes more thread breaks will occur with dark colors because the excess dye required to achieve the color may make them too thick for the needle, or the extra thickness may be too tight for the tension setting used with other colors. To remedy this, try a slightly larger needle or less tension. Similarly, white and other light colors can break easily because of less dye in their fibers, making them weaker than the darker colors. Again, loosening the tension will probably solve the problem. If that doesn't work, try a different container of thread.

Care of embroidered goods is very important because of the thread. Rayons, especially dark red shades, may bleed or fade if proper laundering instructions are not followed. Here are the proper laundering instructions, which you may wish to share with your customers:

1. Colored embroideries should be machine-washed separately.
2. Do not allow starch build-up.
3. Do not allow embroidered garments to lie crumpled up while wet.
4. Avoid bleach and brightening agents. This is less critical with polyesters.
5. Embroideries on wool should neither be machine-washed nor spin-dried.
6. For ironing, dampen slightly, then iron on wrong side. Use low settings.

7. The combination of certain dry cleaning chemicals mixed with starch may damage embroidery.

Color selection is extremely important in the embroidery business. Most thread color charts are arranged in groups of the same color. This provides ease in color blending. The choice of colors or shades can mean the difference between getting an "ah" or "ugh" from your customers! The nature of high-sheen embroidery thread causes it to change shades depending upon the stitch direction and the light in which the work is seen. Natural sunlight is the best light for color selection, particularly when trying to match thread to fabric color.

Mixing directions of thread patterns in a design can create a beautiful and artistic effect. It can even look variegated (varying shades within a single piece of thread) when used in different directions to simulate such elements as grass, leaves, fur, scales on a fish and so on. Of course, variegated threads are also available, and can add interest to florals and detailed designs. Avoid using variegated threads in column stitches, however, unless you like stripes!

The selection of thread colors can be a detriment to getting your work done. If you offer too many choices for putting a name on a garment, your customers may take considerable time to choose. For this reason, many embroiderers limit choices for simple jobs. Also, don't be afraid to help hesitant customers. Sometimes those who are not used to working with embroidery have a difficult time imagining what it will look like. They will most often appreciate your telling them, "I think this would look great on that." Another trick is to have a sample sewn of the various colors you offer, and if possible, sewn on the various colors of jackets or shirts you offer.

When embroidering certain designs, particularly animals, the color selection, as well as the design, must be realistic. If you are unsure, it is worth a trip to the library or bookstore to locate a color photo of the real thing. Humorous embroidery can be the exception. I once took a fur-bearing Colorado trout to a seminar!

If you really want to know your colors, consider taking a seminar on color. Some embroiderers who have taken such a course, now display their threads according to warm shades and cool shades and so forth. This is just one more way you can become an expert in what you're doing.

Here are the major thread brands and sources in the United States:

Accessory Resource Co. (ARC) 471 E. 124th Ave. Thornton, CO 80241 (303) 451-0420 (800) 877-4272	ARC rayon Isafil rayon Isacord polyester Metallic Rasant cotton bobbin thread - assorted Polyester pre-wound bobbins -assorted
Coats & Clark P.O. Box 670 Toccoa, GA 30577 (404) 886-2141 (800) 241-4312 (800) 342-6770 Georgia	Trusew® polyester Ready-wound bobbins
Gunold + Stickma Of America Inc. Suite 112 2140 Newmarket Pkwy. Marietta, GA 30067 (404) 955-7968 (201) 595-0029 New Jersey (312) 691-1303 Illinois (714) 751-0481 California	Sulky rayon Cotty cotton Mety metallic Bobby-fil pre-wound bobbins
Madeira USA Ltd. P.O. Box 60687 30 Bayside Court Laconia, NH 03246 (603) 528-2944 (800) 225-3001	Rayon Metallic Cotton Polyester
Madeira West Suite #145 2727 N. Grove Industrial Drive Fresno, CA 93727 (209) 454-8173 (800) 462-3347	

Robison-Anton Textile Co. P.O. Box 159 175 Bergen Blvd. Fairview, NJ 07022 (201) 941-0500 - New Jersey (212) 695-3347 - New York (800) 932-0250	Rayon Cotton Metallic Pre-wound bobbins
Sew Art International 412 South 425 West Bountiful, Utah 84010 (800) 231-2787	DMC (Cotton)

Bobbins

Bobbin thread for computerized embroidery machines is usually cotton, polyester or a blend of the two. Most embroiderers use the prewound disposable type, but bobbin thread is available for those who wish to wind their own. Most Melco machines do not come with metal bobbins or a bobbin winder built in. The Stellar 1 model is an exception. Barudan machines include metal bobbins and a bobbin winder. Some people have bobbin winders on their home sewing machines and will use them to wind their own bobbins. If you do, be sure to use bobbin thread. Using top embroidery thread for the bobbin may cause tension and quality problems.

Although most embroideries are done with white bobbin thread, colored pre-wound bobbins and bulk bobbin thread are available. They add a finished look to the back of embroiderable goods for use on items such as towels, scarves, sheets, blankets and handkerchiefs—anything where the back of the garment may show. You won't find a big assortment of colors, but it is acceptable to use black with navy and dark brown, for example. Give them a try—you might like the look and your customers may be impressed with your attention to detail.

Backing

Backing is one of the six basics needed to achieve good quality embroidery (the other five are hooping, needles, tension, design quality and sewing speed). There are other factors, but poor quality is most often due to one or more of these. Walter Floriani, Jr. calls these the ingredients, which need to be altered in amount to concoct the best recipe for each design.

Appropriate backing is essential for embroidering most fabrics. Only a few fabrics need no backing. These include heavy denim and canvas, heavy nylon bags (unless they are slippery) and pre-backed patches. You may discover a few others, but count on using some type of backing for most everything you embroider. This is not a place to skimp on money or time—it's too important if you really want to turn out top quality work. Still, people do cut corners. If you're one of them, consider the thousands of dollars you have spent on equipment capable of producing excellence every time. Skimping on backing defeats the purpose of that investment.

Without backing, fabrics can slip, even when they are hooped tightly. The fibers will move, preventing even stitching. Also, the threads of the garment can sink into the needle plate opening. Backing solves these problems, adding firmness to flimsy material, steadiness to slippery fabrics, and thickness to thin goods.

There are two categories of backing: (1) cut-away and (2) tear-away, so named because of the method for removing the excess after stitching. There are various weights available in each category. It would be advantageous to have a light, medium and heavy weight of each kind. Refer to the Applications section of this book for simple guidelines, then experiment when you test-sew designs and fabrics to find the right backing for each job.

Backings are also available in various colors. These give a professional look to sheer fabrics or loosely woven, colored garments where a white backing would show. Some people prefer to buy backing by the roll and hang it on a special wall dispenser, similar to those in gift wrap departments. They cut only what they need per job. Others prefer to buy pre-cut sheets the size of their largest hoop. Smaller pieces cut for sweaters, shirts and so on are also available.

Shop around among the various suppliers of embroidery accessories to find the type, weight and size you prefer. And, when selecting cut-away for garments worn next to the skin, keep in mind that it must be comfortable to wear.

Topping

Topping, also known as facing, is used on top of the garment being embroidered to hold down a nap. It is advisable to use topping on such items or fabrics as towels, terry cloth, corduroy, fur, bulky knits and blankets. It helps the thread to lay flat and evenly distributed.

Solvy™ and Saran Wrap™ are the most commonly used toppings. Solvy is a water-soluble plastic. What can't be torn off the design after stitching can be lightly misted away with a spray of water. Saran Wrap must be picked off with a seam ripper or some other sharp object.

Needles

The needle is extremely important to good quality embroidery. After penetrating the fabric, the needle causes the top thread to form a loop. The loop is then caught by the hook as the hook revolves, thereby creating a stitch. Quality stitching is dependent upon correct loop formation.

In addition to a defect-free needle, correct formation of the loop involves using the correct needle and thread combination. If the thread is too thick for the needle, no loop or too small a loop will result. Too thin a thread for the needle causes irregular loop formation or fallen loops.

The timing of the hook is also critical to proper loop formation. During a stitching cycle, the hook must pass through the scarf of the needle, just above the eye. Thus, needle height must be properly set to enable the hook to pass through.

Different needle brands may vary slightly in height. If you use a brand other than what your machine manufacturer recommends, be sure you adjust for the difference by raising or lowering the needle for proper alignment with the hook.

Use only the type of needle recommended for your machine. Most require an industrial type. However, some machines, such as the Stellar 1, require a household type.

The common range of needle sizes for computerized embroidery machines is listed below with both the American and European numbering systems, from smallest to largest:

American	**9**	**10**	**11**	**12**	**14**
European	**65**	**70**	**75**	**80**	**90**

In choosing a needle size, there are two factors to consider: the weight of the thread and the structure of fabric (how densely it is woven or knitted). As a guideline, use #50 thread with either a #65 or #70 needle for finely woven or knitted garments. Use a #65 needle with this type of thread on lingerie or other sheer fabrics. For the majority of applications, sizes #70 and #80 needles are used with #40 weight thread. Use a #70 on lightweight fabrics, and a #80 on medium to heavy fabrics. A size #75 may also be used for medium weight fabrics. Use a #90 needle for #30 weight thread and most metallics. There are some metallic threads that will work with a #80 needle without having to slow the machine down to prevent thread breaks.

There are also various types of needle points. A sharp point will pierce through the fabric, which is desirable for most woven goods. A ball point should be used on knits because its rounded point will slide between the fibers, rather than cut them. There are light, medium and heavy ballpoints. Use a light ball for fine knits, heavy ball for bulky knits, and medium ball for everything in between. Ball points are also preferred by some people for use with bathing suits, Lycra®, Spandex® and nylon satin.

A controversial needle point is the wedge, which is a three-edged cutting needle. It is designed for leather, but some designs with heavy stitch density will cause the needle to make too many cuts, thereby slicing and damaging the leather.

Teflon-coated needles are also available. They have the advantage of reducing the amount of friction, which is helpful when sewing on Cordura®, Lycra® or Spandex®.

Many embroiderers limit their needle selection to two or three, but most agree on the need for ball points for knits and sharps for most wovens. The needle recommendations I have given represent those of the needle manufacturers who have designed different needles for specific uses. Those who are meticulous about quality will appreciate the importance of using the correct needle for their applications.

When do you replace a needle? Some people try to schedule it after so many hours of sewing, or after so many days or weeks have passed, or when they hit a hoop with the needle. The only common sense approach is to change the needle when it needs to be changed! If it has a burr or imperfection, get rid of it—even if it's never been used. If it's dull from use, replace it. Take the time to examine your needles with a magnifying glass to look for burrs. An experienced operator can tell by feeling a needle's point if it is dull and needs to be replaced. The most obvious indication is the deterioration of sewing quality. You will not get an even line of stitching with a dull needle.

Color coding your needles by marking a horizontal line across the shaft with a permanent marker will enable you to tell at a glance which size and type of point it is. This sounds time-consuming, but in the long run, it will make selection quicker and easier. It will also be a sure way of letting you know what kind of needle is in the machine at any given time.

Here's another needle tip: Marilyn Reichenberg of Initial Stitch in Boulder, Colorado, keeps needle #1 of her six-needle, single-head machine a constant size and point type for monogramming. If any of the operators need to use that machine for other work, they use only needles #2-5.

Scissors

Melissa J. Thompson Maher, editor of Stitches Magazine, did an excellent job of summarizing the various types and uses of scissors for the embroidery industry:

Sewing scissors may range in size from about 4-1/2 to 6 inches. They are good for trimming cut-away from garments and other general cutting.

Dressmaking shears are designed for cutting fabrics, such as backings, on a table. The bent handles allow the fabric to lay flat. Sizes generally range from 7 to 9 inches.

Pinking shears can be used to give a finished decorative edge to sample sewouts or when cutting applique fabrics that have a tendency to ravel.

Trimming scissors range in length from 5 to 6 inches and are designed for detail cutting. This is one of the most popular choices for embroidery trimming.

Embroidery scissors range in size from 3 to 4 inches. These products were originally directed at the hand-embroidery and needlework market, but their size makes them useful for trimming in commercial applications, particularly where smaller trimmers are preferred.

Curved embroidery scissors are just like the straight-nosed type, but with a gentle curve to their tips. They further minimize the danger of leaving a tiny hole in the garment you are trimming.

Cuticle scissors are fast replacing the basic trimmers as a staple in embroidery shops. The small tips make close trimming less dangerous.

Applique scissors have a "duckbill" blade, which enables the scissor blades to glide between the layers of fabric. This allows trimming of appliques without danger to the garment.

Thread clips, snips and nippers are tools designed for severing threads with a quick squeeze. Their spring action makes them popular for quick trimming to get the machine unloaded for the next run. There are many different designs of this tool on the market, but the function is fairly universal. Use for close work only at your own risk. They are not designed for error-free trimming.

Good quality scissors are worth the investment. The cutting action should be smooth and clean to the tips of the blade. The blade points should meet precisely, without any overlap. Scissors should also be selected on the basis of comfort.

As with anything, your scissors will last longer with proper care. Periodically wipe lint from the blade surfaces. Lint from synthetics, particularly, can have an abrasive effect. Wipe handles to avoid build-up of acidic skin oils. Periodically oil the pivot area, around the screw head and between the upper part of the blades. Use white sewing machine oil and a light touch. Wipe with a soft cloth.

When cutting, don't use force. If you're trying to cut through several layers of heavy bodied cut-away and the shears have stalled, take it one layer at a time.

Avoid dropping scissors. Have a place for such tools so that they will not be mixed up with other things and inadvertently dropped. Proper storage also helps prevent loss.

Have your scissors sharpened periodically.

Miscellaneous

There are many more helpful accessories you will need or want to have. Rulers and measuring tapes are essential for proper placement, although with experience many placement jobs can be "eye-balled." Invisible marking pens or white chalk and straight pins are also important to have for placement.

Spray adhesives are available for attaching applique fabrics and for adhering fabric to backing when garments cannot be partially or fully hooped. Sometimes using a spray adhesive with backing, even when the garment can be fully hooped, adds sufficient stability to use a tear-away instead of a cutaway backing, or less layers. Choose one that is not permanent so that backing can be removed after stitching. KK-100® is an excellent spray adhesive, available from Gunold + Stickma and ARC.

Fray Check® is a popular product for securing embroidery. It is commonly applied to the beginning and ending points of the design or lettering, and on wide stitches to prevent raveling in case of snags or trimming so closely that a lockstitch is removed.

Anti-static sprays and mats are also available. They are recommended in areas of low humidity or where computers are on carpeted floors.

Stain removers should be on hand in embroidery shops. Excess oil can cause stains during sewing, although test sewing should be done after every oil application to prevent this. Sometimes garments may be received with stains and it's a nice touch to remove them before delivering to your customer. And there will be accidents such as spills, and garments that become soiled by handling. Test stain removers on remnant fabrics first to determine if they do the job without leaving additional stains, or removing the dye of the fabric. Some stain removers are specifically for dry cleanable fabrics; others are for washables.

Contact the major embroidery supply companies for brochures, prices lists and product information. You will find a wide selection from ARC, Madeira, and Gunold + Stickma (see the section on thread for complete information on these companies). As the embroidery industry matures, new and improved supplies are coming into the market to make your work faster and easier. And if you have an idea for a product, by all means suggest it to your supplier or market it yourself!

CHAPTER 11

APPLICATION TECHNIQUES

Hooping

To produce top quality embroidery, the garment or fabric must be taut and flat, and the weave or knit must be aligned straight. This is accomplished with careful hooping.

Always use a flat surface. A hooping device will stop the hoop from moving about when inserting the garment, thus preventing crooked placement. Never hoop on the machine. It's hard on the hoop and the hoopholding bar. It also wastes production time.

Select the smallest hoop that will accommodate the design or lettering to be sewn. Round hoops are preferable because they provide the most even tension. Barbara Chmara of Barbara's Embroidery in Tucson, Arizona, recommends holding a set of circular hoops up to the light and sliding the inner hoop around until the position of most even tension is located. (The little crack of light between the inner and outer hoops will be even all around the edges.) Then mark the top center of the inner hoop so that each time it is used, you can easily align the inner and outer portions of the hoop at this point where the least amount of slack will occur. Oval hoops are next best, followed by square and rectangular hoops. When you do use hoops of a shape other than circular, check the outer limits for slack. If a hooped garment slides even slightly, you could have registration problems; or in other words, a design where the stitches fail to come together as planned. Examples of this include adjacent columns not meeting, or a fill pattern not meeting an outline. To take up such slack, there are several techniques available to you.

1. Wrap the hoop with "twill tape", a non-adhesive fabric tape found in fabric and notions stores.
2. Use extra backing.
3. Insert pieces of paper between the fabric and the inner hoop at the outermost edges. Use anything from tissue paper to tag board, depending upon the amount of slack you need to remove.
4. Before hooping, use a spray adhesive to adhere the backing to the fabric. This provides more stability.

Smooth out the garment as much as possible before hooping, including any linings and backings. It may even be necessary to iron excessively wrinkled garments before hooping. Then lay the garment over the outer hoop and insert the inner hoop, using both hands. Press down on the inner hoop, starting at the top and working down towards the bottom. Be sure the inner hoop is fitted well into the outer hoop so that the garment will lay flat during stitching. Michelle Marino of Macpherson Monogram, Greensboro, North Carolina, recommends tapping the inner hoop at various points around the circumference or perimeter of the inner hoop after attaching to the machine to assure evenness of tension.

Always check the back of the garment after hooping to be sure there are no wrinkles and to see that you're not inadvertently sewing other parts of the garment together. This is an important habit to form and will save hours of ripping out or dollars in ruined garments.

Be innovative about your hooping methods if you are not getting good results. For example, Barbara Chmara says hooping satin jackets or windbreakers over a bar stool helps her get them smooth!

When inserting wooden hoops into your machine or similar hoopholding device, hold it as close as possible to the metal bar so as not to put undue stress on the wooden hoop itself and its rivets. Many a wooden hoop has been broken because this procedure was not followed.

How tightly should fabrics be hooped? It depends upon the fabric. As a general guideline, tightly woven fabrics should be hooped rather tightly. This applies to nylon satin jackets, dress shirts, sheets and so on. Loosely woven fabrics and knits require a little less tightness in hooping.

Once the fabric is inserted into the hoop, you may add tautness or smooth minor wrinkles by pulling gently on the fabric. Do this with care. *Never* pull against the grain or against the direction of a knit. Pulling too hard or rubbing some fabrics against hoops—particularly wooden hoops—can tear or otherwise damage the fibers of the fabric. Also, be careful not to overly stretch the fabric. If more or less tightness is needed, and you're using the kind of hoops that can be adjusted after hooping, simply adjust the hoop screws.

Some experts in the industry, however, recommend that hoop screws never be tightened after the garment is inserted. Consultants Deborah Jones of Data Stitch Inc. in Fort Worth, Texas, and Barbara Chmara of Barbara's Embroidery in Tucson, Arizona, subscribe to this theory, except on nylon satin jackets. They warn that such tightening wears out the screws, is hard on the hands and can easily damage fabrics.

However, if you don't tighten hoop screws after hooping, then you must become very adept at pre-setting the proper space between the inner and outer portions of the hoop to accommodate the garment. And if you misjudge it, you must start all over.

Your hooping technique must be perfected. If you hoop too tightly, puckering will occur. If your hooped garments are too loose or the weaves or knits are not aligned straight, registration will not be correct. Practice, practice, practice!

Sometimes hooping is made difficult by the size, shape or construction of the garment or the desired placement of the embroidery on the garment. In such cases, experiment with the various directional stitching features of your machine. Shirt collars and cuffs, towels and sheets are easier to sew upside down because the bulk of the garment or item can then hang loosely in front of the machine rather than be bunched up around the sewing head. Because of the traditional placement for monograms on coat linings, these garments are easier to hoop and sew if turned sideways.

There are times when the area to be embroidered cannot be completely held by a hoop, such as jobs on some collars, cuffs, plackets, shirt pocket hems and some cap panels. There are also items too small to completely be held by a hoop, such as ribbons, bookmarks or patches. In such cases, hoop some backing and adhere the garment or fabric to the backing with a spray adhesive or pins. This technique can also be handy in working with such delicate fabrics as sheers, velvet, velour and suede.

Gwen Osment of Gwen's Embroidery in San Antonio, Texas, uses this technique a lot. She embroiders suede boot bags, and does not want hoop marks or any damage to the suede fibers. First she hoops backing, then pins the lining of the bag to the backing material. The hoop never touches the suede.

In my early years of involvement in the embroidery industry, I was taught that anything that can be hooped can be embroidered, and it was commonly believed that if it couldn't be hooped, it couldn't be embroidered. But, that theory has been proven wrong by such creative people as Gwen. I now subscribe to the idea that if a needle can penetrate it, and it can fit between the needle bar and the tabletop of the machine, it can be embroidered on a computerized machine.

If you do hoop fabrics that are susceptible to hoop marks, be sure you don't pre-hoop garments too long in advance of stitching. Temporary hoop marks on some fabrics, such as corduroy, can then be brushed away. A light misting of water may be needed to completely restore the nap. Steam also helps to remove hoop marks from some fabrics.

One other tip on hooping: Be sure to remove or push aside all unwanted obstructions from the garment, such as collar stays in shirts and nylon mesh stays in caps. Stitching over the stays can ruin the garment or cause poor quality embroidery.

Placement

Placement of embroidery on garments requires some thought, measurement and marking. The goals are to satisfy the customer's preference, to make the embroidery attractive and to align the design proportionately to the garment.

Size is an important factor—not only the size of the design or lettering, but also the size of the garment. For example, let's consider placement of a name on the left chest of a jacket. First, find where the shoulder seam meets the collar line, and measure down. For women's sizes, you will mark approximately 7 inches to 8 inches down. For men, measure down about 8 inches to 9 inches. This vertical line is then bisected by a horizontal line based on the jacket placket or closure. Jackets with snaps are usually marked across from the second snap down from the neck. However, if you're working with a much larger jacket, say size XXXL, your intersection point between these two lines may need to be adjusted over and down further. Conversely, names on children's jackets will be placed higher and closer to the center placket so that they are not hidden by the sleeve when worn.

Where the markings meet is the proper starting point. However, again consider the size. Long names will have to be sized down in height or possibly moved toward the placket to avoid any letters being hidden by the sleeve. Yet, allow at least 2 inches between the snap and the beginning of the lettering, or 2-1/2 inches between the center placket edge and the beginning of the lettering.

Knit shirts with four-button plackets are also easily marked for proper placement. Again, measure down from where the collar meets the shoulder seam to a point between the bottom two buttons. Always be sure the plackets are straight. On a knit shirt with a three-button placket, use the bottom of the placket or the bottom button as a guide.

For V-neck sweaters, use the bottom of the "V" as a guide.

Generally, the same guidelines apply for a design as for names; however, the size of the design may require special adjustments. For designs over shirt pockets, allow at least 1/2 inch between the pocket edge and the lower edge of the embroidery. Center the design's width over the pocket. If you are embroidering on both sides of the shirt front, align them across from each other.

For jacket backs, measure horizontally between the sleeves to find the center. Measure from the collar to the bottom of the underarm portion of the sleeve to find the vertical center mark. That is where the center of the design usually goes. Again, depending upon the size of the design, you may have to adjust. If lettering goes above the design, be sure to leave about 2-1/2 inches between the bottom of the collar and the top of the embroidery. If lettering goes below the design, you may need to move the design up higher on the jacket to achieve a balanced look. If lettering goes above and below a large design, re-hooping may be necessary. Plan ahead to avoid having to re-hoop in the middle of the design or a line of lettering.

Placement for monograms on shirts is largely a matter of preference, but some guidelines apply. Here are some popular choices:

On shirt cuffs, the vertical measurement should be either 1/4 inch to 1/2 inch above the lower cuff seam or centered between the top and bottom seams. Horizontally, start the monogram 3/4 inch to 1 inch from the center, towards the button hole. To be absolutely accurate, have the customer try on the shirt and mark the cuff so that the monogram will be centered over the top of the wrist. Don't forget to fold the cuff up before monogramming French cuffed shirts!

Shirts can also be monogrammed on the pocket, either centered between the top edge and the top seam, or centered on the body of the pocket. Some prefer a monogram just to the right side of the pocket (as the shirt is worn).

On collars, some put a monogram in the center of the diagonal towards the collar tip, with the final initial ending 1/4 inch to 1/2 inch from the tip. Others prefer a straight line along the top edge, about 2 inches from the center.

A European style shirt monogram involves placing the monogram 8 inches to 10 inches above the lower edge of the shirt on the left (as it is worn), in line down from where the collar and shoulder seam come together.

See Exhibit 7 for illustrations of monogram placement on jackets, shirts, cuffs and collars. Here are recommendations for monogram placement on other garments:

Towels	Place the monogram on the opposite side from the label and centered on the opposite end. (Measurements are from the bottom of the monogram.)
Washcloths	1 1/2 inches above hem or 1 inch above border.
Hand towels	2 inches above hem or 1 1/2 inches above border.
Bath towels	4 inches above hem or 2 inches above border.
Bath sheets	4 inches above hem or 3 inches above border.
Sheets	The bottom of the monogram should be centered about 2 inches above the wide hem line of the top side of the sheet.
Pillow cases	The monogram should be centered between the edge of the open end and the stitching on the hem or the border design.
Ties	Place 1 1/2 inches to 2 inches up from the bottom tip, or 9 inches to 11 inches up from the bottom tip when worn with a vest.
Men's sweaters, robes	8 inches to 9 inches down from where the left shoulder seam meets the collar, and 4 inches to 6 inches over from the center.
Ladies' sweaters	3 1/2 inches to 4 1/2 inches down from the collar and centered on the front.
Ladies' robes, blouses	4 inches to 6 inches down from the left shoulder seam and 3 inches to 5 inches over from the center.
Sweatshirts	Place 3 inches to 3 1/2 inches down from the bottom of the crew neck edge, either centered or over the left chest.

Women's fur coat linings	Right side (as it is worn) at waist level.

Traditionally, when the center letter of a 3-letter monogram is larger, that center letter is the surname initial. When all are the same height, the letters are in the same order as the name—first, middle and surname.

You must develop an eye for garment construction. Some shirts have pockets that have not been sewn on straight. Plackets are usually straighter than pockets, so some people align against the placket. Others remove the pocket and sew it on straight. Still others have learned which shirt manufacturers consistently sew pockets on straight and only embroider on those brands.

Barbara Chmara cautions, "When embroidering on the center chest of crew neck sweaters, count the ribbings of the neckline on the left and the right. If they aren't the same number of knitted rows, the design will not look straight. It is better to go with left chest placement."

Striped fabrics can be tricky. If the stripe isn't straight, the embroidery won't look straight. In such cases, it's OK to refuse to embroider on garments that will yield less-than-top-quality work.

At some point, you will likely encounter a complex placement challenge where portions of the design or lettering will need to be straight while another portion may need to be angled. Some people have an eye keen enough to visualize it and they just angle the garment. Others use patterns for precise placement.

Marian Zink of Initial Artistry in Dearborn Heights, Michigan, makes patterns for angled designs. She cuts a piece of backing the same angle as the design. Then markings are made on the garment at the beginning of each line of lettering. She sews the straight line of lettering first, then lays her pattern over the garment, properly angles it to fit and begins at the mark on the garment. (See Exhibit 8.)

People with programmable machines can combine the two lines into one operation. Those with a screen monitor can view it before sewing. Any of these techniques will save hours of trial-and-error experimentation.

You can also make templates for hoops, using Mylar® or plastic sheet protectors. By carefully and accurately cutting the plastic to fit the inner portion of the hoop, you can then find the center of the plastic and mark it with a pinhole. Then, when you insert the hoop into the machine, align the needle over the pinhole. Then place a mark on your machine's tabletop at the edge of the pantograph. Use tape, or as Deborah Jones recommends, plastic-covered graph paper held down with double-sided tape. This marking will enable you to align the machine so that the starting point will be at the center of the specific hoop you are using. (See Exhibit 9.)

Arcing

Most machines enable you to choose between "arc from center" or "arc normal." Selecting the amount of arc you want is a matter of knowing the degrees on a circle. A helpful tool to have for this is a radius chart, which some machine manufacturers and accessory suppliers have available. It saves time and helps you visualize the amount of arc in increments of degrees. The following chart will also help you select the appropriate radius for the size of lettering used. These are figured from the "arc normal" setting, in inches.

Letter Size	Radius
.25	2.00
.50	3.00
.75	5.00
1.00	7.00
1.50	7.50
2.00	8.00
3.00	9.00
4.00	10.00
5.00	11.00
6.00	12.00

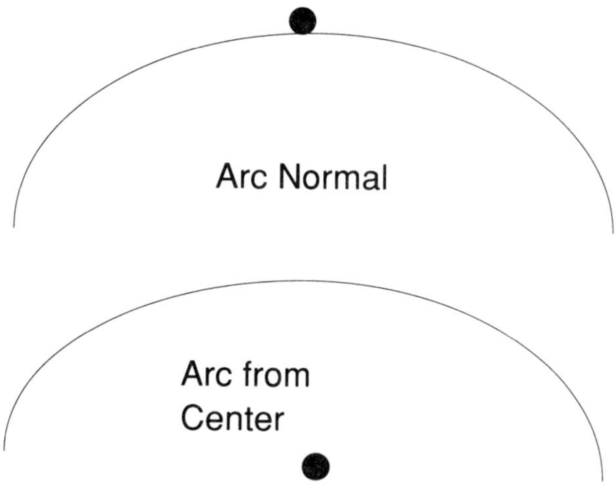

Tension

It definitely causes many headaches! It is difficult to describe and easier to see and feel, but here are some guidelines:

Tension is the amount of resistance on the thread when pulled through the needle or the bobbin casing. When the tension is too tight, the stitching on top will become uneven and, in severe cases, the thread will break. The underthread, or bobbin thread, will pull out easily. When the tension is too loose, looping may occur. When the underthread is loose and top thread tight, you will see bobbin thread in the top stitching. Therefore, not only is proper adjustment of both threads important, but the relationship of top tension to bottom tension can also make a difference.

Ideally, when proper tension is achieved, approximately one-third to one-half of the thread showing in the column width on the underside should be bobbin thread. Less bobbin showing in a fill pattern is normal. Less bobbin showing when the bobbin is full is normal, but some people will loosen the top tension slightly to compensate, tightening it again after the first 8 to10 revolutions of a new bobbin. (I cannot imagine actually taking the time to count the revolutions of a bobbin, even if my eye *were* quick enough!) If you notice that much of a difference using a new bobbin, simply cut off a foot or two of bobbin thread.

Run a test pattern using a 1 inch column on different fabrics, with appropriate needle and thread for the fabric, and examine your tension and sewing quality. If it does not meet your standards, adjust the tension in increments of 1/4 turns on the top thread adjustment mechanism, and very small increments on the bobbin thread adjustment mechanism until you achieve proper tension. Practice pulling and feeling the resistance for different tension adjustments, examining the sewing quality with each, until you arrive at your desired quality level.

Consultant Frank Gawronski observes that most people with tension problems tend to over-tighten the bobbin tension. He recommends using the standard bobbin test:

With the bobbin in its casing—but before threading the pigtail—hold the end of the thread and give a slight, quick, vertical jerk of the wrist. The bobbin thread should lengthen approximately 1 inch to 2 inches. Once this amount of bobbin tension is achieved, leave it at that setting for all fabrics. Adjust the top tension as needed for different fabrics and threads.

Thicker garments require more tension. The resistance from added backing, topping, glue or stronger thread requires tighter tension.

It is important to keep the bobbin casing clean by using canned air or by flossing with thread. Never use needles or other objects to clean the bobbin case, as you could damage the spring. If the spring is damaged, replace the bobbin case or you may experience uneven bobbin tension.

Quality Embroidery

Melco Industries Inc. established a committee of employees from its various departments to define top quality embroidery. The committee consisted of engineers, manufacturing people, service representatives, quality assurance people, trainers and customer representatives. Here are the conclusions of that committee:

Top quality embroidery has smooth edges. For a column sewn straight or on an arc, across two adjacent endpoints, there can be no more than .004 inch (one embroidery point) variation in distance from the centerline of the column.

Top quality embroidery has good repeatability, defined as the ability to repeat any previous needle penetration at the same programmed point, within .004 inch.

Good registration is another factor, which means the alignment of adjacent features must be within .004 inch.

Top quality embroidery has no skipped or missed stitches. There can be no failures of the upper thread to pick up the bobbin or lower thread.

There should be no gaps in the stitching. A gap is a lack of thread over .004 inch of where thread should be.

Width variation is another factor affecting the quality of sewing. For a column sewn straight or on an arc, there can be no more than .004 inch variation in distance from the centerline for a 1.0 inch column length.

When addressing bobbin consistency, the committee determined that the appearance of the back is acceptable as long as there is no visible looping or bird-nesting (wads of built-up thread), and all other quality parameters are within tolerance. Also, there should be no unwanted bobbin pull-through on the top side of the embroidered material.

Puckering is not acceptable in top quality embroidery. There cannot be wrinkles caused by stitches.

Looping is not acceptable in top quality embroidery. The top thread cannot have stitches that are distinctly looser than other stitches.

In addressing head-to-head repeatability, the committee determined that the position of a needle penetration measured relative to the fabric-holding device must be consistent within .10 inch from any sewing head to any other sewing head. However, this standard does not provide for good embroidery quality when the same piece of fabric is moved from one head to another head to complete a design.

Recipes

Walter Floriani, Jr., Tehachapi, California, has coined the term "recipe" for the combinations of techniques that determine sewing quality. Just as in cooking, you will find many variations of recipes in embroidery. Through experience, you will determine your own, adopt those of others, and hopefully continue to experiment. There are few absolutes in technique, but the differences in the recipes determine poor or excellent sewing quality and every level of quality in between.

One of these basics is sewing speed. Most top quality work is done at around 550 stitches per minute. Some jobs, such as simple names on stable fabric, can be run at higher speeds. Some jobs—those on delicate fabrics, or with certain threads, or with poorly planned or heavily detailed designs—may need to be run at slower speeds.

Another basic is backing. In addition to standard tear-away and cut-away fabrics, some embroiderers experiment with other fabrics, sometimes combining them with the standards for a sandwiched effect. For example, Marilyn Reichenberg sometimes uses broadcloth as a backing to help stabilize knits. Melco trainer Sandy Behr has used polyester sheer curtain material as a backing.

Again, the importance of test sewing cannot be overstated. This is an opportunity to develop the correct recipe for a job so that production will run smoothly and the look will be top quality.

For a general guideline, here are some popular "recipes" for stitching common embroiderable garments:

LETTERING/ DESIGN (Heights)	BACKING/ TOPPING	NEEDLE	WIDTH	DENSITY
Knit Golf Shirts				
.25"-.50" Letters	1 Cut-away or 2 tear-away	Ball point #70	2-4	55
.51"-1" Letters	Cut-away	Ball point #70	2	55-60
Design	Cut-away Solvy as topping	Ball point #80	N/A	55
Shirts/Blouses/Ties (Cotton/Polyester)				
.25"-.35" Letters	Cuff—none Pocket— tear-away	Sharp #70	2	55
Design	Tear-away	Sharp #80	N/A	55-60
(Silk)				
.25"-.35" Letters	Cuff or pocket— 2 layers tear-away	Ball point #70	2	55-60
Design	2 layers tear-away	Ball point #80	N/A	55
Wool/Acrylic Sweaters				
.25"-.50" Letters	Cut-away, Solvy	Ball point #80	4	55-60
.5l"-1" Letters	Cut-away, Solvy	Ball point #80	2	65-70
2.5"-3" Letters	Cut-away, Solvy	Ball point #80	2-3	70
Design	Cut-away, Solvy	Ball point #80	N/A	60-65
Nylon Satin Jackets				
.25"-.50" Letters	Tear-away	SES Ball point #80	1-3	55
.51"-1" Letters	Tear-away	SES Ball point #80	0	60-65
1"-2" Letters	Tear-away	SES Ball point #80	0	65-70
2"-3" Letters	Tear-away	SES Ball point #80	0	70-80
Design	Tear-away	SES Ball point#80	N/A	55

(Use double-height hoop on jackets.)

Sheets

2"-4" Letters	Tear-away	Sharp #80	0	70-85
Design	Tear-away	Sharp #80	N/A	55-60

(Must be hooped tightly.)

Towels

2"-4" Letters	Tear-away	Sharp #80	0-3	70-80
Design	Tear-away Solvy as topping	Sharp #80	N/A	65-80

Lingerie/Nylon

Letters up to 1"	1 layer tear-away	Ball point #70	2-4	45-55
Design	2 layers tear-away	Ball point #70	N/A	50

Bathing Suits/Lycra/Spandex

Letters up to 1"	Cut-away	Ball point #70 or #80	2-4	50-55
Design	Cut-away	Ball point #70 or #80	N/A	50

Solvy may be used as topping.

Leather

.25"-.50" Letters	Tear-away	Sharp #70 or Wedge #80	2-4	40-45
.51"-1" Letters	Tear-away	Sharp #70 or Wedge #80	2-4	45-50
Design	Tear-away	Sharp #70 or Wedge #80 or Teflon #80	N/A	45

Heavy Denim/Canvas

.25"-.50" Letters	None	Sharp #80 or #90	2-4	55
.51"-1" Letters	None	Sharp #80 or #90	2	55-60
Design	None	Sharp #80 or #90	N/A	55

Vinyl

.25"-.50" Letters	Tear-away	Ball point #70	2-4	40-45
.51"-1" Letters	Tear-away	Ball point #70	2-4	45-50
Design	Tear-away	BP #70	N/A	45
		Teflon if thread breaks reoccur.		

Patches

.25"-.50" Letters	None	Sharp #80 or #90	4	50
.51"-1" Letters	None	Sharp #80 or #90	4	55-60
Design	None	Sharp #80 or #90	N/A	55

(If thread breaks occur, try 1 layer tear-away and Teflon #80 needle.)

Hats
(Foam-backed front panel)

.25"-.50" Letters	Tear-away	Sharp #80	4	50
.51"-1" Letters	Tear-away	Sharp #80	2	55-60
Design	Tear-away	Sharp #80	N/A	55

Corduroy

.25"-.40" Letters	Tear-away	Sharp #80	2-3	50-55
.40"-.60" Letters	Tear-away	Sharp #80	2	55-60
.61"-.65" Letters	Tear-away	Sharp #80	2	60-65

Poplin or Heavy Broadcloth

	Tear-away	Sharp #80	N/A	50-65

(If hat has buckram backing, use no other backing and increase width to 1.)

Soft Cotton/Polyester

	2-3 layers tear-away	Sharp #80	1	50-65

Satin

	1-2 layers tear-away	SES Ball point #80	1	50-65

(Never stitch through nylon mesh stays. Roll them up and out of the way or remove.)

In the "olden days" when computerized embroidery first began, we were taught that T-shirts were too flimsy for embroidery; they had to be screen printed. However, people like Janie at Business Boosters in Park Forest, Illinois, who hadn't heard of this, found the right recipe. Janie uses two layers of stiff tear-away backing attached to the shirt with KK-100® spray adhesive, making sure that the backing is the full size of the hooped area. She cautions against pulling the material. She sets the bobbin tension tight and the top thread rather loose. 1/2 inch to 3/4 inch is the preferable letter height, with density set at 54 to 58. She uses a #80 ballpoint needle and #40 weight thread.

Here are a few other tested recipes and helpful hints from individuals around the country:

Freida Coonrod of Cedar Rapids, Iowa, uses two layers of cut-away backing on sweaters if the letter height is .40" or above. For smaller heights, she uses three layers. Density is set at 75 and a #80 needle is used. Her sewing speed with the extra layer of heavier backing can be increased to 650-750 stitches per minute. For Orlon sweaters, Freida uses four layers of cut-away and hoops loosely.

Janet Hamlin of Initial Artistry, Dearborn Heights, Michigan, uses two layers of cut-away backing on sweatshirts. She also increases the stitch width to +1.

Cindy Sutherland at Creative Threads Embroidery, Santee, California, suggests pulling the sleeves of jackets inside out for ease in smoothing the lining. She uses a tear-away backing on satin jackets and a #80 needle. She recommends loosening the tension and sewing at medium to fast speeds. When sewing a large design on the jacket back, the speed is lowered.

Dave Reeves of Uniform Fashions in Statesville, North Carolina, embroiders names on lab coats. He uses .40" letter heights set at 55 density. Two layers of backing are used if sewing on a thin fabric. He uses a #70 ballpoint needle and sews at 550 stitches per minute.

Mary Newton of Uniquely Yours, Edmond, Oklahoma, uses one layer of tear-away on denim jackets. For 2" fill stitch letters, she uses a 70 density setting, a #75 sharp needle, and sews at 650 to 700 stitches per minute.

Julie Talley of Abcets Inc. in Blue Island, Illinois, gives her recipe for 50/50 knit bowling shirts. She uses two layers of tear-away, #40 thread and a #80 ballpoint needle. When using a script style at 3" height on the back of the shirt, she sets her density at 70-72 and sews at 600 stitches per minute. Fill stitch lettering could go as high as 4". She cautions against hooping knits too tightly or having too much density to prevent putting holes in the material. When the bowling shirt is not knit, she hoops tightly and uses a tight tension on the upper thread.

Sandy Behr uses Solvy® on sweatshirts to prevent the stitches from sinking into the fabric. She says, "When using Solvy®, it helps to lick your finger, touch the topping and press on the fabric to avoid slipping."

I've also heard it's wise to store Solvy® in ziplock storage bags to prevent it from drying out and becoming brittle.

Barbara Chmara has had good results with a #60 needle and #50 thread for small lettering or fine details on shirts. The #60 needle, available through Madeira, comes in a sharp point only. "It doesn't matter on the knits because the needle is so fine that it will work its way around the fiber rather than cutting through it," says Barbara.

One of the many tips I've heard at seminars is that you may not need a topping on corduroy hats that have buckram backs because the nap usually isn't too high.

Gwen Osment of Gwen's Embroidery in San Antonio, Texas, has found that widening the column width helps the quality when embroidering on foam hats.

Stitches Magazine published a guide based on recommendations from Denise Bierworth of Jasper Textiles Inc. in Lumberton, North Carolina, and Lance R. Sabo of The National Embroidery Company in Gilbert, Arizona. Here are some of their recipes:

For coated or waterproofed fabrics, use a #80 sharp point or light ball point Teflon® needle and one layer of tear-away, although heavyweight fabrics may not require any backing.

Golf shirts will look better if a topping is used for high detail designs and for pique knits. Cotton and polyester blends need one layer of tear-away. 100% cotton golf shirts will need two or three layers of tear-away.

Reducing the sewing speed will help the quality on leather goods and vinyls. Use the smallest needle possible for the weight of leather to avoid the formation of large holes that could cause the embroidery to tear out of the garment. One layer of tear-away is recommended for most leathers and vinyls, but lightweights could require more.

When stitching on Lycra® or Spandex®, use a round hoop and stretch the garment to wearing size in the hoop so that the finished embroidery will not be distorted when the customer is wearing it. You should explain to the customer that the embroidery will look puckered when not being worn, but will stretch into shape with the garment when it is worn. Use a #70 or #80 ballpoint needle and one layer of cut-away backing.

Applique

The use of applique has become quite popular in the last couple of years. It reduces the stitch count of a design (yet, it may not save time in the long-run, depending upon the complexity and the number of stitches reduced). It does add a unique and decorative touch to designs, giving more texture and variety to the embellishment.

There are nylon applique fabrics available, such as Step Stitch®, which give the appearance of embroidery. Colors can usually be matched to threads, if desired. To prevent fraying of the edges, cut with pinking shears or a hot knife.

Virtually any fabric can be used in an applique. Satin applique material is attractive when used with the high sheen rayon embroidery threads. Furs give a realistic and fun look to animal designs. Polka dotted materials or lace make nice clown collars. Metallic fabrics over seashell designs are very attractive on towels. I once saw an oak leaf design done with a leather applique on a lady's knit top. Here's one area where your creativity can really be put to use, especially for the small shop specializing in one-of-a-kind items. People love uniqueness—something that no one else can buy. Visit a fabric store and create some unique appliques of your own!

Make a pattern out of heavy paper such as file folder scraps. Remove the thread from the needle and stitch the outline of the design with the needle. Then carefully cut the pattern on the outline's needle penetrations. For large volume production, it is best to have your pattern die cut. Then cut your applique fabric to fit the pattern.

Designs for applique should have a walk-stitch outline. Stitch the outline on the garment. Then stop the machine and apply the applique with spray glue, or iron on if you're using adhesive backed fabric. Trim any excess applique fabric. The embroidered design should then finish with a column stitch to hold the applique more permanently and give it a professional, finished look.

Walter Floriani, Jr. introduced me to three-dimensional applique. An embroidered flower design was cut out, then stitched to embroidered leaves, then stitched to the background material.

Trapunto

Trapunto is a puffed effect using embroidery. There are two approaches. First, using a bean stitch or a very low density fill pattern, the design should stitch around and in between, leaving the portion that is not embroidered to create the letters or design. By stitching down the fabric in this manner, the untouched area puffs out more. This is shown to best advantage on thick fabrics such as fleecewear.

The second method, for flatter fabrics, is to shoot a filler into the lining in back of the design. This filler is shot into the areas to be puffed only. It can be done with string shot out of an air compressor or by stuffing a filler by hand, using foam, batting, thermal lamb or some similar filler. Only the area to be puffed is left open. The rest is held down with the bean or loose fill stitch.

Shadowing

This technique adds interest to embroidery. To create a look of movement, sew out lettering with low density, then move slightly to the right and, increase the density and sew the lettering again. For more movement, slant slightly. For color shadowing, use regular density and sew out. Then move over and down slightly, change colors and resew. Use shades of the same color for the best effect in color shadowing. Colors will blend more if Solvy® is used.

Michelle Marino discovered that shadowing can be used effectively with lettering on an arc. To do this, set your first line of lettering at the radius degree you want, and your second line (using the same letters) at 1-2 degrees less. After the first line has finished, stop the machine and using your arrows, move slightly to the right.

Free Standing

Linda Burney of Gunold + Stickma has several unique designs using free standing embroidery or applique. One example is a mouse with fabric ears that are tacked to the shirt at the base of the ears, but not stitched down flat. They are free standing. Another example is a butterfly sewn on either a heat soluble or water soluble fabric. Dissolve the background fabric with an iron or water, then stitch the design to the garment in the middle. The wings of the butterfly are free standing.

The techniques used for embroidering on the heat or water soluble fabrics are:

- Be sure the design has interlocking stitches.
- Heavy underlay is required.
- Use of a low-melt bobbin thread enables the embroidered design to be ironed on.
- Bobbin tension should be loosened and top tension tightened so that more bobbin thread than normal is showing.

Boring

(No yawning allowed.) Boring is making holes. There are special boring attachments for some machines, but you can be creative without such attachments. For example, knits and sheers can be pierced through with your regular needle. In fact, you may have inadvertently done this already. Wedge point needles can be used or a die punch. Just be sure when you do use boring that you have circular stitching around the hole so that it doesn't ravel or tear the parts you want to stay intact.

Boring can be used to create a lacy effect. Another use is when you want to insert diodes to light up a design.

More Hints

When large letters are needed, it is best to use a fill stitch. Stitches won't pull out so easily. If you have an alphabet style where the outline only can be used, an applique in the center portion of the letters will also prevent snags. When neither of these is appropriate and column stitch letters are needed, sew them with normal column width and density first. When finished and it returns to the center, re-run the same lettering at a lower density and narrower column width. The result produces wider columns that are secured by the last narrower column of stitches. Apply Fray Check® along the bobbin stitches for extra security.

Changing column width on your lettering can be a useful tool, and is often recommended for certain garments where stitches can get "lost" in the fabric. However, not every style is conducive to narrowing or widening. Alphabets that combine horizontal and vertical stitching will look disproportionate if widened or narrowed, especially when sewn next to a letter with all vertical stitching. Take the time to analyze the stitching of the letters before changing the column width. Be sure to sew a sample first.

Sometimes it is necessary to adjust spacing between letters for names. An optical illusion may occur when certain letters are placed next to each other. A good example of this is the name "Tom". You will probably want to move the "o" closer to the "T" to close the gap. Usually, there is nothing wrong with the way the letters were designed. It will just look that way when capital letters have nothing in the lower right portion to balance the upper right portion. This illusion will occur with letters such as "F", "J", "P", "T", "V", and"Y".

Use Scotch-Guard® on all weather exposed embroidery such as umbrellas, wheel covers and hats, to name a few.

The bottom line is, whatever works for you to produce quality embroidery in a smooth and efficient manner, is the best method. Experimentation will lead you to the best methods for you. Practice will bring you the confidence of knowing you're putting out your best work. As you discover new techniques, I encourage you to share them with others, as so many have done for this book and other educational functions within the industry.

Exhibit 7

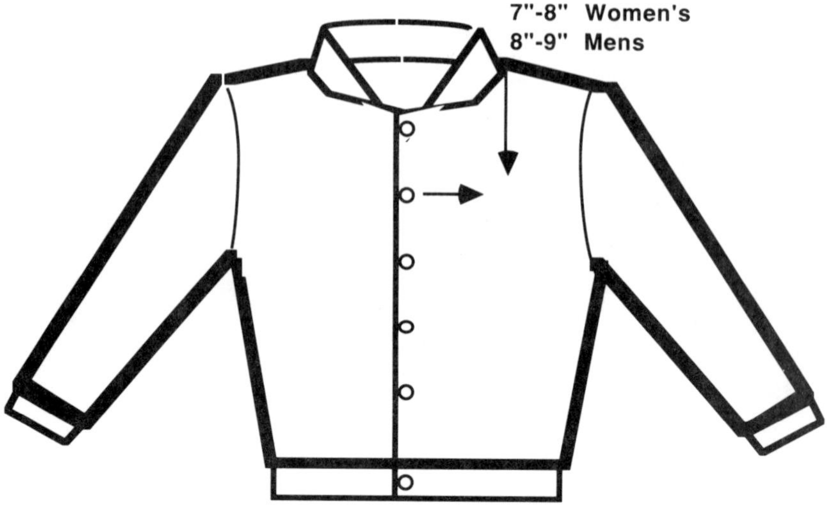
7"-8" Women's
8"-9" Mens

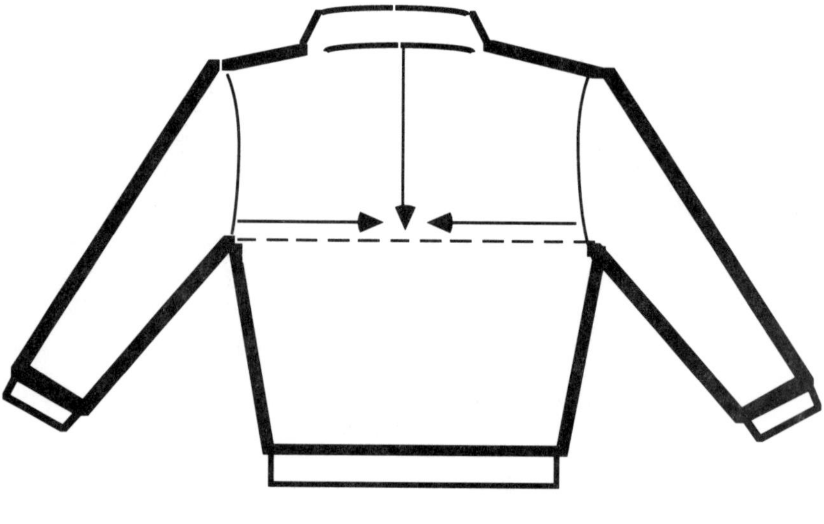

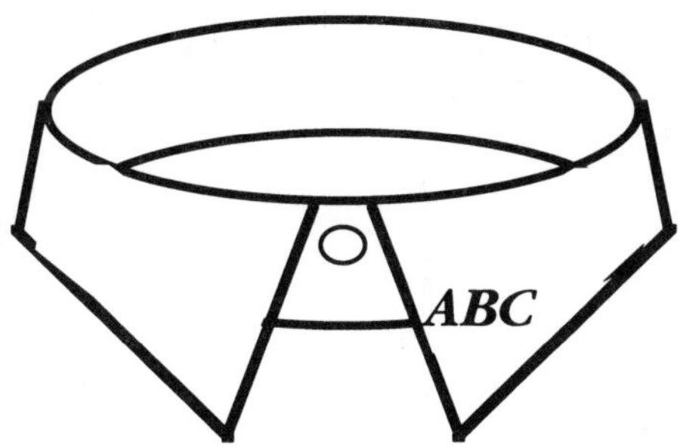

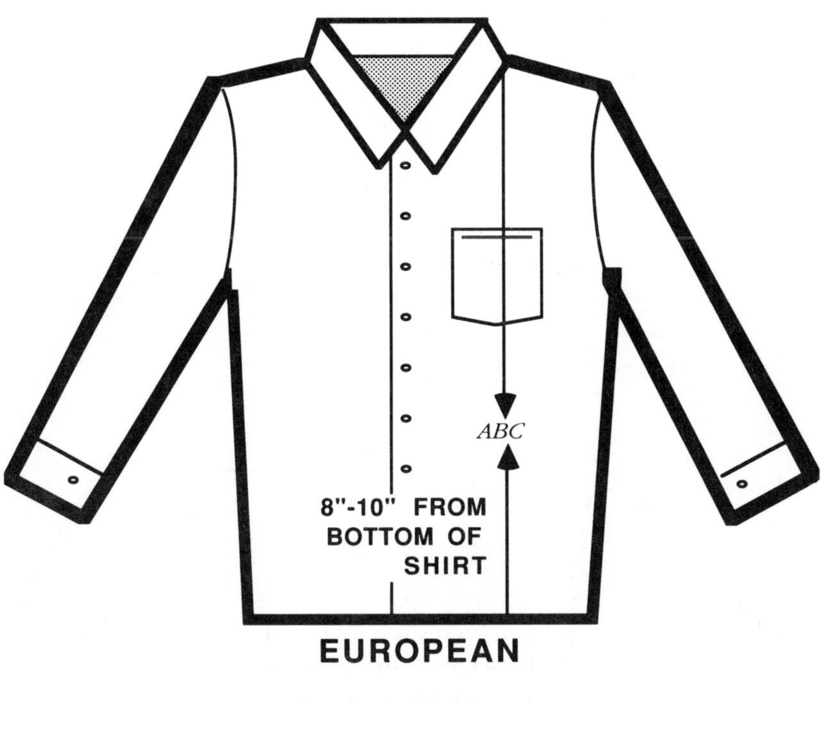

EUROPEAN

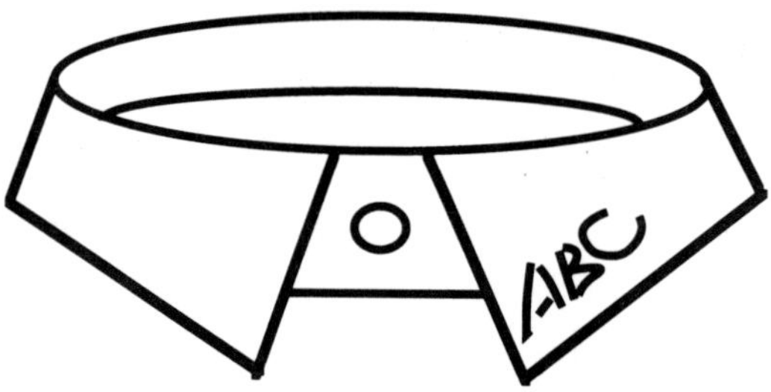
ABC

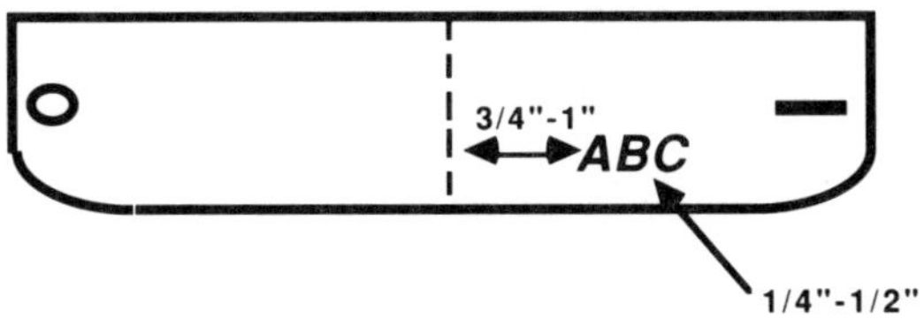

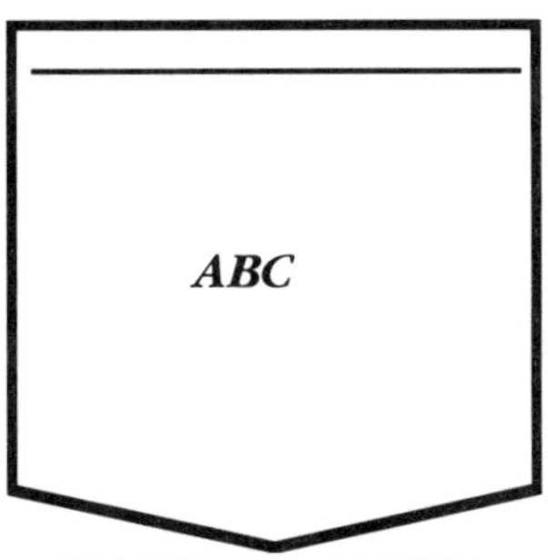

CENTER OF POCKET

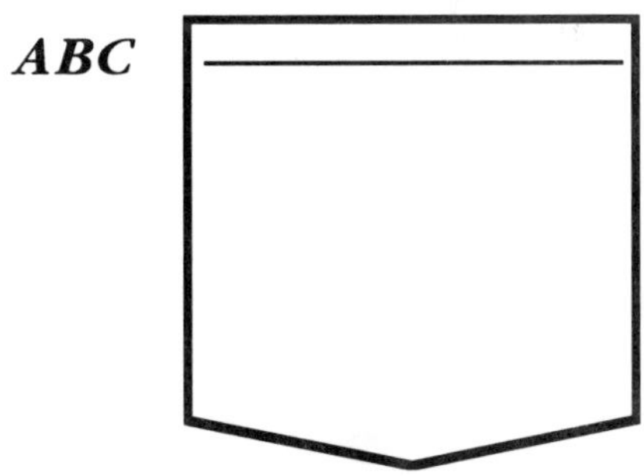

SIDE OF POCKET

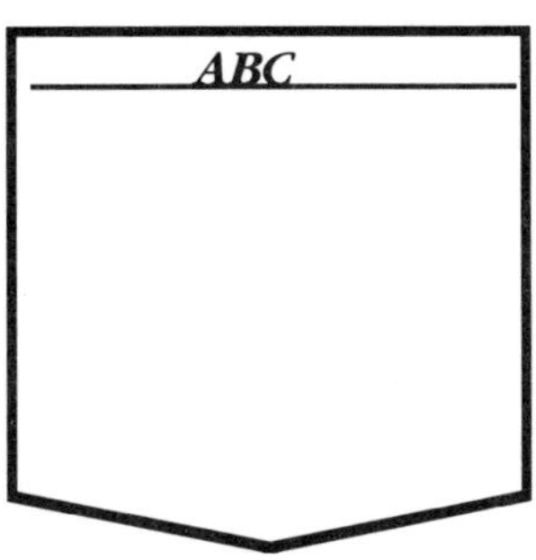

TOP OF POCKET

SIDE OF POCKET

Exhibit 8

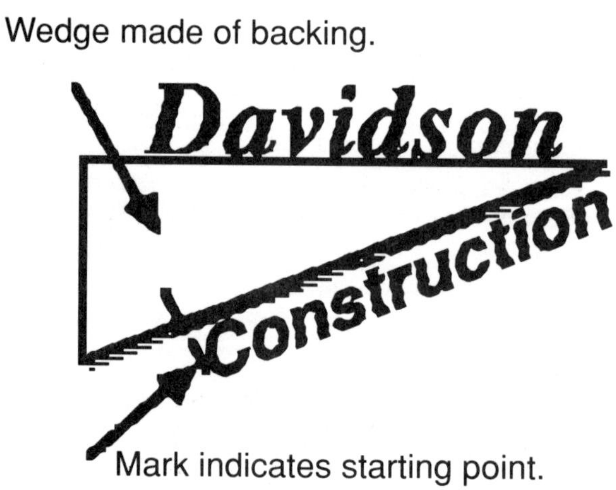
Wedge made of backing.
Davidson
Construction
Mark indicates starting point.

Exhibit 9

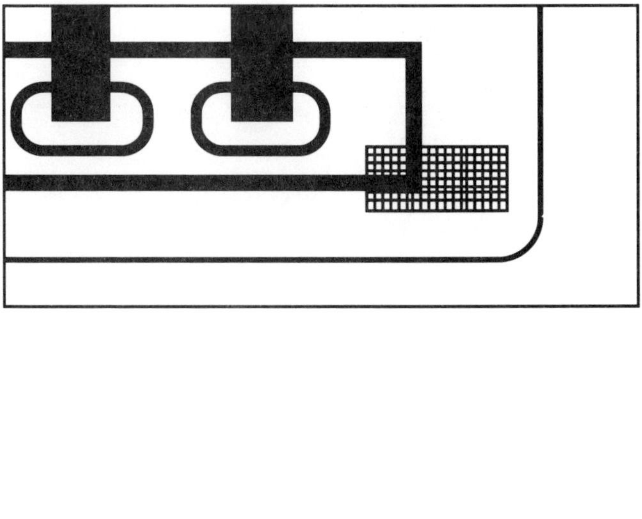

CHAPTER 12

CUSTOM DESIGNS

Designing embroidery is an art and a skill. There are many designers, commonly known as punchers, in the industry. Disappointingly, there are only a few really good ones who understand the finer points involved in creating designs that look good and run smoothly for production embroidery.

In-House Designing

If you are digitizing your own designs, I highly recommend investing the time and money to learn the finer points from one of the consultants in the industry who specialize in embroidery design. You will learn everything from preparing artwork to digitizing techniques. You will also learn how to fully utilize the time- and effort-saving features of your equipment.

Editing equipment is also a very worthwhile investment for designers, as well as production embroidery shops. Designs can be quickly and easily changed to enhance quality, run more smoothly, or for other applications.

You should consider producing your own custom designs in-house if:

1. You're losing business because your customers can't afford the cost of designs for small volume orders.
2. The turnaround time to obtain designs is causing you to lose orders.
3. You could increase sales by preparing logos in advance to use as a marketing tool.
4. You or an employee have the time and the interest, or if you can afford to hire someone to design.
5. You could profit by also designing for other embroidery shops.
6. You're consistently spending as much or more for designs per month, as the monthly payments would be on design equipment. If an additional employee would be needed to handle the extra workload, add the cost of that employee to the cost of the equipment, then compare the total to what you're spending on designs.

7. You want total control over the quality of your designs.

Selecting A Design Center

If you prefer to use a design center, either exclusively or in addition to generating some of your own designs, shop around. Check the trade magazines for ads, talk to other embroiderers, or obtain some recommendations from your equipment sales representative. Find out such basics as price structure, normal turnaround times, whether rush service is available, and if they can produce the language or format for your particular equipment. Also, can they produce it in the medium you need; i.e., tape, correct disk size and so forth?

If you select a design center that also runs production embroidery, you may need to protect yourself against that firm competing with you for your customer's business. If your design is to be kept confidential, a signed agreement to that effect is justified. It's also a good idea to give the design center written instructions as to whether your design is to be considered exclusive for your use only or if it can be added to its stock designs for sale to other embroiderers. (See Exhibit 10 for a sample agreement that covers both situations; however, you should consult with your attorney to determine if this form will work for you.) Of course, if a design is copyrighted, the owner of the copyright can authorize use of the design by others.

This also becomes a question of ethics. Some design centers will charge you custom prices, then add your design to their stock catalog and sell it for much less than what you paid. Richard Fryer of Franklin Mills in Franklin, Indiana, says this is a rip-off for customers. His firm treats every customer order as a custom design and never includes a customer's order in its stock catalog. Somerset Embroidery of Englewood, Colorado, creates original work for every customer, even if it is a design that has previously been done. The owner, Pat Somers, also views the practice of charging different prices to different customers—custom for one, then stock for all others—as highly unethical.

There is a wide variety of stock designs available from many design centers. It would be a good idea to collect their catalogs and "stock up" on those designs you think would appeal to your market. Stock designs are less expensive than having original artwork digitized.

Price structures will vary. Most charge per 1,000 stitches, but it is becoming more the practice to charge by level of difficulty or the time involved in creating the design. What you receive for the price will also vary. Some design centers provide complete sew-outs, while others run a low density sample or none at all. Some provide backup disks, and some automatically provide a tape and a disk.

Working With A Design Center

The more complete the information you provide your design center, the better your chances are of receiving what you need the first time. Fill out the design center's order form as completely as possible. It needs to know what equipment will be used, the language or format and the medium. Indicate if your machine has thread trimmers.

Be specific about sizes. Give the desired height and width of the overall design, as well as any portions of the design that must meet size specifications, such as lettering. Most designers recommend a minimum letter height of 1/4 inch, and column widths no smaller than 1/8 inch. If a portion of the design looks as if it will be a problem, let the design center know that you will accept enlargement in that area. Also, let the designer know if there is a limit on the number of stitches that can go into the design.

In addition to language formats, which coincide with machine brands, there are the technical formats of expanded and condensed. Expanded format means individual stitches have been specifically digitized. Condensed format means a proportionate number of stitches have been placed between two points. If your machine can read condensed format disks, then you have the ability to scale down a design, including the density. Expanded format designs cannot be changed more than about 10% to 15% without distortion because the density remains constant. Therefore, if ordering a condensed format design, you will also need to specify maximum and minimum size ranges for the design.

This feature is very beneficial, but much to the dismay of design centers, its practicality has been grossly exaggerated. As a general rule, a 50% to 75% reduction is the maximum attainable for most designs without causing distortion, even with the density scaled down. Therefore, it is not realistic to expect designs created for a jacket back to look as good when reduced for a pocket logo. You may have to purchase another version of the design.

Another misconception is to expect a design to look good on all fabrics. A good designer will compensate for fabric pull when digitizing. This will vary with different fabrics. A design created for a nylon satin jacket will not look the same on a knit shirt or a corduroy cap or a leather bag. Informing your designer of the fabric to be used is extremely important. Whenever possible, it is best to provide a sample of the fabric so that the designer can see it, feel it, work with it, or even run a sew-out on it.

Other important information to provide your designer includes the type thread you will be using, the number of colors desired, where those colors should be in the design, any preferences for type of stitch, and the best artwork you can obtain. If there is to be an applique, the design center needs to know where it will be placed in the design. If an applique is to have loose stitching over it, indicate this.

Consider the design from a production standpoint. Would it be helpful to have it stitch in such a way that you can hand-trim during production? Do you need the design sectioned so that parts can be used in other jobs? If so, discuss these matters with your designer. Your machine operators may be invaluable in providing input for instructions about a design to be created. Encourage them to make suggestions. Many designers have no production experience, and operators usually are not designers, yet communication between them is important. Remember the goal: to obtain a design that looks good, yet sews smoothly and efficiently.

If you experience difficulty with a design, first check your hooping, backing, needle and thread compatibility, tension and other variables. If a sew-out was provided by the design center and it looked good, ask your designer what "recipe" was used. You need to determine if the problem lies in the design or the way it is being stitched. For example, if you are experiencing too many thread breaks, does it always occur in the same place of the design? If so, it's probably too many stitches in that one area. Slow the machine down. If that doesn't solve the problem, you may need to have a few stitches removed from that portion of the design. On the other hand, if thread breaks occur randomly or intermittently, it is probably due to the sewing technique or a problem in your machine.

Don't always assume that a problem with a design is inherent in the design. Study what is happening and work with your designer to understand the problem, rather than just assume the design is wrong or needs to be redone. It may be, but often it is just a matter of changing the recipe for sewing.

Understanding the Language

Terminologies in this industry can be quite confusing. Some terms from the Schiffli industry and some from hand embroidery have been used. What makes it difficult is that there is no universal agreement on definition of some of the terms. I spoke with consultants Lance Sabo, Frank Gawronski, Walter Floriani, Jr., Walter Floriani, Sr., and Melco's Helen Jorgensen. In an effort to simplify the language for computerized embroidery, here are descriptions of the most common stitches used. (See Exhibit 11 for samples of these stitches.)

Bean stitch—This is formed by three (can be more, but usually three) running stitches on top of each other between two points, all on a straight line.

Chain stitch—Triangular stitches with locks in the middle to form a chain.

Cross stitch—This consists of stitches that cross at the center axis and look like an X.

Fill stitch—This is a series of single running lines broken at different increments and at a certain angle. These stitches lay side-by-side and can be digitized at a tight density for solid coverage, or more loosely for a less dense look.

Jump stitch—This stitch is used when connecting one area to another, and the connection point is too narrow for easy trimming. No needle penetration takes place.

Lock stitch—This stitch is used when entering or leaving a jump stitch and during a change of thread colors. It ties the ends down so that the embroidery doesn't pull out. It is a series of three to five stitches crossing or close to each other. This is a very important stitch, for without it, the embroidery will unravel.

Running stitch (also known as walk stitch)—This is a single, manual stitch or line of stitches. It is used to show fine detail or outline a specific area. It is usually stitched twice so that it stands out better.

Satin stitch (also known as column stitch)—These stitches lay side by side, in a single direction, at a certain density to achieve a certain coverage.

Underlay—These stitches are laid down before the stitches that will form the exposed, or finished, embroidery.

Copyrights & Trademarks

There are some true horror stories of copyright/trademark infringements within the embroidery industry. Companies, schools and other organizations—prime customers all—are sensitive to unauthorized reproduction of their names and logos. Embroiderers can take steps to protect themselves from legal action. The first step is to know the law.

A trademark relates to any word, name, symbol or device that is used in trade to distinguish goods and to indicate the source of those goods. A trademark registered and visible on the product protects you from others producing something similar and fraudulently marketing it as the original.

Large corporations, such as The Walt Disney Co., and Anheuser Busch Inc., are strict in enforcing their trademark privileges. It is also highly risky to use names and symbols of sports organizations without permission or licensing (i.e., professional football, baseball, and basketball teams), as well as amateur groups such as the Olympics. Universities are also taking steps to ensure only authorized outlets reproduce their trademarks.

Again, review the list of what a trademark protects. Even reproducing the *name* of your favorite team is prohibited.

Copyrights protect the literary, dramatic, musical and artistic works of an author or artist. The copyright goes to the form of expression, rather than to the subject matter. This means you cannot recreate someone else's picture or design without their permission.

The second step is to know how to get proper authorization to create or sew protected designs. If you're initiating the request, ask for exclusive rights in writing. Large corporations will have legal forms for this purpose and may grant exclusive rights for a particular design, garment, marketing area, or some combination. If not, for protection, ask your attorney to prepare a license agreement for you. (Exhibit 12 is a sample license agreement; however, consult your attorney to see if this form will meet your needs.)

It is not uncommon to be awarded a contract for a single specific application on a quantity of articles. Some will stipulate that all materials related to that job be returned or destroyed, including tapes or disks of the design, sample sew-outs and rejects. It is also common practice for large corporations to require a signed agreement of confidentiality, which means that you cannot reveal the work you are doing or any details concerning such work.

Universities sometimes request copies of records or sales orders to be sure they are collecting royalties on all work sold with their name, logo or mascot.

Granted, there are corporations and organizations that don't mind if their trademarks or names or logos are reproduced. They view it as free advertising. Still, don't settle for verbal authorization. Ask for a letter granting permission. A change in personnel within the corporation or organization may change the attitude toward the protected works.

There are also some designs that are assumed to be protected, when in fact, they're not. One example of this is a snowflake that was widely used to promote a particular skiing association in the Colorado Rockies. It became a status symbol and its use was so widespread that it was finally declared a public design because no one had registered it. If your customer does not provide authorization forms for a design he wants to have reproduced, seek legal advice to draft one that protects your rights to produce the design. A generic, fill-in-the-blanks type form may work or you may need to specify detailed terms for each customer, depending on the nature of the job.

If you want to obtain the rights to specific licensed designs, investigate what's available through the U.S. Licensing Industry Buyer's Guide. Contact the Licensing Industry Merchandisers Association (LIMA) in New York. Another source is *The Licensing Letter*, P.O. Box 1665, Scottsdale, Arizona 85252.

The third step in protecting yourself against infringement is notification. The appropriate symbol for protected designs should be sewn with the design, if your customer will agree to it. ™ denotes a trademark has been established, but not registered; ® identifies a registered trademark; and © is the symbol for copyright, whether or not it is registered. If the customer will not permit notification on the sewn design, it would still be a good idea to label your tape or disk so that you do not inadvertently sell the design to an unauthorized user.

The fourth step is to protect your exclusive authorization. As previously mentioned, give your design center written notice that your design is for your use only. Otherwise, it may be included in a stock catalog for anyone to order.

An alternative is to request all copies of the media. However, this may prove costly to reproduce in the event of loss or damage. Some embroiderers keep a backup copy of tapes and disks in a fireproof safe.

Design centers may request a copy of your authorization before agreeing to produce a protected design. Others may simply require a signed indemnification form stating that you agree to incur any expenses of any proceedings arising from the use of the design.

What are the risks or penalties for trademark or copyright infringement? Usually, a letter or legal notice to cease and desist in the use of the design is sent to a first-time offender. If use continues, a suit could follow. There have been cases, however, where it was probable that the offender knew he was reproducing a protected design and the warning letter did not precede a lawsuit.

So, when weighing the risks, consider the time and money needed to defend such a suit. Also consider the unfavorable reputation you could acquire in the industry for being a known violator.

If you want to establish a trademark or copyright, or if you encounter a situation concerning protected designs and need more information, research it at the library; or write the Commissioner of Patents and Trademarks, Washington, D.C. 20231. For copyrights, write the Copyrights, Information and Publications Section, LM-455, Copyright Office, Library of Congress, Washington, D.C. 20559; or seek legal counsel. The fees for registering a design are nominal. You will have to provide a copy of a sewn sample for their files.

Another fact to know is that an employee of yours who creates a design on your time or on your equipment, or on behalf of your business, has no right to that design when he/she leaves your employ. This fact also holds true for any instructional or other confidential information you or they may have prepared that could be used later in a competitive situation.

Integrity breeds confidence and trust in your business relationships. Know the law and do your part to honor protected designs.

Ownership Of The Media

A design center may rightfully sell a protected design to anyone who has authorization to use that design. So, even if you request all copies of a tape or disk, chances are the design center may still save a copy or retain it in machine memory. After all, if the center does get another order for that design, it may not want to recreate what has already been created. The design center also may copy-protect a disk to prevent embroiderers from duplicating them.

So, now we know that the one who has the copyright or trademark owns the design, logo, name and so forth. But, what about the disk or tape? Usually, your customer orders it from you, you order it from a design center, and money is exchanged in both transactions. Once the design center sells you the disk or tape, it can no longer claim ownership, even though it still can access the design to produce another disk or tape.

How you handle the sale of the embroidery to your customer determines whether you or the customer own the tape or disk. If you charge for the tape or disk and so state in writing on your sales order or invoice, then the customer bought it and owns it. If, however, you charge for the service, in language such as "set-up charge," then you own the tape or disk, unless you've signed a contract or agreement agreeing to turn over all materials related to the job. Retaining ownership of the media usually assures that your customer will use your business for all repeat orders of that design. Most likely they will not want to pay for the design twice by taking their business elsewhere.

Some customers have been known to contact design centers directly, then take the disk or tape to the lowest bidding embroiderer for the sewing. In such a situation, clearly the customer owns the media.

Exhibit 10

NONDISCLOSURE/NONCOMPETE AGREEMENT

THIS AGREEMENT, made and entered into on this ____ day of _____, 19__, by and between ____________________(hereinafter referred to as "________(1)_________"), and ____________________ (hereinafter referred to as "_____(2)_________").

WITNESSETH:

WHEREAS, _____(1)_________ and ____(2)_________ have contracted as more fully described in Exhibit A hereto; and

WHEREAS, ____(1)_________ possesses certain confidential and proprietary information (the "information"), including but not limited to designs, plans, specifications, potential or existing customers, contacts and contracts; and

WHEREAS, the information has been and will be necessarily divulged by _______(1)___________ and/or its agents to ____(2)___________ and such disclosure will place _______(1)__________ and _____(2)__________in a confidential and fiduciary relationship; and

WHEREAS, ______(2)____________acknowledges the highly confidential nature of the information and that the confidentiality of the information must be protected to the benefit of ______(1)___________;

NOW, THEREFORE, in consideration of the premises, ________(2)___________, for and on behalf of itself and any of its employees, agents, representatives, successors and assigns, agrees to maintain the confidentiality of the information, and will neither use the information commercially or otherwise for the use or benefit of _______(2)_____________ or any third party, nor disclose the information under such circumstances to any person who is not an officer or employee of _____(2)__________, except as authorized by _______(1)___________ in writing.

_______(2)____________ will take all reasonable and necessary measures to prevent disclosure and use of the information to any and all third parties, except as authorized by ____(1)________ in writing.

________(2)__________ further agrees that _______(2)________, its successors and assigns, will not, directly or indirectly, compete with _______(1)_______ or engage in any activities involving or relating to the information for a term of _____ years from the date hereof.

__________(2)_______ further agrees that in the event of actual or threatened breach by _______(2)________ of the provisions of this Agreement, _______(1)________ shall be entitled to an injunction restraining ________(2)___________ from activities constituting a breach of this Agreement. Nothing herein stated shall be construed to prohibit _______(1)_______ from pursuing any other remedies available to it for such breach or threatened breach, including the recovery of damages, costs, and attorney fees.

_______(1)_____ and ______(2)_______ further agree that:

(1) This Agreement shall be governed by the laws of the State of _______, both as to interpretation and performance;

(2) This Agreement shall not be assigned without the written consent of both parties; and

(3) This Agreement shall be binding upon the parties, their successors and assigns.

______________(1)________________ ___________________(2)________________

By:________________________________ ____________________________________

Exhibit 11

Underlay

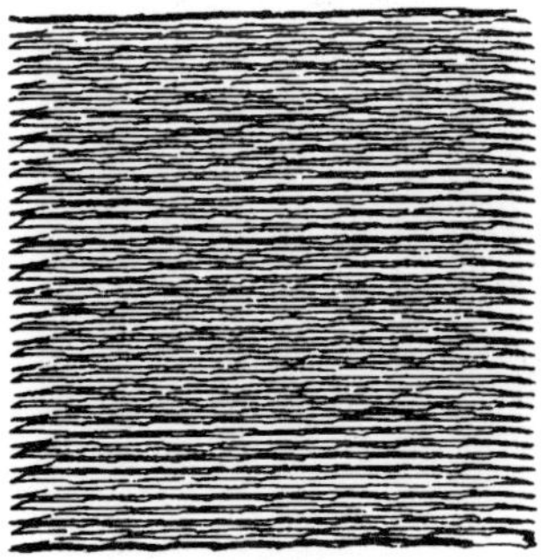

Fill

Cross

Bean

Running

Statin
Stitch

Chain
Stitch

Lock Stitch

Jump
Stitch

Exhibit 12

License Agreement

THIS AGREEMENT, effective as of the ____ day of ____, 19__, by and between:
___________________, thereinafter called OWNER, a __________ organized and existing under the laws of ___________, ____________, located at ____________, and _____________________ thereinafter called USER, a ______________, organized and existing under the laws of ___________, ______________, located at ___________.

WHEREAS, OWNER is the owner of the trademarks and service marks (hereinafter called Marks) and registrations thereof listed on Schedule A and

WHEREAS, USER is desirous of using the Marks in connection with its business:

NOW, THEREFORE, in consideration of the foregoing and of the mutual promises hereinafter set forth, the parties agree as follows:

1. GRANT OF LICENSE
OWNER grants to USER a nonexclusive, nontransferable license to use the Marks in its name and in connection with the goods and services covered by the registrations referred to in Schedule A and USER accepts the license subject to the following terms and conditions.

2. OWNERSHIP OF MARKS
USER acknowledges the ownership of the Marks in OWNER, agrees that it will do nothing inconsistent with such ownership and that all use of the Marks by USER shall inure to the benefit of and be on behalf of OWNER, and agrees to assist OWNER in recording this Agreement with appropriate government authorities. USER agrees that nothing in this License shall give USER any right, title or interest in the Marks other than the right to use the Marks in accordance with this License and USER agrees that it will not attack the title of OWNER to the Marks or attack the validity of this License.

3. QUALITY STANDARDS
USER agrees that the nature and quality of all services rendered and goods sold by USER in connection with the Marks shall conform to standards set by and be under the control of OWNER.

4. QUALITY MAINTENANCE
USER agrees to cooperate with OWNER in facilitating OWNER's control of such nature and quality to permit reasonable inspection of USER's operation, and to supply OWNER with specimens of use of the Marks upon request. USER shall comply with all applicable laws and regulations and obtain all appropriate government approvals pertaining to the sale, distribution and advertising of goods and services covered by this License.

5. FORM OF USE
USER agrees to use the Marks only in the form and manner and with appropriate legends as prescribed from time to time by OWNER, and not to use any other trademark or service mark in combination with any of the Marks without prior written approval of OWNER.

6. INFRINGEMENT PROCEEDINGS
USER agrees to notify OWNER of any unauthorized use of the Marks by others promptly as it comes to USER's attention. OWNER shall have the sole right and discretion to bring infringement or unfair competition proceedings involving the Marks.

7. TERM
This Agreement shall continue in force and effect for the terms of the registrations issued for said Marks listed in Schedule A and all renewals thereof, unless sooner terminated as provided for herein.

8. TERMINATION FOR CAUSE
OWNER shall have the right to terminate this Agreement upon thirty (30) days written notice to USER in the event of any affirmative act of insolvency by USER, or upon the appointment of any receiver or trustee to take possession of the properties of USER or upon the winding-up, sale, consolidation, merger or any sequestration by governmental authority of USER, or upon breach of any of the provisions hereof by USER.

9. EFFECT OF TERMINATION
Upon termation of this Agreement USER agrees to immediately discontinue all use of the Marks and any term confusingly similar thereto, and to delete the same from its corporate or business name, to cooperate with OWNER or its appointed agent to apply to the appropriate authorities to cancel recording of this Agreement from all government records, to destroy all printed materials bearing any of the Marks, and that all rights in the Marks and the goodwill connected therewith shall remain the property of OWNER.

10. INTERPRETATION OF AGREEMENT

It is agreed that this Agreement may be interpreted according to the laws of the State of _______, United States of America.

IN WITNESS WHEREOF, the parties hereto have caused this Agreement to be executed as of the day and year first above written.

OWNER	USER
______________________________	______________________________
BY__________________________	BY__________________________

CHAPTER 13

MARKETING

Market Position

Though still in its infancy, computerized embroidery has grown to the point where real market structures can be seen. And embroiderers should plan where they want to be positioned in the market.

Most products and services can be categorized into three quality and price categories. The top of the line is usually the best, the most expensive, the name brand. At the opposite end is the lower quality, no frills, off-brand. Somewhere in the middle are all others, which make up the major market.

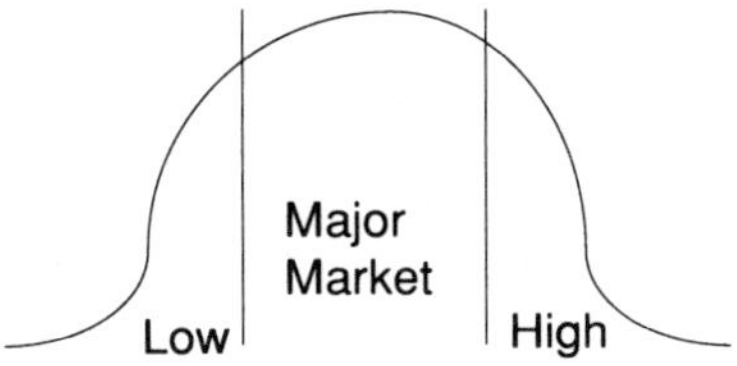

All three categories have a market. Usually, the extremes have limited markets, but can still be quite profitable. In the high end, you have to provide only the best quality work and service, and you'll charge top dollar, even though you may have fewer customers or have to work harder to find customers. At the low end, you will likely cut corners or skimp on quality, provide few extras and charge discount prices. After all, customers in this category are looking for the lowest prices available.

Image

Once your desired market position is determined, you must take steps to create the appropriate image for your business. Everything you do must stay within character to develop company reputation, recognition, ethics, quality and service. Any merchandise you carry, the name and logo you choose, your letterhead, vehicles, manner of dress, advertising, displays—*everything*—should be consistent with your projected image and market position.

The name you choose for your business should first be checked through the office of your Secretary of State if you are incorporating; or through your local or county office if you are operating as a sole proprietorship. Search the Yellow Pages before even submitting a name request. If there is another business with the name you are considering, change it to try to avoid delays in obtaining a business license or legal incorporation. Your attorney can help you in this matter.

If you're starting an embroidery business without many initial contacts, you may fare better in selecting a name that describes your business. However, there are many successful embroiderers whose names do not reflect what they do. It is most important, though, to include what you do on your business card.

An attractive logo is important to your image. If you are artistic, you may wish to design your own logo. Otherwise, hire an advertising agency or consider a local art student. Have the business cards professionally printed, selecting a style of print that is clearly readable. A few companies in the industry have embroidered logos on their business cards and/or letterhead! Your letterhead paper stock and color should match your business cards, although the cards will be on heavier paper. If you are adding embroidery to an existing business, consider adding a line about embroidery to your business cards.

Advertising

Many embroiderers have built successful businesses with little or no advertising other than word-of-mouth, and possibly a listing in the Yellow Pages. But with the industry expanding and competition becoming more keen, we see an increase in advertising dollars being spent by embroiderers. Also, word-of-mouth advertising takes time because you need satisfied customers before they can spread the word about your business. Advertising can be an effective way for a start-up business to gain customers, or supplement the workload in slow seasons, or for any existing business to increase sales in general. Advertising should occupy a deliberate part of your budget, rather than be limited to whatever funds are left over.

How much should you spend on advertising? Certainly no more than you can afford. As a guideline, retail apparel shops spend an average 2.5% to 3.5% of their sales. But, more important than the dollars spent is what benefits you will receive. This will depend on whether your ad is clear, targeted to the market you seek, and long-running enough to be certain the market has absorbed your message.

Let's back up to what you can do without spending much. First, make use of those business cards. If you're after business from anywhere and anyone, always carry them with you and ask family members and friends to help you distribute them. Everytime you meet someone new, give them your card. Take your cards to club and organizational meetings. Post them on bulletin boards, at grocery stores, bowling alleys, bingo parlors, health spas—anywhere that has a bulletin board for business ads. Take them to flea markets, conventions, special events where other businesses are showing their wares. Some retailers enclose them with every embroidery order they fill so that their customers will remember them for repeat business. If you are a wholesaler, think twice about this, however, because your retail store clients might feel you're trying to cut them out by encouraging their customers to buy directly from you.

Try to take advantage of free advertising through your local newspapers. They frequently will print an article about unique businesses, or businesses that do something unique. Pat Steely of the Monogram Centre in Buffalo, New York, was successful in getting free advertising this way. A reporter for *The Buffalo News* brought a photographer to Pat's shop and conducted an interview. The reporter was so fascinated by computerized embroidery that she devoted almost a full page of the business section to the Monogram Centre, describing how the equipment works, what's popular in embroidered designs and monograms, what garments are fashionable for embroidery, prices, and the fact that Pat had 500 steady shirt customers. The article also elaborated on Pat's prom business, wherein more than 1,000 tuxedo handkerchiefs were personalized with the couple's names and the theme and date of the prom. The boys give them to their dates as a memento of the evening.

Beverly Fiebelkorn, of Punkin Patch Factory, in Vinton, Iowa, received a big spread and two color photos on the front page of the Lifestyle section of *The Gazette* newspaper in Cedar Rapids.

Having had a doll business for some time, Beverly added computerized embroidery and created the Hayden Fry doll to commemorate the University of Iowa football coach. The dolls sold for $75 and orders poured in from California to New York, and from Missouri to Minnesota.

Because there are still many people who have never seen a computerized embroidery machine, your business may capture the interest of a local reporter. Give it a try, and ask them to bring a photographer so that you can show their readers something of interest. Establish rapport with the reporter and keep him or her informed of anything your business does that is newsworthy: a unique new product, a well-known customer you have served, a service you performed for the community, your sponsorship of events and so forth. Keep your name and that of your business in the public eye as much as possible.

Carolyn Henson of Custom Monogram & Embroidery in Toccoa, Georgia, not only captured the attention of her local newspaper for an article, but also the local TV station. A reporter visited her shop and interviewed her about her business. The TV camera showed close-up shots of the embroidery and focused on Carolyn as she explained the computer processes. The intereview closed with the machine stitching the TV station's logo.

Another vehicle for getting this type of free advertising is the press release. In order of importance, type an article in third person narrative or formal, about your business or an event, answering the standard who, what, where, when, and why questions. Include your name, business name and phone number and send it to a specific person's attention. Follow up with a phone call. If timeliness is important to the article, request a specific date for release.

Karen Fox, Melco's director of advertising, suggests writing a press release whenever you have news to report.

"News can be defined as anything of interest to people. When you upgrade or develop new products or services, write a press release. Tell the reader what it is, who can use it, and why it is bigger or better or less expensive. Tell how your new equipment has increased productivity, decreased turnaround time, and made you the largest embroiderer in town.

"When you hire or promote key employees, write a press release. Include the employee's name, position, background, college, marital status, number of children, current or past community involvement and organizational memberships. Also include any unusual hobbies or accomplishments.

"When you sponsor an embroidery contest or donate 50 jackets to the children's hospital, or if you plan to give every customer a free hat on President's Day, write a press release.

"The press loves a good human interest story. Perhaps your family members are fourth generation embroiderers, or your custom work is designed by your 90-year old Apache grandmother. Write about it."

Limit each release you write to one product, person or event. The tone of your release should be straight and factual—the copy should be clear, simple and clean. Make sure your facts are accurate and avoid adjectives like "terrific."

Photographs should accompany your press releases whenever possible. Black and white, 5 inches x 7 inches photographs are preferred. For personnel releases, include a head and shoulders picture of your employee. Plan to take photographs at your sales promotions. Be sure to give the photographer a photo credit. Ask all the people in your pictures for permission to use the photos with news releases, and be sure to identify them in captions attached to the photos.

Send press releases to the editor or business editor of your local newspaper. You may also send them to trade publications and local radio stations. See the sample press release in Exhibit 13.

Probably the best investment in advertising is the Yellow Pages. Some say bigger is better; some say size doesn't matter. There are those who believe the first name listed in a given category draws the most business, while others believe it's your business location or the content of the ad that is most important. I believe the most important points of your Yellow Pages ad are to place it under the appropriate headings and to adequately describe what it is you offer. The best headings for placement are both Embroidery and Monogramming. Of course, if this is not your primary business, then your ad should also appear under the correct heading for your primary business.

Those who have used red print in the Yellow Pages say it has increased their responses, probably because it makes their ad stand out more. Take a look at competitors' listings in the Yellow Pages. See what they deem important to include. Then examine what you offer that they do not mention. Perhaps you offer credit card convenience and no one else lists it. It doesn't mean they don't have it, but you gain the edge by advertising the service they didn't. Give as much information as you can about what you offer. If you offer custom designs, say so. If you sell garments, say so, and possibly list some well-known brand names. If you specialize, state your specialty. You also may want to consider giving your business hours, or directions to your site if your business is difficult to find. You may wish to state whether your business is wholesale or retail, and whether you offer volume discounts. If you offer "while you wait" service or pick-up and delivery, consider mentioning those services in your ad. Perhaps you want to advertise your niche, such as uniforms or team jackets and so on.

Additional business directories are also becoming available, such as directories for more concentrated areas or directories for businesses owned by women and other groups and minorities. You may wish to expand your advertising into such other publications if you receive business resulting from the Yellow Pages, if any of these other directories available in your area appear to be gaining acceptance by your targeted market, or if you qualify to be in a more exclusive directory in which your competitors could not advertise.

Experiment with trade and business papers if your market is business logos. A trip to the Chamber of Commerce may help you locate other suitable publications where inexpensive ads can be placed.

Many organizations publish newsletters and magazines for their members. These are worthwhile for ads, as well as direct mail-order campaigns.

Small businesses nationwide have found classified ads in major newspapers to be effective. They are relatively inexpensive, and those who respond usually are looking for a specific product or service. This has been overlooked in the embroidery industry, but may be worth testing. A few companies have placed classified ads in the screenprinting magazines.

Paid advertisements placed in newspapers, newsletters and magazines can be used to promote your business, products and services in general. They can also be used to promote items that are timely because of seasons, holidays, events, or national advertising by manufacturers and producers. The latter may be a way of obtaining cooperative advertising dollars. Manufacturers of certain garments or embroiderable goods may make funds available if you give them a plug in your ad.

When producing printed ads, mention your specific offer in your headline and restate it in your subhead. Say something to differentiate your business from others who advertise in the same publication. It's also helpful to add a sense of urgency to your ad, which can be done by placing a deadline on your offer. Use short words, short sentences and short paragraphs. Borders around ads, especially small ads, are proven attention-getters, as are photos. Above all, be sure to include your business name, address and phone number, preferably at the bottom of the ad. Make it easy for customers to find you.

Be sure your ad is in character with your intended market. The placement is also important for targeting the right market. The news section is the best, of course, because it is the most widely read. The next most frequently read section of the newspaper is the astrology page. If you're advertising personalized household linens, it should be located in the women's pages. Male-oriented offers may do best in the sports section. If your target is businesses, consider the financial section.

Fund-raising projects, such as cookbooks, are frequently done by organizations. Many welcome advertisements for nominal fees, and it has been my experience that they usually limit their advertisers to one per category—one embroidery shop, one dry cleaner, one dentist and so forth. There is also paid advertisement space available in special-event programs such as ice shows, circuses, theatrical performances and rodeos.

The average American has five radios in his household, plus another in each car. Have you considered radio advertising?

There are two kinds of radio advertising: foreground and background. Foreground radio includes news shows, talk shows, public radio, sportscasts and religious shows. Because it's verbal, foreground radio requires active listening, and commercials are often integrated into the shows. Foreground commercials are most effective when you go on the air and talk about your business yourself. You could even consider hosting an event and inviting the radio station to hold a remote broadcast at your place of business. This encourages customers to stop by, participate in the excitement, and see what you have to offer.

Background radio includes music shows. With background radio, you must consider your market and choose the station or program that appeals to that market—senior citizens, women, kids, men, cooks, office workers, and fans of rock and roll, country, oldies, jazz, heavy metal, classical or easy listening. The type of music dictates the type of rate. Rates in the Denver area, for example, range from $10 for one minute on a religious station, to $300 for one minute on a classical station.

Lee Caroselli, now owner of Balboa Threadworks Inc. in Balboa, California, formerly had a retail embroidery shop. She doubled her proceeds with radio advertising. Lee's market was the Baby Boomer generation, which primarily led the trend from printed T-shirts to direct embroidery. Based on the results of a questionnaire completed by her local clientele, she chose the station that played oldies music, and ran her commercials in the mornings—5 spots per day, 7 days per week. The radio advertising was so successful that Lee took it a step further. She sponsored a trivia contest, based on old rock and roll songs. The winners received an embroidered shirt, which they had to pick up at her shop. This gave Lee and her staff the opportunity to sell additional merchandise to the winners.

How long should a radio spot run? A 30-second spot is usually far more than 50% of the cost of a 60-second spot, but in most instances, you can say in 30 seconds what can also be expressed in 60 seconds. So go with the shorter spots even though they're not great values. In the long run, they'll give you more value for your money. If, however, you have a complex promotion, you may need to run it longer. Most announcers speak at the rate of 70 words per 30-second spot, but according to studies done by Columbia University, people will listen more attentively if the announcer talks faster, up to about 90 words per 30-second spot.

Many stations have the capability to produce your ad. If they do, and you want to use their service, check out their equipment. Listen to their announcers. They may also be able to write your copy. If you have a flair for words, do it yourself. If you use the station's writers, work with them because you know your business far better than they do. You don't want your ad to sound like all the other ads, stressing just your name, location, courteous and friendly service. These are all important, but what you really want to stress is the embroidery—it's beauty, it's uniqueness, it's functionality for the target market and the fact that you can create anything the customer wants. Perhaps you'll want to mention the various types of garments you have available or maybe even mention brand names.

The personal interview method works well also. As the owner, arrange to be interviewed by the announcer or talk-show host. Let the interview go on for 20 or 30 minutes, then use small sections of the interview for future commercials. You could even arrange for the announcer or talk-show host—whoever will be doing your commercial for you—to visit your shop and let him give a personal testimonial to the quality and creativity of your work.

Sound effects can enhance your radio ad, especially appropriate music or jingles. Try to avoid annoying sounds such as car horns or crying babies.

Television commercials are very effective. The cost of advertising on television varies dramatically. The rates for the Denver stations, for example, range from $10 to $10,000 for a 30-second spot. It depends primarily upon the time of day the advertisement runs and how many people are watching. The broadcast day is divided into specific time segments called "dayparts." Some common examples of television dayparts are:

1. Morning	- Monday through Friday	6 a.m. - 9 a.m.
2. Daytime	- Monday through Friday	9 a.m. - 3 p.m.
3. Early Fringe	- Monday through Friday	3 p.m. - 6 p.m.
4. Prime Access	- Monday through Saturday	6 p.m. - 7 p.m.
5. Prime Time	- Monday through Saturday	7 p.m. - 10 p.m.
	and Sunday	6 p.m. - 9 p.m.
6. Late News	- Monday through Sunday	10 p.m. - 10:38 p.m.
7. Late Fringe	- Monday through Sunday	10:38 p.m. - 2 a.m.

Reaching your best customers has different price tags. Usually the larger the number reached, the higher the price. Buying frequency to a smaller number of your best customers can carry a bargain price. TV rates are negotiable in most cases.

Charles Ellison is owner of Ellison's Western Wear in the rural town of Franklin, Texas. He pays $100 for a 30-second spot during prime time; half that price for daytime drama spots (the "soaps"). These are package prices and will vary depending upon your location and how much time you purchase. Charles has three or four various ads running over a one- to three-week time period. Of the 30 seconds, 10 seconds is devoted to embroidery. The ads are shot at his store and the embroidery portion shows a close-up of his machine stitching a large embroidered design. The other 20 seconds feature his best-selling garments: jackets, caps, shirts and towels.

Charles has found that his TV ads work best when used for special occasions such as Christmas, back-to-school, rodeos and the beginning of ball seasons. After much trial and error, he has narrowed his marketing approaches to direct mail, newspaper ads, TV commercials and word-of-mouth. According to Charles, "So much depends upon your location. I can afford TV ads here, whereas in a major city it would probably be cost-prohibitive. Yet, in a major city, the Yellow Pages are probably effective, but in my rural area, it's the most expensive method with the least amount of response. You just have to keep trying different approaches until you find what works best for your business and your location."

One of the most modern techniques of TV advertising is known as the "informercial," which is a 30-minute TV show that is really one long commercial. The program should be closely tied to the products and services you offer. Informercials are available through satellite networks, cable stations or directly from TV stations. Some are available for as little as $200. This buys nonprime time, but at all hours of the day and night, many people are watching that tube!

When producing a TV ad, again, get involved in the writing of the script because no one knows your business and its value to your customers better than you do. The message of the script should be product oriented. Talk about the embroidery and the garments you offer. Then, when choosing samples to be worn or shown, note on the script what is to be seen when particular paragraphs are spoken. TV is a great medium to advertise such a visual art as embroidery. Yet, nothing is worse than being impressed by what you see and not knowing where to get it. So, be sure your business name and location are mentioned frequently, at least at the beginning, middle and end of the commercial.

Selecting the concept for your commercial is important. You can use a storyline or playlet to act out how embroidery is used in normal living—the pride of an employee wearing a uniform with an embroidered logo, an elaborate jacket back design and the response of people seeing it, the joy on the face of a child who received a personalized toy and the thrill of a bride seeing her new initials monogrammed on her linens. Another concept would be to emphasize the wide selection of designs available and how they are produced. A few seconds of the embroidery machine stitching a colorful design could be shown.

It's a good idea to add action or movement to your ad. You can hire a video producer or use the TV station's production department. They have the equipment and expertise to handle the cameras, lighting, direction and even the actors or actresses. Hold planning meetings with the key people involved in the production of your TV ad. Also schedule rehearsals so that the final product can be done right the first time.

You can use tape or film for the ad, but tape has the advantage of allowing you to view the results right away. Changes can then be made accordingly. However, if film is used, you will have to reschedule a take after the film has been developed and reviewed.

It's usually more effective for small businesses to concentrate on one good commercial and repeat it often, rather than spend the money doing a variety of ads. In all forms of paid advertising—newspapers, magazines, radio, and TV—it is important to run your ad frequently. This helps to establish your business as legitimate and successful. The repetition will also help the customer remember your company's name. According to *Sales & Marketing Digest*, a study analyzed more than 175,000 inquiries generated by advertisements in five selected publications with 10-week inquiry processing cycles. On the average, the greatest number of inquiries are generated in the last four weeks of processing—practically 50% of the total. The first three weeks represent the least activity—less than 20%.

Direct Mail

In a 1987 study, 46.6 percent of retailers said direct mail was their most effective marketing method. In contrast, only 32.4% said newspaper advertising was best. The goals of direct mail are to get your letter opened, get it read and get the order.

Focus your mailing on a single idea and state it at least three times. Long copy seems to work better than short copy. There is a saying in marketing that the more you tell, the more you sell. Of all things that people dislike about marketing, the first is a feeling of deception, and the second is lack of information. Be sure all claims are true, and tell your readers all you can about what you're selling.

Feature your biggest customer benefit in your headline. After the headline, the first line of a letter is what is read first. Therefore, it needs to be enticing enough to make the reader want to know more. The next thing read is the postscript and the signature, followed by the rest of the first paragraph. Then, most readers will look at the subheads, and if they are still interested, they will then read the rest of the letter.

Keep paragraphs short and sentences easy to read. Underline a few key words to draw attention. Testimonials from satisfied customers may help add credibility. If you're making a special offer, put a time limit on it. Also, it helps to include a brochure or something visual with the letter. Those who don't take the time to read what you have to say may look at what you have to show.

Having the right mailing list is crucial. The best is a list of your own customers. Such a list should be developed from the start (but it's not too late to start now if you don't already have one). It should be updated regularly and kept current with key contacts, correct address and phone numbers. It should be added to regularly and used for marketing purposes. Some embroiderers even ask all customers who visit their shop to sign a guest registry.

For prospecting, there are many lists available for purchase. Refer to your Yellow Pages under "mailing lists" for a broker who can help you. Any directory is a good source for names—city directories, Dun & Bradstreet, trade associations of other types of businesses, organizational rosters. If you want to compile your own, start with the newspapers. As Linda Engelhaupt of Bellefontaine, Ohio, points out, "The business section is full of news about local companies and their events, personnel and products. Funeral homes are listed daily. There are restaurants and car dealers galore mentioned in the papers. And don't overlook the club news. All of these are excellent sources of prospective customers."

If you have a small business, you can send a few letters or postcards each day or week, signing your own name for a more personal touch. The best times to send a direct mailing are in the months of January, February and October. These mark the beginnings of something: the new year, the coming of spring, and our industry's best season, the winter months.

Be sure to include a method of response—a card, form, or coupon to return, a number to call, or a deadline to meet, to name a few. However, don't assume that no response means no interest. Your investment in a mailing deserves follow-up. A telephone call following the mailing will usually yield higher results. The most effective sales people rely upon persistence. They follow up as much as five or six times or until the prospect says, "I'm not interested." This is another form of direct marketing: telemarketing. Of course, telemarketing does not require a mailing to precede a call, but the mailing enables you to include more information and, in particular, something visual such as a brochure or sample sew-out.

Promotional Events

Sponsoring an event will give you more opportunity to put your company's name before the public. Any kind of event has merit, even if it has no direct relationship to your type of business, because *everyone* is a prospective customer. However, being in the embroidery business gives you an added advantage for sponsorships because you can also promote by having the participants wear advertising of the event (embroidered, of course). If you're sponsoring a walk-a-thon, the participants could wear embroidered shirts, shorts, hats, socks or headbands. If you're sponsoring a fashion show, be sure fashions with embroidery are highlighted. (Of course, you could hold your own fashion show of embroidered garments.) By sponsoring a bowling team, you gain access to the entire league of bowlers and possibly all bowlers at the lanes where your team bowls.

A popular event for start-up businesses is to hold an open house and invite all prospective customers in your targeted market or niche. However, this is not limited to start-ups. Established businesses can hold open houses to show what's new in the way of designs, lettering styles, garments, or to show off a remodeled store. If your market is made up of women who don't work outside the home, consider an afternoon tea. For those who do have 8-to-5 jobs, consider evening and weekend at-home parties similar to the Tupperware® method.

Think about sponsoring a contest or offering a drawing. The drawing could even be tied in with a sales promotion; for example, all those who purchase XYZ brand of fleecewear with embroidery are eligible.

You could also plan a joint venture with other neighboring businesses. This could be anything from a lip sync contest to a German Octoberfest.

Anything that brings customers to your place of business or puts your business name in the limelight is an excellent marketing tool, so long as the event is viewed favorably. It is best to avoid controversial events or promotions, unless they are handled with humor or both sides of a controversy are represented.

Brochures & Catalogs

A brochure is an informational piece about your product, service, or your business in general. It can also be used to present ideas to your customers. Simple flyers can be produced inexpensively and easily, especially if you have a personal computer. Flyers can also be printed relatively inexpensively. According to Jim Norland in an article that appeared in _The Press_, you can print 500 copies of a single 8 1/2 inch x 11 inch flyer for about $20 to $25, on colored stock. If art and typesetting are needed, it may cost $100. A professionally printed brochure will project a more attractive image and be more attention-getting, but it is more expensive and generally requires the help of an advertising agency. Because embroidery is highly visible and needs to be seen to be appreciated, color photos in your brochure are preferable. Consider full garment shots as well as close-ups of the embroidery. Models will greatly enhance the professionalism and image of your brochure. To reduce the cost, consider photogenic friends or relatives.

Catalogs are used to show your complete line of products and services, and to facilitate direct mail sales. Each item (garment, design or lettering style) would have a catalog number and price. Sales would be via phone order or mail-in order form. Again, a professional advertising agency should be employed for such a project. It will cost, but it is becoming more acceptable to charge customers for catalogs, which would help recover some of the expense.

Ann Chapman of Galena, Illinois, has a very successful catalog business with her screenprinting and embroidery business. Her catalog features various styles, sizes and colors of jackets with prices listed for embroidery and screenprinting. Director's chairs, place mats and matching dinnerware, clocks, laundry bags, pillowcases, log carriers, trophy items, wine bags, tote bags, shirts, towels, caps and patches are other items featured in the catalog. Several pages are devoted to available designs and lettering styles. An order form and ordering information is included, along with a statement about the value of their customers. The cover of the catalog shows a picture of their retail store; the toll-free numbers are printed across the bottom.

Catalog and direct mail sales are very popular because people like the convenience of shopping in the comfort of their own homes or at the office. The wider your range of products or services, the better suited you are for catalog sales.

If you're a wholesaler, encourage some of your retail customers to include your products and services in their catalogs. Having at least one advertising specialty firm as a client is particularly helpful for wholesalers wanting to capitalize on catalog sales.

Evaluation

You need about six months to see the effects of your advertising efforts. The basis for evaluating can be the number of leads received. Some people only track sales. However, if you captured the customer's attention but failed to make the sale, you must determine if it was a poor lead or a poor sales job.

The best method of tracking responses is through a coupon return program. But, for an overall evaluation, make a list of all advertising and promotional campaigns. Put this on a clipboard next to the phone and at the place of purchase. The last question you ask every customer is, "How did you hear about our business (event, design)?" Then mark the response. You'll soon have the beginning facts on what media have been most effective.

By dividing the cost of the campaign by the number of leads received, you will know the cost per lead. Your account ledgers for all customers who resulted from your advertising campaign will tell you the total sales generated by that campaign.

Some businesses measure the success of a marketing campaign solely by the number of leads or percentage of response. Of course, they are usually with big firms that are so departmentalized that they view the responses received as the final step, content to let the sales department worry about the revenue generated. Others will measure the success of a marketing campaign solely by the resulting sales volume. This is more difficult to determine because other factors besides a specific ad or promotion may have influenced the customer to buy; perhaps a salesperson, another customer or a window display was also instrumental.

I think you need to measure a campaign's success from both vantage points. Immediate sales generated by a marketing effort are great, but they are not the final result of the campaign. Those who responded to a marketing campaign are now a more important lead than just another name on a list. They have shown an interest in what you offer. Even if a sale is not immediately transacted, respondents to a marketing campaign become good prospects for regular follow-up sales calls.

Once you gain a handle on which advertisements, which media, which promotions worked best for your market in your area, then you can plan your future marketing efforts with the experience and knowledge of a pro. Continue to experiment and be flexible with changes in market trends.

Store & Window Displays

Make a special shopping trip or two just to study how others display their goods. Take paper and pencil along and jot down ideas—both good ones you'd like to try and bad ones to avoid. More importantly, try to determine why some displays attract customers and why others are easily overlooked.

As consumers, most of us like to shop in well organized stores where garments are easy to select either by size, style or color. Display similar items together—all shirts, all sweaters, and so forth. Don't hang a shirt next to slacks unless they are being sold as a set. Be sure you use hangers that hold the garment. It's so frustrating for customers to have to bend over and pick up items that easily fall off. Also, leave room in aisles for people to move about without knocking garments off racks and onto the floor.

Many shops decorate their walls with embroidery, either directly on the garments they sell or as wall hangings. Inexpensive hand-embroidery hoops make nice frames for displaying monograms, lettering styles and designs.

Window displays require special care. First, check your window at various times of the day for glare or special lighting needs. Perhaps an awning or overhang is needed to reduce reflected light during certain hours. You need to have the level of light on the display stronger than the light reflected on the window.

Small embroideries, such as monograms on shirt cuffs, should be enlarged for window displays. Also, use contrasting colors rather than tone-on-tone. Customers cannot see the embroidery close-up; therefore, exaggeration is needed. Light colored merchandise shows better close to glass than dark colors. Avoid combining colors that clash. Groupings are more appealing in odd numbers rather than even numbers. Balance in heights is important for eye appeal. Experiment with the use of mobiles or fans to create movement, which attracts attention. And, of course, clean windows are a must.

Strive for a theme by using props. For example, when displaying embroidered towels, add a towel rack, some colored and sculptured soaps, a matching rug, and perhaps a shower curtain for a backdrop. Or, when featuring golf shirts, add clubs, bags (embroidered, of course), tees and balls. A piece of green indoor/outdoor carpet would complete the look. Be creative—many household items make excellent props.

Trade Shows, Exhibits, Fairs

If you're considering going on the road with your machine, again it's important to identify your niche. Browse through the *Tradeshow/Convention Guide*, at your library, or order a copy from Budd Publications, P.O. Box 7, New York, N.Y. 10004. Your local Chamber of Commerce is another good source for shows coming to your area. Find out who to contact about particular events, usually a local association or promoter.

According to Lance and Cindy Sabo, it's important to know something about the type of show you're attending. Customers will buy more if you know the language. And, being able to converse with your customers about something they know and love helps build a good relationship. "Before going to an air show, we bought books on planes," says Lance. "I studied them and designed a few in embroidery so that I would know the differences between airplane models."

If you have a hobby or area of interest, see if there is a publication or association involved and find out if it sponsors such events. Your natural enthusiasm will spark ideas and give you an edge for marketing to others with the same area of interest.

It would be wise to visit a show before participating as a vendor.

This will give you the opportunity to study the attendance, buying habits of the attendees, competition, layout, booth sizes and displays. Perhaps you'll even meet another exhibitor you'd like to team up with and share expenses and space at the next event. Another idea, if you're primarily a wholesaler, is to talk to other representatives who may be interested in carrying some of your embroidered garments in their stores back home, and you may find items you can use in your business. Don't overlook the bartering possibilities!

Once you've determined a particular show to work, request an information packet and necessary forms. You will need to know booth costs, booth size, locations available, deadline dates for registering, and what is included in the way of carpet and electricity. Also find out when and where equipment should be shipped, and the set-up and tear-down times. Can you handle your own set-ups or must union personnel be employed? If so, at what cost?

You will need a display. The choices range from make-shift, home constructions to elaborate and expensive models available from display vendors. A sign or large banner is a must for attracting business and acquainting people with your business name.

Plan what you will take in the way of machines (some people rent additional machines for shows). Also, plan what garments, designs and samples to bring along. Kathy and Les Bueling of Bueling Monograms in Fargo, North Dakota, reserve a booth every year at the National Western Stock Show in Denver. They take 600 to 700 jackets, but only five or six sewn samples. Sewing jackets on the spot keeps the machines running, which always attracts more people to their booth.

While many jackets can be stitched during the 10-day show, many more orders are taken. In fact, the orders and repeat business from that single show keep the Buelings busy for the entire year until the next show!

Good sales and repeat business is reported by most who travel the shows, fairs and conventions. Phyllis Collins of Circle C Western Shop in Xenia, Ohio, has a traveling Western store. A furniture van was converted into a store on wheels. It has a hardwood floor, paneling on the walls, and patio doors with steps for easy access. The van is equipped with air conditioning, heat and an embroidery machine. Wall decorations consist of embroidered placemats with samples of their animal designs and their lettering and monogramming styles.

When showtime is near, be sure to give your machine a thorough check-up and take along spare parts. You don't want to be inoperative at such an event. Clean your machine thoroughly each day while at the show. Dust and dirt are usually excessive at show locations.

Take along plenty of business cards, brochures (if you have them), sales orders and price lists. The less time you must spend explaining how much everything costs, the more time you'll have to write those orders. Consider accepting major credit cards for purchases, and be somewhat leery of checks if you or the customer are out of your own area.

Wear comfortable shoes and get plenty of rest at night so that you will be physically up to heavy business activity for the duration of the event. Also, staff your booth with enough people to help, selecting only those who are knowledgeable, personable and willing to work.

Giveaways

Everyone likes something free, so giveaways are an excellent public relations tool. For those who choose to give their embroidered goods, it has the added advantage of exposing more people to embroidery. Thus, it would make sense to give something that will be highly visible to many—a jacket or cap—rather than something seen by few, such as lingerie. Be sure to include a business card so that the recipient of your gift knows who to contact when additional embroidery is needed.

Marilyn Reichenberg of Initial Stitch, however, never gives embroidery. She will give other items such as coffee mugs, but she believes that giving embroidery lessens the perceived value of the embroidery. Other embroiderers give items that bear their business name and address. Pens, calendars and many other such items are available through advertising specialty firms.

Summary

Marketing is simply a way to inform people about your business, your products and your services. It should be an ongoing effort because those customers you have now may not always remain loyal. They may have to be replaced. Also, if growth is your goal, marketing is the surest way to succeed. Perhaps marketing will serve to change your customer base from those who can't pay your prices to those who can. If you're one of those who have fallen into the trap of lowering your prices and not making a profit, marketing to a different clientele may cure that. Then again, it could be that you need to learn how to price more profitably.

Exhibit 13

SAMPLE PRESS RELEASE

NAME
ADDRESS (Or send on company letterhead)
PHONE

FOR RELEASE: (Give the date the release can be used or write "FOR IMMEDIATE RELEASE")

CONTACT: (Name of contact person and phone number)

HEADLINE
(Your headline should tell who, what, why, when, where)

PARAGRAPH 1: (Should reiterate and expand your headline. Always doublespace all paragraphs. Keep the tone of the release straight and factual. Avoid adjectives like "terrific.")

PARAGRAPH 2: (Give additional information about important points.)

PARAGRAPH 3: (Identify your company and its past activities.)

Photographs: Available upon request.

CHAPTER 14

PRICING FOR PROFIT

Theory

Profit is the difference between revenue and cost. If you followed the guidelines in Chapter 7, you already know your projected costs for the remainder of the year, and you know your actual costs if you've been in the business a month or longer. If you haven't followed the guidelines, you must take the necessary steps now to determine your costs. You cannot price for profit without knowing your costs, and then monitoring those costs regularly to maintain profitability.

Convert your costs to an hourly rate. To do this, examine your business operation time as follows: 1) months or weeks per year; 2) days per week or weeks per month; and 3) hours per day or week. Be realistic. If you're working 12-hour days regularly, figure your costs accordingly.

Once you know your cost per hour of doing business, then figure the number of units you can produce per hour, add in your profit and price accordingly. If you're pricing on a per-job basis, then you must analyze that job to determine how many you can produce in an hour or fraction of an hour. One approach is to add the sewing time at the speed you intend to sew, the time needed for preparation, such as unpinning, unfolding, unbuttoning, measuring, marking, hooping, pattern making, trimming and repackaging. Also figure the changing of needles and threads, and time needed for programming the machine. This sounds like a lot to go through to price, but as you gain experience, you'll be able to quickly analyze such things and give realistic price quotes.

Realize that a name may take two minutes to sew, but the total time spent preparing, sewing and finishing may stretch to four minutes. That's 15 names per hour on a single-head machine. If your hourly rate is $60, you must charge $4 per name to make that $60 per hour.

Another approach is to base your price on stitch count. If your average production rate (determined only by logging previous production) is 250 stitches per minute in an eight-hour shift, that is an average of 15,000 stitches per hour. If your rate is $60 per hour, then you must charge $4 per 1,000 stitches. If you average 400 stitches per minute, that's 24,000 per hour and your rate at $60 an hour is $2.50 per 1,000 stitches.

Businesses with single-head machines must realize the pricing edge multi-head shops have. If an average of 400 stitches per minute can be maintained on 12 heads, that's a total of 288,000 stitches per hour. Even if we double the costs and figure $120 per hour as a rate, that's $ .416 per 1,000 stitches. At 250 stitches per minute, it would be 180,000 stitches per hour, or $ .67 per 1,000 stitches. This becomes an alarming revelation to single-head shops trying to compete with multi-head shops, and mathematically it proves the benefits of networking! Subcontract those volume jobs out to the larger embroidery shops. There's enough profit for both of you, and meanwhile, you're doing more of the "right stuff" on your single-head machine for additional profit.

Stitch count is important for estimating operating time on your machine, but it is really less accurate as a pricing method because some jobs take longer to prepare than others. Many jobs include appliques. This may drastically reduce the stitch count, thereby reducing the price in stitch-count pricing. However, it does not take into consideration the time needed to make a pattern, cut the applique fabric, position, glue, stitch and trim. That's why I prefer the per-job method of pricing. Often though, when bidding on a contract job, stitch-count pricing is required. Exhibit 14 is a sample form that could be used to help you determine a bid. It would also be helpful for planning production.

Along with knowing your cost of doing business, an equally important part of profitability is production. At $60 per hour, every minute wasted is $1, and those dollars add up over a period of a day, week, month and year. Efficient production will be addressed in a subsequent chapter, but it is also a vital part of operating a profitable business and, therefore worth mentioning here. In fact, profitability is directly determined by cost, price and production. If you want more profit, you must either lower costs, raise prices, produce more or combine these strategies in such a way as to achieve profitability.

When adding profit to cost to determine your price, it's important to understand the terms "markup" and "margin." Markup is the difference between your cost and selling price, expressed as dollars or a percentage of the cost. If your cost per hour is $42.90, the difference between your $60 rate and the $42.90 cost is $17.10. Divide the markup amount of $17.10 by the cost of $42.90 to arrive at the markup percentage of 39.8%.

Margin is the percentage of the markup in dollars to the selling price. In the above example, divide the markup of $17.10 by the price of $60 to arrive at the margin percentage of 28.5%.

How much markup or margin should be added? There is no single answer to that question. We live in a free enterprise system where price fixing is unlawful. However, the McGuire Fair Trade Bill of 1952 reinstated the binding effect of the single-contract agreement whereby one individual agrees to subscribe to a fair trade price. In this way the individual manufacturer or wholesaler compels all other distributors of the product to adhere to the price fixed under the fair trade agreement. Supply and demand ultimately dictate price. In some industries there are averages to use as guidelines. In checking for averages, no studies have been done specifically for the embroidery industry; however, most embroiderers I have interviewed price their retail goods at 30% to 35% over wholesale prices. In retail apparel, the average markup is reportedly 50%, but more are demanding closer to 100% and sometimes even more. Retail markup in general is estimated to be between 30% to 40%.

Geographic location and area competition will play an important factor in determining your markup. Prices are higher on the East and West Coasts than in the Midwest or the South. Prices may vary from city to city within the same state. This is why it is important to keep abreast of what your competition is doing.

Another factor to consider is the uniqueness of the garment or design you are selling. If there is no competition, yet a strong demand, you can and should charge more. On the other hand, if you're selling something readily available most anywhere, you will probably have to accept much tighter margins.

Retail & Wholesale

Once again, let's understand these terms. Retail is selling to the end user. Wholesale is selling to retailers who, in turn, sell to the end user. Wholesalers cater to the small retail shops, ensuring both parties are profitable. Large retailers will often buy garments direct from the manufacturer, if possible, eliminating the middle-man wholesaler.

The role of the wholesaler should be:

1. To sell retailers goods at prices that permit them to compete.
2. To sell small quantities to retailers.

3. To deliver quickly.
4. To ease retailers' cash problems by extending credit terms.
5. To help retailers anticipate and meet demand.
6. To help retailers price their merchandise.
7. To help retailers merchandise their goods through promotions, advertising and displays.
8. To help retailers with their buying.

Few garment manufacturers embroider their own goods. That is why there is such a need for wholesale embroidery shops. So, even when retailers purchase garments direct from manufacturers, they rarely can obtain embroidery from the same source. Therefore, I believe it is valuable to differentiate between garments and embroidery when looking at pricing methods.

Garments are typically keystoned; that is, the cost is doubled to determine retail price. Yet, if a wholesaler is involved with the garments, he needs a profit too. As a wholesaler, you can determine retail price and discount 30%, if the retailer will agree. In this case, a shirt which costs you $4 from the manufacturer would carry a retail price of $8 (keystoned), and you would discount that price by 30% or $2.40, and sell it to the retailer for $5.60. Remember, *this* is for the garment only. The price for embroidery is additional. If this is unacceptable to the retailer, then you must determine if that shirt can sell for a higher retail price or if you can accept a smaller margin. Some retailers and wholesalers will use the markup on the garments as a cushion and give the embroidery away in order to sell more volume, be more competitive, or sell goods more quickly. Of course, only you can determine what is an acceptable profit rate for your business.

When pricing the embroidery, use your standard rate. Wholesale pricing should be less than retail pricing by 30% to 40%. Again, the reason for this is the added costs of operating a retail store. So, if we have $2.50 worth of embroidery added to the $5.60 shirt, our price to the retailer is now $8.10, and the retailer sells it for about $11.50. Your price of $2.50 already includes a profit margin for the embroidery. The retailer marks up the $2.50 by 30% to 40% and adds it on to the retail price of the shirt.

Some consistency is needed in pricing, especially if you are a retailer and need to develop a price list. There are embroiderers who charge a flat rate for names, often charging more per letter over five letters. They will also charge per color, especially those with single-needle machines. Others will charge by letter height, with a separate price listed for each size offered, in increments of 1/2 inch or 1 inch. Too much of this can become cumbersome, so you may want to consider standardizing by garment. For example, charge for lettering per line on a jacket front; have a set price for monograms on washcloths, hand towels, bath towels and the complete set; or ask a flat rate for left-chest logos where the stitch count usually averages 4,000 to 6,000 stitches. You may also want to set a minimum price.

When using flat rates, you're really job averaging. You'll make more on some jobs than on others. Notice I didn't say *lose on some and profit on others*. Plan to be profitable on every job. As Frank Gawronski says, "You don't need the practice!"

Exhibit 15 lists some flat rate prices for embroidery on certain garments. Use it strictly as a guideline; this is not meant to be a standard price list because correct pricing for your business will depend upon your cost, your production rates and your markup.

Pricing Custom Designs

While this book is mainly written for embroiderers rather than design centers, I believe it is appropriate to address the subject of pricing designs profitably. The time has certainly come (and is probably overdue) to restructure the methodology for pricing embroidery designs. As a carry-over from the days of hand punching, the standard has been to charge according to stitch count. The range varies from about $12 to $40 per 1,000 stitches. Some centers offer discounts for large stitch-count designs, and stock designs are typically priced less than custom designs because of repeat sales on the same design.

But, consider these problems with stitch-count design pricing:

- Automation enables quick and easy digitizing of columns and fill stitches (no longer do we "punch"); therefore, embroiderers and their customers could be paying high prices for the simplest jobs.
- Some designs, though low in stitch count, may take the most time to create because of difficult detailing, or adjustments for fabrics or small lettering, for example. Yet, because of the low stitch count, designers are not being paid adequately for such designs.
- The use of applique has created pricing problems because, while it lowers stitch count, it requires additional work for

designers and embroiderers alike. Yet, because the stitch count is lowered, the price goes down.

- Stitch-count pricing does not usually cover the time spent on sew-outs, written instructions, consultation and collection efforts.
- Stitch-count pricing makes no allowance for extra effort required in preparing artwork. A design with many color changes, complex patterns or detailing takes longer to prepare than a simple, one-color, solid fill where the original artwork is simply enlarged and marked.
- The potential exists, in stitch-count pricing, to encourage designers to add unnecessary stitches in order to charge a higher price.
- There is no way to control forthcoming orders of large, simple, profitable jobs vs. small, complex, unprofitable jobs. Therefore, having a profitable week or month is left to Lady Luck!
- With editing equipment available, design centers have a new market in converting and changing tapes and disks. This service would be difficult to price on a stitch-count basis.

Design centers who want more control over profitability should take the same approach as outlined for embroidery shops; that is, add up your costs, add in a profit and reduce it to an hourly rate. Then start analyzing the designs you create in terms of time. There is no substitute for experience here, but some guidelines to consider are consultations, artwork, the actual digitizing process, sew-outs and follow-up.

Forget estimating and provide quotes for your work. This will eliminate the temptation to overcharge due to poor planning on your part. Customers will become dissatisfied and go elsewhere if the price exceeds the estimate significantly or often. Also, quoting a firm price should force you to strive for accuracy and efficiency from your staff.

However, I do not recommend quoting your hourly rate. As you will see from the example that follows, the rates can vary drastically, yet still have a competitive bottom-line price. Quote only the price of the job or customers will shop around for the lowest price per hour and think they're getting a deal. Perhaps they are, but not necessarily because of the hourly rate.

At a digitizing seminar, I once asked two designers to estimate their costs, add in their profit, and then come up with an hourly price. Then, upon showing them a single design, moderately complex and containing 23,000 stitches, I had them estimate the time they thought it would take from start to finish.

Shop A—a one-man operation—was using a small digitizing tablet and a single-head embroidery machine as a verifier, and a simple artwork enlarger. His hourly rate, with a 100% markup came to $24. He estimated the design would take 16 hours to complete. His price for the design would be $384.

Shop B was using a much larger digitizer, an editing system and a single-head verifier and was redrawing all artwork. His hourly rate, with a 100% markup came to $88. He estimated the design would take four hours to complete, and the price was quoted at $352. There is not much difference in the two bottom-line quotes, yet the hourly rates are substantially different.

Many design centers have begun to charge by the level of difficulty. I believe this to be a wiser course, more fair to all. Let's hope this trend catches on nationwide.

Most embroiderers pass along the cost for custom designs to their customers. A few charge a price slightly higher than what they paid, and this is perfectly acceptable. After all, they spent time coordinating and communicating between the customer and the design center and that is a reasonable service to provide for a fee.

Estimating Stitch Count

As you build a library of designs and study them, you will learn to approximate stitch counts based on other designs with similar stitch counts. To be more precise, a ruler that shows square inches, available at art supply stores, would be helpful. Then refer to the following chart:

GUIDELINES FOR CUSTOM DESIGN ESTIMATES

Fill stitch @ 60 SPI/4.2 PT. with length of .15"/38 PT.

SQUARE	WITH UNDERSTITCHING
1"	1,200 Stitches
2"	4,500
3"	10,000
4"	16,000

CIRCLE	WITH UNDERSTITCHING
1"	950 Stitches
2"	3,600
3"	7,500
4"	14,000

BLOCK LETTERS	WITH UNDERSTITCHING
0.20 High @ 55 SPI/4.6PT.	80 Stitches per letter
0.25 High @ 55 SPI/4.6 PT	140
0.35 High @ 60 SPI/4.2 PT	200
0.50 High @ 63 SPI/4.0 PT	225
0.75 High @ 65 SPI/3.9 PT	375
1.00 High @ 70 SPI/3.6 PT	475

SCRIPT LETTERS	WITH UNDERSTITCHING
0.20 High @ 55 SPI/4.6 PT	80 Stitches per letter
0.25 High @ 55 SPI/4.6 PT	125
0.35 High @ 60 SPI/4.2 PT	180
0.50 High @ 63 SPI/4.0 PT	275
0.75 High @ 65 SPI/3.9 PT	450
1.00 High @ 70 SPI/3.6 PT	650

COLUMNS, BORDERS, LINES	
1" Long x 1/16" Wide	125 Stitches
1" Long x 1/8" Wide	140
1" Long x 1/4" Wide	196
1" Long x 3/8" Wide	240
1" Long x 1/2" Wide	285

Note: SPI = Stitches per inch
PT = Points

Pricing Strategies

Pricing in a complex and competitive market is not simple. In fact, it presents one of the most difficult problems in management. If the price is set too low, the business cannot remain solvent for long. If set too high, the product may be priced out of its markets, cutting sales volume below the break-even point. Therefore, setting prices is a compromise between what the producer would like to get and what the buyer is willing to pay.

You may price different garments and different designs with different profit margins—those that are highly competitive will force a lower margin and those that are unique will provide a greater margin. Over the years, if a business is to prosper and grow, 10% or better must be maintained as an average annual net profit (after taxes).

Alertness and flexibility should be the keynotes of your pricing activity. Often, establishing and commanding a price from your customers is more a matter of perceived value, individually from your business and collectively from the industry. Salesmanship is necessary in many instances to persuade the customer that the product has value equal to or more than the price. If you underprice embroidery, you have not only robbed yourself of profit, but you have also contributed to lowering the value of embroidery in the marketplace.

Sometimes you can't afford not to lower your prices. If you have a large inventory that must be moved quickly, this is usually justification to lower your prices. It would have been better to have planned your inventory more carefully.

A common pricing strategy is to use a leader—something priced under your normal markup to attract buyers who, hopefully, can then be sold additional merchandise or add-ons to the leader. For example, you may run a campaign to embroider names on jackets for $4 instead of your usual $5. Then, when you get an order, aim to sell an additional design under the name. Another version is the loss leader—pricing at a loss to attract increased sales, again with the intent of selling additional items.

Discounts are sometimes used as a way of improving cash flow. You offer a discount for prompt payment, in 10, 20 or 30 days from the date of invoice.

Suppose you are unfortunate enough to have a spoiled run, too time-consuming to rip out, yet unacceptable to the customer who ordered the job. If the goods can be sold to other customers, perhaps a discount would be appropriate. There have been times when the only things wrong were color or placement or size of garment, making it an excellent bargain for someone else who likes the color, placement, size and so forth.

Discounts are also quite common for volume orders. I would stress the importance here of discounting garments, rather than embroidery. Garments can be purchased from the manufacturer at volume discounts, and those discounts can be passed on to your customers. However, with embroidery, what you're doing is lowering the value of embroidery and where is it coming from? Are you saving enough time to warrant a discount in running 500 pieces of one job over running 100 pieces of five jobs? Hardly. All you're saving is programming time and a few minutes in rethreading. One exception would be if it saves you sales time. In other words, if you can save a day of calling on customers to get additional orders to fill the production time, then perhaps it's worth a lower profit to you.

When you negotiate your prices, terms, delivery or any other standard—whether for volume orders or to gain a prestigious account—you are in effect doing contract embroidery. Contract embroidery involves doing a specific job at specific terms other than your normal wholesale or retail price or terms. It is a compromise between what you normally receive and what you're willing to do for a specific job. However, don't get trapped into some common game-playing. For example, your customer asks you to quote a special rate on a job of 1,000 pieces. You quote a lower price based on that volume. Then, all of a sudden 250 pieces arrive at your shop with the customer expecting the price based on 1,000. Be firm. Let your customer know that the price quoted was discounted for volume and the 250 pieces would have to be priced at a higher rate. Better still, insist on a signed sales order for the full 1,000 pieces.

A word of caution here: The Robinson-Patman Act states that price differences must be specifically traceable to the differing volume or character of your transactions with customers that compete with each other. What it amounts to is marking up the cost of each transaction by the same percentage for each customer. This applies to the same garments or same design going to different customers.

Seasonal pricing strategies are common. Retailers may increase their prices during the Christmas holiday buying season, and sell any leftovers at a discount after the season.

Extra services can command higher prices. If you pick up and deliver, even if you don't charge directly for the service, it is acceptable to incorporate costs for this service into your price. Rush service should certainly be priced higher. After all, the customer is expecting you to drop everything and work on his order immediately. Giftwrapping can be an add-on service for a higher price. Even using colored bobbins and backing, which give a higher quality image, are justification for higher prices.

Limited editions of a licensed design are worth more. Timely designs centered around an event can command premium prices. When the Statue of Liberty rededication took place, jackets with the statue embroidered on the back were selling for as much as $250.

Price cutting should be thoroughly analyzed before you proceed. It can lead to price wars where competitors undercut you, then you in turn undercut them, and soon no one is making money. This can be dangerous because it is difficult to raise prices back to normal.

Refer to Exhibit 16. It shows the percentage of increase in unit sales that you will need to earn when you cut a price. This is based on gross profit (before taxes). For example, if your present gross margin is 25% and you cut your selling price 10%, you will need to sell 66.7% more units to earn the same margin dollars as at the previous price. So, look at the chart before you lower your prices and decide if you can really afford to do it!

A price may be hopelessly high or low in terms of accounting formulas and still be psychologically correct for maximum sales. As merchandise increases in price, higher markups are taken. Customers for a pair of $15 shoes are less concerned with price than customers for a $5 pair. Fashion embroidery is vulnerable to quick changes in public taste; a dress, which can become old-fashioned overnight, should have a higher markup than a T-shirt. Yet, in embroidery, there is merit in charging a higher markup for lower priced designs, and a lower price for higher priced designs. The elaborate jacket back designs are rarely sold at the normal rates charged for embroidery. If, for example, your hourly rate is $60 ($1 per minute), psychologically you can charge more than $1 per minute for embroidery that takes 1 minute to 7 minutes; charge $1 per minute for that which takes 8 minutes to 17 minutes; and less than $1 per minute for that taking 18 or more minutes.

Additional strategies include penetration and skimming pricing. Penetration is deliberately selling at a low margin in order to gain a larger share of the market from your competitors. Again, be responsible about lowering the value of embroidery in the market and causing price wars. Skimming is being the first to introduce a garment or unique design, taking a very high margin until other competitors come along and sell it for less. You then lower your margin accordingly.

Brian Tracy, a powerful lecturer on sales, states that price is a determining factor in making a sale only when identical goods and services are sold by more than one source. If anything whatsoever is different—the garment, the design, the quality of workmanship, the services rendered—then price is not a factor because you can sell on the basis of value. With that positive thought in mind, let's proceed to the next chapter—Successful Salesmanship.

Exhibit 14

In-House Pricing Worksheet

Garments

Item: (Specify brand, style, colors, and sizes)
Quantity: (Per color, per style, per size) Total no. garments: _______

Cost: $________
Shipping $________
Total $________
Markup $________

Total price for garments $_______

Designs

Design cost $_____
Handling $_____

Total $_______

Embroidery

Stitch count: _______
Machines needed:_____ # Hours:_____
Operators needed:_____ # Hours:_____
Type thread: __________ Sewing speed:_____
Backing:______________
Topping:______________
Pinning/measuring/patterns needed:_____________
Appliques____________
Counting in/out_________
Garment
preparation____
Sewn sample_________
Finishing____

Individual names_________
Style lettering__________________
Machine & operators needed___________________ # Hours:____________
____

Total hours______________
Total machines___________
Total operators___________ $_______

Total quote for job $_______

Exhibit 15

PRICES FOR 5-LETTER NAMES AND 3-LETTER MONOGRAMS

Item	No. per hour per head	Wholesale	Retail	Revenue per hour retail	Revenue per hour wholesale
Sheet	8	$5.50	$8.00	$64.00	$44.00
Pillowcase	10	3.50	5.00	50.00	35.00
Hand Towel	10	3.50	5.00	50.00	35.00
Bath Towel	8	5.50	8.00	64.00	44.00
Napkin	10	3.50	5.00	50.00	35.00
Table Cloth	6	7.00	10.00	60.00	42.00
Cuffs, Collars	15	3.00	4.50	67.50	45.00
Ties	15	3.00	4.50	67.50	45.00
Robes	8	5.50	8.00	64.00	44.00
Pajamas	12	3.50	5.00	60.00	42.00
Sweater	10	4.25	6.00	60.00	42.50
Lingerie	10	4.00	5.50	55.00	40.00
Jacket, shirt front	10	4.25	6.00	60.00	42.50

Exhibit 16

Price Cutting Chart

If You Cut Your Price	IF YOUR PRESENT GROSS PROFIT IS..................							
	5%	**10%**	**15%**	**20%**	**25%**	**30%**	**35%**	**40%**
	To achieve the same gross profit, you will need to increase your sales units by:							
1%	25.0%	11.1%	7.1%	5.3%	4.2%	3.4%	2.9%	2.6%
2	66.6	25.0	15.4	11.1	8.7	7.1	6.1	5.3
3	150.0	42.8	25.0	17.6	13.6	11.1	9.4	8.1
4	450.0	66.6	36.4	25.0	19.0	15.4	12.9	11.1
5	--	100.0	50.0	33.3	25.0	20.0	16.7	14.3
6	--	150.0	66.7	42.9	31.6	25.0	20.7	17.6
7	--	233.3	87.5	53.8	38.9	30.4	25.0	21.2
8	--	400.0	114.3	66.7	47.1	36.4	29.6	25.0
9	--	1000.0	150.0	81.8	56.3	42.9	34.6	29.0
10	--	--	200.0	100.0	66.7	50.0	40.0	33.0
11	--	--	275.0	122.2	78.6	57.9	45.8	37.9
12	--	--	400.0	150.0	92.3	66.7	52.2	42.9
13	--	--	650.0	185.7	108.3	76.5	59.1	48.1
14	--	--	1400.0	233.3	127.3	87.5	66.7	53.8
15	--	--	--	300.0	150.0	100.0	75.0	60.0
16	--	--	--	400.0	177.8	114.3	84.2	66.7
17	--	--	--	566.7	212.5	130.8	94.4	73.9
18	--	--	--	900.0	257.1	150.0	105.9	81.8
19	--	--	--	1900.0	316.7	172.7	118.8	90.5
20	--	--	--	--	400.0	200.0	133.3	100.0
21	--	--	--	--	525.0	233.3	150.0	110.5
22	--	--	--	--	733.3	275.0	169.2	122.2
23	--	--	--	--	1115.0	328.6	191.7	135.3
24	--	--	--	--	2400.0	400.0	218.2	150.0
25	--	--	--	--	--	500.0	250.0	166.7

CHAPTER 15

SUCCESSFUL SALESMANSHIP

Sales is asking for the order, making the sale and closing. Read that again—it's important!

Asking for the order is self-explanatory, yet often overlooked. Many sales have been lost because the salesman didn't simply ask for the order. Making the sale means giving a presentation—explaining all the reasons your prospect needs the product, discussing how the product will solve problems or enhance his business or image and overcoming all his objections. Closing is getting your prospect to make the decision to buy.

Salesmanship, however, also includes seeking out prospective buyers, creating or meeting a need or a desire and gaining your prospect's trust—both in you, as well as that which you're selling.

Say the word "salesman" to 50 different people, and you'll likely get 50 different reactions. Unfortunately, many of those will be negative. Personally, I have a very high regard for salespeople. Sure, there are some bad ones, as in any profession, but they usually don't last. Let's analyze the good ones and what it is that makes them good.

Because salesmanship relies upon good communication, evaluate yours. For oral communication, use a tape recorder and listen to your enunciation, speed and pitch of voice, tone, continuity, confidence and choice of words. For written communication, look for clarity, conciseness, tone and content. Then, practice in front of a mirror. How's your body language? Facial expressions? Appearance? There is no substitute for practice and polish in these areas. To help you further develop the skills of successful salesmanship, visit your local bookstore. There are some excellent publications that could turn you into a supersalesperson. There are also cassette tapes available on the subject—an excellent way to spend lengthy driving time to work or en route to give a sales presentation. Sales video tapes are also readily available, and if you're near a large metropolitan area, you may have the opportunity to hear a lecture by one of the country's leading sales motivators. There are also seminars and courses designed to help people learn to sell. The Dale Carnegie course is one of the best.

One of the best salespeople I've ever known is very much

involved with embroidery—Rick Gelman of Hirsch International in Hauppauge, New York. This industry is especially fortunate to have many knowledgeable and talented sales representatives, and certainly Rick can be and has been outsold, but not often.

Rick practically admitted to being born with a sales order in hand, but it is his belief that anyone with the desire can sell. When asked what it takes, it was obvious he had thought about this considerably. He replied without a moment's hesitation:

"Persistence—polite persistence. That's what separates the excellent from the mediocre salesman. You make as many calls as it takes to qualify the prospect and progress until the customer stops you. With experience, you become able to tell whether you're progressing with each call or whether the customer is stringing you along."

As far as basics are concerned, knowledge is most important, according to Rick. "You have to know your product. If you don't, find out. It's also important to know your competition. I spend as much time keeping informed about my competition as I do my own line of products."

People who know Rick may think he's a fast-talking New Yorker, but another important practice he follows is to *listen.* It's important to hear what the customer wants, what he needs, what concerns or objections he has. Only by listening will you know; once you know, your direction is set. You don't start talking price if the customer is concerned about delivery.

A couple of factors Rick didn't mention that I think are major contributors to his success are his inward drive to succeed and his enthusiasm and pride in what he sells. On the wall of Rick Gelman's office hangs a caricature of him, with this message: "I'm gonna be a big millionaire—I'm promoting a little machine that embroiders love messages on the seat of your jeans!"

And, when you hear him say, for openers, "You plug it in and it makes you money," the tone is set and you want to know more. Few people are disappointed.

So where do you begin? Wear embroidery as often as possible and always have a supply of your business cards with you everywhere you go. If you're seeking business from anyone and everyone, talk about embroidery and your business at every opportunity. Even if you're specialized—catering to only businesses, for example—anyone you meet may lead to an important account for you. Perhaps it will not be directly with the person you met, but maybe that person has a neighbor, a relative or someone he does business with who can use your services. Even if you're shy, you'll gain confidence as you practice this habit and become experienced at it. Most importantly, learn to handle rejection. It's a way of life for everyone who sells. You must remember that it is not *you* being rejected, but rather what you're selling. Another mind-set worth noting is to think of it in terms of playing the odds. When you contact large numbers of people, some will buy and some won't. Every time you come upon one who won't, statistically you're that much closer to finding the one who will. But, you must continue the search. Also, heed the advice of Rick Gelman and be politely persistent. Perhaps a rejection just means not now, but later.

Mary Newton of Uniquely Yours in Edmond, Oklahoma, agrees. "All you have to do is open your mouth. You can't wait for everyone to come to you—you've got to go after business. When I first located my store in a strip shopping center, I went to the other businesses surrounding me. For example, I sold personalized aprons to the Muffin Shop next door. I try to have lunch with other people in business at least once a week. This method works. I was profitable immediately and in just three weeks, my sales were $12,000."

Now let's focus on some sales ideas and approaches commonly used in the embroidery industry.

In The Retail Store

Remember the first time you saw a computerized embroidery machine running? It captures the fascination of most who see it and they immediately want something embroidered for themselves. So, when customers visit your store for the first time, if they can see the machine in operation, share their excitement. Tell them a little more and show them a little more. Chances are, you can make a sale right then and there if you suggest something. Pay attention to which particular designs or lettering styles attract them. Tell them how nice it would look on a shirt or jacket, or whatever. Tell them the benefits. "This will really add elegance to your dress and it will last a lifetime." Then ask for the order. This can be done with many different approaches: "Would you like me to embroider one for you?" or, "Do you prefer it in red or white?" Or, "I can have it ready for you in 15 minutes."

In effect, you've shown them, made them feel good about it and persuaded them to buy. That's salesmanship, and if you love embroidery and can appreciate how proud it makes your customers to wear something elegant and personalized, you won't have any guilt hang-ups or reluctance about selling. Most people just need to practice being assertive in asking for the order or closing the sale.

Marlena Krueger of Monograms to Go in Denver, Colorado, found that she must take an assertive approach to people seeing the machine for the first time. Their initial reaction is oriented towards the technology—"Wow, look what computers can do today!" It's up to you as the salesperson to bring that back around to what the machine can do for them.

When customers come into your store, they should not be ignored. A friendly smile and a warm greeting go a long way. Put your personality to work for you. The standard, "May I help you?" is polite, but it sounds more dutiful than sincere. Why not strike up a conversation instead? Designer Lee Caroselli once had a retail store in Vail, Colorado. She greeted her customers by asking them how the skiing went. Freida Coonrod has an old-fashioned popcorn machine in her shop. After introducing herself, she offers popcorn to her customers. Such approaches naturally lead to conversation and establish rapport.

Some customers prefer to browse on their own, while others want full attention for the duration of their visit. Be sensitive to such preferences, but always find a way to let the browsers know you are available to them, and be sure they are aware of the embroidery services you offer.

If you have garments already embroidered in various sizes and colors and ready for sale, your job as salesperson is easier. But, if the embroidery is to be added, your customers may need more guidance in making a decision, particularly those who are buying from you for the first time. They may not know appropriate fashion trends, such as where to place a name or color coordination. They certainly won't know peculiarities about your available lettering styles. One style may be too wide for the length of their name, while another style may have upper case letters only. Judging size of lettering is another area of difficulty for most customers. Your suggestions will usually be appreciated and save time in finalizing the sale.

Marlena Krueger suggests, "Guide them through it. Perhaps they want a gift. Ask if it's for a man or a woman. If they want a shirt, find out if they want a dress shirt, a golf shirt or a T-shirt. What size, what color? Do they want a name or just initials? Then suggest two choices for everything. For example, 'I think this red or this burgundy thread would look great on that. Would you like this formal style of lettering, or the more casual look of that one?' By leading them through each step, you can reduce the amount of time per sale to 5 to 10 minutes per customer. Then, when they come back for more, they usually have a good idea of what they want and it goes even faster.

"I always use an order form and write down everything pertinent to the sale. Then I have the customer sign it. That way I eliminate a lot of mistakes and customers saying they thought they were getting something else." Exhibit 17 is a copy of Marlena's order form.

If you're offering designs, a picture is worth 1,000 words. Have your sample sew-out book on display.

Suppose you've got a hot new item or an overstocked inventory on a particular item. Encourage or require your staff to wear a sample every day for a week or two to help promote that item. (You'll incur the expense of the garments, of course.) Let each employee select appropriate embroidery to be added. Customers will notice and, again, the power of suggestion helps create the desire.

Don't be afraid to sell add-ons. If a customer wants a name on a shirt, suggest a design as well. Use buzzwords such as fashion, elegance and custom-look to help create the desire. Also, if your customer is selecting something for himself or herself, suggest another item for a gift idea and remind them of an upcoming holiday, or suggest something for birthday, anniversary, graduation and so forth. Always mention any special promotions or new designs. Turn those single purchases into multiple purchases through good salesmanship.

Selling To A Retail Store

First, visit the stores on your prospect list. Take along pencil and paper and make notes about what type of items are sold, price ranges, type of clientele and window displays. If the store sells garments, find out the size ranges, quantity and color selection per item. Then go back to your shop and plan a presentation. Develop a couple of different ideas and prepare samples of exactly what you intend to sell. They need to see and feel the actual garment. They also need to see your exact colors. Know the fabric content and any special care needed. Be sure you talk to the garment supplier to get needed information about quantities, sizes and colors available, pricing, shipping, delivery time and payment terms.

Cheri Schembrie of Custom Monograms by Cheri, Issaquah, Washington, stresses the need to have all your facts and figures together for your presentation. "Know your costs for the garment and the embroidery, then add shipping and your markup. Also, be prepared to suggest a retail price. The stores I sell to mark up an additional 50% to 100%, depending on the item. I buy the merchandise ahead and have it shipped C.O.D. to me. Then, when I have the order ready, I present the bill to the store's buyer or executive officer and usually I'm paid in 30 to 60 days."

Verna Schembrie, Cheri's mother, is also involved in the business. Mrs. Schembrie advises planning well ahead when selling to department stores. "Their buying season is six months in advance, so if you're planning a Christmas item, June is your deadline for negotiating a sale to them. Once you've made the sale, you *must* deliver on time. Failure to deliver can be a very costly mistake."

Both Cheri and Verna like coming up with new and unique designs. They buy popular styles of garments and dress them up with embroidery. Some stores prefer to provide the garments themselves. Their stores like the creativity—not only in the different designs and colors, but also in different placements. Examples include a garland of holly leaves around the hem of a skirt; patterns embroidered in sets of three for the front of a lady's shirt; neon designs for the younger set. The Schembries find that fashion magazines are a great source for ideas. They also work with artist Harry Jay, Arvada, Colorado, to develop new ideas that sell.

Smaller stores and specialty stores such as gift shops and art galleries (a framed sew-out of a beautiful design constitutes a work of art) may best be sold on a consignment program. You place a few items in the store (be sure to get a receipt for them with the value stated). Then, when the store sells the item, they pay you, and you replace the inventory. Be sure you follow up regularly to monitor the sales activity. This costs the retailer nothing except the space. It also provides you with an idea of what sells and what doesn't. However, you must determine whether it's the item that lacks market appeal or whether the store clerk lacks salesmanship. You can help by informing the clerk about the item and about computerized embroidery. See that the items are properly displayed and encourage the clerk to mention the items to their customers.

Cheri Schembrie recommends talking to sales representatives at local trade marts. "They sell to small boutiques and they're always looking for new or unique items."

Pamela Ross of Fine Details in Garden Grove, California, struck it rich just walking into a mall. "I was just getting in embroidery and was going door-to-door in a mall. I stumbled onto a French linen store and discussed with the manager the idea of putting monograms on their linens. After making a few samples for their displays, the idea caught on and soon I had other sales representatives who visited their store contact me. This led to my getting into doing my own digitizing and soon custom work became the bulk of the business. This particular linen store is rather exclusive and carries high quality brands. Their clientele consists of sophisticated people and interior decorators. Much of my business is to match a wallpaper design or pattern in a rug for the linens. I also match china patterns for placemats, napkins and tablecloths. Now I custom-make sheets and other linens, as well as embroider them, for companies of some of the sales representatives that contacted me."

Fine Details found its niche and grew as a result of a cold call visit to a store in a mall. There is a sales force behind Pamela's products, but not on her payroll!

Business To Business

From your market research and on-going prospect list, plan to do some cold calling regularly. Assign yourself or your salesperson a certain number of accounts to contact per week. Start with a phone call to introduce yourself. State right up front who you are, the name of your business and what you do. Some people find it better to state their business as providing corporate identity items, rather than just stating they do embroidery.

After the introduction, ask for the name of the appropriate person so that an appointment can be scheduled. In very small businesses, the appropriate person is usually the owner or manager. In larger businesses, it may be the head of personnel, public relations, purchasing or marketing. Once you have the name, the initial sales goal becomes scheduling an appointment with that person. This may take some salesmanship. You must capture their interest by letting them know what your service can do for them, yet you don't want to give your entire presentation by phone because it is important they *see* your work. Also, you must convince them to give up a portion of their day for you—and time is valuable to them. Therefore, request only a specific amount of time. Thirty minutes ought to be plenty of time to say what you have to say and show them your samples. You may have to be assertive in asking which day of the week is best and do they prefer mornings or afternoons?

If you are unable to schedule an appointment, ask when you could call back. Unless you receive a definite no with sound reasons, you may benefit by sending a letter, brochure or sample sew-out. State in the letter that you will call again in a couple of weeks.

Assuming you are granted an appointment, begin further research about the company so that you can plan an appropriate presentation. Call the secretary or receptionist again. Find out such details as:

1. Do employees wear uniforms or name tags?
2. Does the company have or sponsor team sports?
3. Is there a company motto, corporate colors?
4. Do they offer promotional or P.R. items or give gifts?
5. How many employees are there?
6. Can a copy of the logo be sent to you?

Answers to such questions will help you present ideas appropriate for the business. Of course, if you have design equipment, the best sample you can show is the company's name and logo. Many put this on an inexpensive garment, such as a shirt or cap, to give away during the presentation. Some give it to the boss and some don't. Bill Beam of American Embroidery in Lexington, Kentucky, says, "I always give a sample garment to an employee—not to the boss. The employee will wear it to work and then everyone else will want one too."

During the presentation, explain the benefits of embroidery. It looks good, and because you have computerized equipment, you have built-in quality control. Embroidery lasts. It won't fade in the wash and it's dry cleanable.

For employee programs, consider these benefits: It enhances morale, pride and loyalty. It's a walking billboard for the business. If on a uniform, it helps their customers remember the name of the business and the employee.

Some companies that do not wish to purchase garments for their employees will still be receptive to the identity idea. Suggest a program whereby each employee receives an order form so that they can purchase their own embroidered jacket, cap or shirt. Be sure to establish one employee to be in charge and leave extra order forms with that person. A special order form with specific choices of garments, lettering styles, placement, size and colors can be developed. Suggest promoting the program through bulletin boards, newsletters, employee meetings and social gatherings.

For wholesalers, a popular and profitable method of selling to businesses is through an advertising specialist such as Pat Hancock of Go Promotions in Frankfurt, Illinois. Pat serves as an advertising consultant for her clients, helping them with ideas on what products to use and how to use them for the most effective market penetration. She works with screenprinters and embroiderers, usually ones that she contacts. Pat says, "I'm interested in quality and cost effectiveness. When someone can provide me a logo that can be used on many different items and includes the price of the tape or disk in the price of the embroidery, that's very attractive. My customers don't like a lot of extra charges.

"On small quantity orders, the embroiderers provide the merchandise. On larger orders, say two dozen or more, I usually purchase the goods direct from the supplier and then have the embroidery added.

"Anything embroidered is popular," according to Pat. "Wearables such as hats are very popular, and unique gift items are good sellers. Recently, I've been selling a lot of desk planters with embroidery. Embroidery is perceived as having high value and I'll be selling more and more of it."

Organizations & Schools

Once you've obtained a contact name for each organization on your prospect list (from friends who are members or from your local Chamber of Commerce or newspaper article), try to make an appointment. Suggest that a flyer and order form be sent to everyone on the roster. (Of course, if you can obtain a copy of the roster, you can contact members directly.)

For a school program, contact the principal or try a district-wide program through the superintendent. Some embroiderers have had success with programs similar to those done for class pictures and class rings. Set up a display in a locked trophy case and see that each student receives an order form. Run the program for two weeks, stating the deadline for ordering. Require full payment in advance or a down payment of at least half and specify the date the orders will be delivered to the school. Again, limit the choices.

When allowing people to fill out their own order forms, it is important the form be simple and easy to complete. Exhibit 18 is a sample school order form, which can easily be adapted for employees or organizations.

Wholesalers can also take advantage of the sales opportunities through organizations and schools. Try selling a fund-raising program. Organizations often have a finance or fund-raising director. For schools, there are PTAs, band boosters and many other clubs that need to raise money every year. You supply the ideas and the products, while they become your sales force.

On The Road

Here's one of my favorite success stories about salesmanship based on meeting a need:

Mr. and Mrs. Oliver Beckett of Palm Harbor, Florida, were a retired couple looking forward to travelling in their motor home. After attending a few camping rallies, they installed an embroidery machine in their mobile home. Their plan was to personalize jackets and caps for other campers—and it was successful. Then, Oliver noticed that the campers brought their own canvas-backed director's chairs to the organized dinners, and with all the socializing going on, people couldn't identify their own chairs. Too many alike! With an embroidery machine so handy, the solution was obvious. The salesmanship was simple, but effective. The Becketts embroidered their name on their chairs and did the same for a couple of friends. They told their friends to send others to their lot. The idea caught on quickly and many of those who came to have their chairs personalized also bought a jacket or cap. The Becketts got their *customers* to sell for them. What a way to retire!

Refer to Chapter 13 of this book for more about trade shows, conventions and fairs.

Closing

Again, the three components of sales are asking for the order, making the sale and closing. The most important of these is closing. Every good salesperson has and uses many types of closes throughout the sales process. Here's a start for your collection of closes:

1. Telephone close for getting the appointment—"Mr. Jones, this is Miss Close. If I could show you a way to increase your sales by 20% to 30% over the next 12 months, would you be interested?" Explain that he has to see it—it can't be fully described over the phone, but 20 or 30 minutes of his time is all it would take.

2. Approach close for the initial appointment—"Mrs. Smith, I'm not going to sell you anything now. I'll just show you the product and tell you why others have bought it and then you tell me if it's something you can use." Afterwards, if she is reluctant to answer, remind her. "Mrs. Smith, you promised to give me an answer on whether this could be useful to you."

3. Demonstration close—"Mr. White, if I can show you the best line of nylon satin jackets with your corporate logo embroidered on them, are you in a position to put $2,000 into it? If no, then $1,000?" The point here is to find out not only how much the prospect can afford, but also to find out if he's able to decide now—today—without checking with someone else.

4. Hot Button close—80% to 90% of the buying decisions are based upon 10% to 20% of a product's features. The key is to carefully ask questions—and skillfully listen to the customers' answers—to find each customer's hot button. Then hit that button over and over again throughout the presentation. The customer will almost always tell you what is important to them, if you will just listen attentively to what they say.

5. Trial close—Throughout the presentation, ask such questions as, "What do you think of this?" and "Is this something you think would be beneficial?" Such questions can produce either a yes or no answer without ending the presentation. By listening carefully to the responses, you can build a picture of what the prospect really wants.

6. Power Suggestions close—The power of suggestion is contagious, just as your enthusiasm about the product is contagious. Use the power of suggestion to get the prospect thinking as if they already have the product you're selling. Create a mental image for them.

7. Ascending close—This is how the most professionally trained encyclopedia sales representatives make a lot of sales. It leads the customer through a series of questions that will be answered yes. If at any point, a no is given, the sales pre-

sentation ends. The key is to carefully plan a one-page presentation that qualifies interested buyers, while building the interest of the prospective buyer. A few suggestions include:

- Are you interested in having an exclusive design for a line of sportswear? Yes.
- Are you interested in increased sales? Yes.
- Are you interested in quality workmanship? Yes.
- Do you like the look of embroidery? Yes.
- Can you devote space in your store for these garments? Yes.
- Can you encourage your store clerks to sell these garments? Yes.

Take some time to prepare your own list of questions suited to different prospects.

8. Invitational close—This close invites the prospect to give it a try. It is best reserved for the end of your presentation. It makes the assumption in the customer's mind that their decision need not be a permanent one. Therefore, it needs to be handled carefully. If you are not in a position to take the product back after a trial period, then you need to be able to offer another easy way out. This could be effective for a consignment program.

9. Price close—Price is not a determining issue. The only exception is when you're talking about two identical products that are equally accessible. Then and only then is price a factor. Therefore, whenever you have any differentiation of product, price is not a determining issue. Keep price discussions at the end of your presentations. If the prospect brings it up, put it off by saying, "We'll get to that, but first I want to tell you the value of having an embroidered garment."

   Never argue over price. If you must negotiate for a contract job, do not let it get to the argumentative stage. Better to get the prospect thinking in terms of price is no object. Say, "Yes, ours is higher priced, and thousands of intelligent people have bought them. Would you like to know why?" Then sell value and quality.

10. Sudden Death close—This is an ultimatum close used when the decision is taking too long. It is reported to work in 50% of cases where it is appropriate to use. Simply write up the order and hand the prospect the pen to sign it. Then be quiet. The longer the silence, the better the chances of the close.

11. Sharp Angle close—This is where you turn an objection around and use it as a reason to buy. For example, suppose the prospect uses screenprinting because his customers never ask for embroidery. Turn it into a positive. "Gee, Mr. Client, it sounds like no one else in your area is offering it, so you'll be the first. It really is popular and your customers just haven't been introduced to it. That's your best reason to buy."

12. Change Places close—When the client won't give you a key issue or a reason for hesitation, change places with him. Don't be afraid to ask, "Is it the money?" Or, if you really don't have a clue, say, "Mr. Client, what else do I need to do to finish this deal?"

13. Alternative close—This is where you assume a purchase, but are asking for a decision as to which product will be purchased. Offer a prospect the choice of the knit golf shirt or the satin jacket. The customer's response will trigger your next move, hopefully to write the order.

14. Ben Franklin close—This close got its name because Ben Franklin reportedly was the first self-made millionaire in our country. His method of selling was to list the pro's, which included all the points made in his sales presentation. He then let the customer write down the con's, knowing that they would usually only make it to three. The close is then, "It looks like you've made your decision."

15. Relevant Story close—Give a success story about one of your other customers who used your services. Create an image in the prospect's mind that he, too, can be as successful with this product. Then ask for the order.

16. Door Knob close—Prepare to leave, then turn around and ask why they didn't buy.

17. Referral close—Never leave without at least two referrals. Trust and rapport come much easier if you were referred by someone the prospect knows.

These techniques take practice. If you try one once and fail, it is certainly no reason to never try it again. Practice breeds confidence and when you're comfortable using different closing techniques, they will become more effective for you. Everyone has some long shots on their prospect list—those who probably won't buy. Use those people as training opportunities for trying out as many closing techniques as possible. Act boldly and close boldly. Studies have indicated that effective salesmanship is based 7% on the words used, 38% on voice tone and 55% on the confidence projected.

Once again I'll remind you of patient persistence. Not all sales can be closed with one attempt. Often it will take up to five or six. So, follow up and keep selling!

Exhibit 17

YOUR LOGO HERE

DATE: ____________________

SALESPERSON ____________________

CUSTOMER'S NAME ____________________ **PHONE:** ____________________

ADDRESS: ____________________

Business Address & Phone

Order No. ____________________

QTY	ITEM	ITEM SIZE	STYLE NO.	MONO SIZE	THREAD COLOR	**PLACEMENT**	**MONOGRAM**	ITEM PRICE	TOTAL

SPECIAL INSTRUCTIONS:

ILLUSTRATION

SET UP FEE	
SUBTOTAL	
TAXES	
TOTAL	
DEPOSIT	
BAL DUE	

ALL OUTSIDE ORDERS WILL REQUIRE 50% DEPOSIT PLUS SET UP FEE

CUSTOMER'S APPROVAL – MUST SIGN BEFORE ORDER IS PROCESSEED ____________________

All sales final.

Customer authorizes the use of the Trademark/Logo to Monograms to Go.

Monograms To Go Inc. will not assume responsibility to customer-provided merchandise due to faulty material or machine-caused damages.

M.T.C. Inc. will assume up to $35 per order for any damage to merchandise.

Exhibit 18

YOUR LOGO HERE

Deadline for Ordering: _________

Name of School________________________________

Name of Student_______________________________

ITEM	QUANTITY	COLOR	SIZE	THREAD	PRICE	TOTAL
1. Nylon Jacket	____	Navy	Ladies:	Navy	$39.50	_____
	____	Burgundy	S M L XL	Burgundy		
(Circle size and	____	Silver		Silver		
thread color)	____	Gold	Men:	Gold		
	____	Green	S M L XL	Green		
	____	Red		Red		
	____	White		White		

PRINT NAME TO BE SEWN ON FRONT__________________ No Charge

MASCOT ON FRONT	YES_____	NO______	$3.50	______
SCHOOL NAME ON FRONT	YES_____	NO_______	$3.50	______

ITEM	QUANTITY	COLOR		THREAD	PRICE	TOTAL
2. Cap	____	Navy		Navy	$ 8.50	______
	____	Burgundy		Burgundy		
	____	Black	(Circle thread	Silver		
	____	Red	color)	Gold		
	____	Neon Pink		Neon Pink		
	____	Neon Green		Neon Green		
	____	Neon Orange		Neon Orange		
	____	White		White		

MASCOT ON FRONT	YES_____	NO_______	$3.50	______
SCHOOL NAME ON FRONT	YES_____	NO_______	$3.50	______

ITEM	QUANTITY	COLOR	SIZE	THREAD	PRICE	TOTAL
3. Sweater	____	Lt. Blue		Navy	$23.00	______
	____	Navy	Ladies:	Burgundy		
(Circle size	____	White	S M L XL	Silver		
and thread	____	Pink		Gold		
color)	____	Red	Mens:	Red		
	____	Burgundy	S M L XL	Green		
	____	Black		Black		
	____	Yellow		Yellow		

MASCOT ON FRONT	YES____	NO____	$3.50	______
SCHOOL NAME ON FRONT	YES____	NO____	$3.50	______
PRINT NAME OF CLUB TO BE SEWN ON FRONT:			$ 3.50	______

____

50% deposit required	TOTAL _______
Orders will be delivered on _______________	DEPOSIT _______
Balance due when delivered.	BALANCE DUE _______

CHAPTER 16

PERSONNEL

Job Description

When you're ready to hire help, the first step is to identify your needs. Jot down the duties you want to assign to the new person. From that, you will be able to develop a written job description. It is important to include all of the responsibilities and duties that may be routinely asked of the employee, but avoid the tendency to state in the job description *how* the duties should be performed. For example, if the job description is for a production supervisor, it would be appropriate to include the responsibility of seeing that all embroidery equipment is maintained in proper working condition. Yet, you do not need to list all that that entails—cleaning, oiling, adjusting, replacing parts or calling a technician. Those specific tasks can be listed in a policies and procedures manual and covered in your training session.

If you expect an operator to sweep the floor at the end of the day, put it in the job description. If your employees are to be cross-trained, state their backup duties. For example, your supervisor may need to relieve the receptionist during lunch, coffee breaks or when absent.

A job description should also include the basic qualifications required or desired. If you want an experienced person, how much experience should they have, and in what areas? Will any work experience do or must they have two years or more on your brand of equipment? It may be possible to find experienced operators, particularly in larger cities where there are usually more embroidery shops. Others prefer to hire people with no embroidery experience so specific methods can be taught from the beginning without having to undo bad habits learned elsewhere. Some employers look for sewing or computer backgrounds, while others want experience in retail, ad specialty or other related businesses.

One important qualification to look for in an employee is the ability to get along well with others. You may even want to specify this in your written job descriptions, as suggested in the sample job descriptions (Exhibits 19 through 21). Emphasizing cooperation in this manner lets everyone know you want minimal conflict. Those employees who talk to customers or suppliers must have particularly good people skills and communication skills, but whenever you have or expect to have more than one employee, let it be known up front that you expect everyone to cooperate with one another.

Having a job description for each position serves several purposes:

- It outlines what is expected for the benefit of applicants, employees and supervisors.
- It enables objective screening of applicants based on qualifications.
- It serves as a useful guide in giving performance evaluations.
- It could protect you in a legal confrontation with a disgruntled employee.

Therefore, if you have employees, take the time to develop a job description for each of them, or ask employees to submit a draft description of their job. Whenever you reorganize or reassign people, update their job descriptions. A current copy should be retained by the employee and the supervisor, and one should be included in the corporate files.

Learning to delegate is often difficult for entrepreneurs hiring their first employee. It's much too easy to fall into the old trap of narrow-mindedness that dictates, "If you want it done right, do it yourself." Sure, employees will make mistakes. Everyone does—if they don't, they aren't working! But, you can minimize the pain by providing everything the employee needs to succeed: training, tools and good management.

Also, be aware of this common mistake and try to avoid it: Don't assign responsibilities without giving an employee the authority needed to handle those responsibilities. For example, if you expect an employee to handle a customer complaint, that employee needs the authority to do something besides give lip service. Perhaps the employee could have the authority to suggest redoing a job, or assigning a higher priority to a job, or issuing a credit memo, to name a few options.

Recruiting

A recent survey of embroidery shop owners indicated that the number one complaint was a lack of good, reliable help. Good recruiting is half of the solution. (The other half is good management to help the employee achieve full potential and to minimize turnover.)

Recruiting is typically done through local newspapers, in the appropriate categories. Openings or job opportunities can be listed under the headings of computer operators, operators, embroidery operators or sewing. Careful thought must be given to writing the ad, and sometimes several versions are needed to bring in the kind of applicants you seek.

Start by glancing through the help-wanted ads in any Sunday edition of a major newspaper. Pick any common category from accounting to computer programmer to secretary to sales, and read how varied the ads are. Some stress duties, while others list detailed qualifications. There are those that highlight benefits; others offer inviting work environments. You'll see some written by work-aholic slave drivers and others flaunting the charm of the manager. Analyze the type of applicants each will draw. Then think about what your business has to offer that would attract the type of employee you want.

If you oversell the job, you run the risk of respondents wanting top dollar and being overqualified. If hired, they'll quickly become bored and leave. Underselling the job may attract non-qualified candidates or none at all.

Different ads will attract different people. Consider these ads for an operator:

Computer Operator
No experience needed. Will train on high tech eqpmt. Aptitude for computers helpful. Learn new skills in growing industry. Apply at 725-1438. EOE

Sewing
Like to sew? Try computerized embroidery. Busy wholesaler will train reliable, take-charge person with good job references for full-time, permanent position. Call 427-6770 for appt.

Embroidery Operator
Needed with experience on Tajima machine. 2nd shift—4-11pm. Team player. Creative. Wholesale Creations, 45 S. Main, Springfield. 222-1010.

Notice that the first ad makes no reference to embroidery. It is appealing to those who want to learn a skill and start a career, yet who probably have little or no training or work experience. It says nothing about characteristics desired, but may appeal to someone ambitious. It also says you want to see them in person, rather than screen by phone first. The EOE stands for equal opportunity employer, which may encourage minorities and females to apply.

The second example is directed towards someone who knows fabrics and who has job experience, but not necessarily in a sewing-related field. It would appeal to a more mature person because of the experience requirement and the characteristic of a take-charge person. Younger people may be the take-charge type, but usually don't know it yet or lack the confidence to respond to such an ad. Inclusion of the word reliable means you need them to be responsible and you need them to be there. The ad offers a new skill and regular work. The word busy may appeal to someone who has worked for failing businesses and wants a more stable job.

The third example is very specific. They want someone who can walk in and do the job with little or no training. It tells the applicants that they will be one of several or many such operators who must work together. It's definitely a production oriented shop.

Other resources for recruiting include minority newspapers, placement centers of high school or college co-op programs, government hiring agencies, organizations for the handicapped and referrals from business associates, friends or relatives. Of these, the most effective is referrals from business associates. It is the best and quickest method of finding the most suitable employees. In fact, it is estimated that 70% of successful hiring stems from business referrals.

Some government agencies offer incentives for hiring certain types of people. Funds are available for on-the-job training. For information about job referral agencies, contact your state's Department of Labor and Employment or your local employers' council. Libraries also have information on employment published by The Bureau of National Affairs Inc.

Embroiderers who have hired people with disabilities and those who have hired immigrants say they are industrious and extremely loyal employees because there are so few jobs available to them. When they find someone willing to give them a chance, they feel grateful and indebted to that employer.

Interviewing

The interview is the most widely used method of employee selection, but studies have indicated it is the least predictive method of determining job success. Interviewing is good, however, for getting to know more about a candidate to see if he is someone you like and can work with and to see if he will fit in with the others in your employ. It's also an opportunity to get more detailed information than what is contained in the applicant's resume or application for employment. See Exhibit 22 for a sample employment application form. With or without a resume, a standardized application form should be on file for each employee. A standardized form can also help you build a file of open applications, which can speed the hiring process next time a need arises.

When considering an applicant for a receptionist's job or any position with heavy telephone responsibilities, it is helpful to have a preliminary interview by phone. This gives you the opportunity to hear the applicant's telephone voice, manners and speech. The telephone interview can also be a timesaver for both you and the applicants for virtually any position, if the basics are covered. A few minutes on the phone can provide sufficient information to determine if there is a good enough fit to warrant proceeding to the next step. Use it to determine if an applicant's salary expectations or hours available are unrealistic within the scope of your job opening.

Prior to an interview, whether by phone or in person, prepare a checklist for yourself so that you can conduct the interview smoothly and learn everything you want to learn about the candidate as well as give information you want them to know about yourself and your business. Develop specific questions, including some that are open-ended—that cannot be answered with a simple yes or no—to gain more insight. A sample checklist might include these topics or questions:

- Appearance—Jim Sales of The Angelica Uniform Group in Alamo, Tennessee, places heavy emphasis on this. He believes appearance tells a lot about a person's attention to detail, a quality he seeks in embroidery machine operators.
- Career interest or job objective—If you're hiring for an operator's position and the candidate clearly wants to be a supervisor in six months, will this be a problem or will this fit into your growth plans? What if you're looking for longevity and

the applicant just wants to earn extra income until a spouse can find work?

- What is your idea of the ideal job, supervisor and company? The answers to such a question will enable you to further determine an applicant's fit with the job, the supervisor and your business. Often details about former jobs will come out, which can either alert you to a potential problem or confirm your positive impression of the applicant.
- Attendance and availability—Are there any current situations that would prevent the candidate from having good attendance on the job, such as child care, transportation or health problems? The fact that you include such a question in an interview stresses the importance you place on being at work. It may also alert you to potential problems. Questions involving such matters as child care must be asked of both male and female applicants to avoid being construed as discriminatory.
- Major personal strengths and areas for concern—These may be assessed by you or you can ask the applicants for their response, preferably both.

Richard Fryer, CEO of Franklin Mills in Franklin, Indiana, has two main criteria for selecting employees: intelligence and a willingness to work. Similarly, Carl Moritz says, "The ideal employees are those who have common sense, commitment, honesty and loyalty. The rest can be taught."

Harvey Mackay, author of Swim With The Sharks, offers an acid test for hiring: "Ask yourself, how would you feel having this same person working for your competition instead of for you?"

Sometimes an item on a resume or application form will prompt a question for more details or further explanation. Review these forms before the interview to make notes about such items. When interviewing someone with specific job skills or experience, get more information about those skills. For example, if an applicant's work history seems to lack longevity with any single employer, find out why. Is the candidate a job hopper or are there sound reasons for leaving each previous job?

The best method for determining specific job skills is a work sampling. If the candidate says he can operate your machine, have him show you. If he is applying for a job involving typing, give him a simple test. David Greenberg, production manager for Barth & Dreyfuss of Los Angeles, California, looks for good manual dexterity and eye/hand coordination. How? He takes the applicant out to a machine and asks him to thread a needle. If the applicant can't do it in a reasonable amount of time, he knows the job will certainly be too frustrating for that person.

The questions you ask must be relevant to the job. Of course, you must avoid any questions that may be construed as discriminatory in the areas of race, color, creed, national origin, ancestry, sex, age and physical handicap. This also applies to the wording of job advertisements and application forms, pay and benefits, promotion and termination. However, if an applicant is a minor, you may require proof of age in the form of a work permit or birth certificate. You may not make inquiries relating to arrests, but you can inquire about any convictions that are substantially related to the applicant's ability to perform a specific job. You may ask if there are any physical or mental handicaps that might affect work performance. The law requires that you make reasonable accommodations to hire those with handicaps. A physical examination may be required, if it is required of all applicants.

Classification

Each state varies in job classifications with regard to compensation. There are salaried people who earn a stated amount per week, month or year. Some are exempt from overtime pay if their status can be classified as professional, supervisory or management, in accordance with state regulations.

Contract workers (sometimes known as independent contractors) are not considered employees. They are self-employed. However, there are employers who classify their employees as contract workers in order to avoid paying Workmen's Compensation, providing other benefits and withholding taxes. An individual is an independent contractor if you, the employer, have the right to control or direct only the result of the work and not the means and methods of accomplishing the result. There are 20 factors that indicate whether an individual is an employee or an independent contractor:

1. Instructions—An employee is required to comply with instructions about when, where and how to work. Even if no instructions are given, the control factor is present if the employer has the right to give instructions.
2. Training—An employee is trained to perform services in a particular manner. Independent contractors ordinarily use

their own methods and receive no training from the purchasers of their services.

3. Integration—An employee's services are integrated into the business operations because the services are important to the success or continuation of the business. This shows that the employee is subject to direction and control.
4. Services rendered personally—An employee renders services personally. This shows that the employer is interested in the methods as well as the results.
5. Hiring assistants—An employee works for an employer that hires, supervises and pays assistants. An independent contractor hires, supervises and pays assistants under a contract that requires him or her to provide materials and labor and to be responsible only for the result.
6. Continuing relationship—An employee has a continuing relationship with an employer. This indicates that an employer-employee relationship exists. A continuing relationship may exist where work is performed at frequently recurring although irregular intervals.
7. Set hours of work—An employee has set hours of work established by an employer. An independent contractor is the master of his or her own time.
8. Full-time work—An employee normally works full-time for an employer. An independent contractor can work when and for whom he or she chooses.
9. Work done on premises—An employee works on the premises of an employer, or works on a route or at a location designated by an employer.
10. Order or sequence set—An employee must perform services in the order or sequence set by an employer. This shows that the employee is subject to direction and control.
11. Reports—An employee submits reports to an employer. This shows that the employee must account to the employer for his or her actions.
12. Payments—An employee is paid by the hour, week or month. An independent contractor is paid by the job or on a straight commission.
13. Expenses—An employee's business and travel expenses are paid by an employer. This shows that the employee is subject to regulation and control.
14. Tools and materials—An employee is furnished significant tools, materials and other equipment by an employer.

15. Investment—An independent contractor has a significant investment in the facilities he or she uses in performing services for someone else.
16. Profit or loss—An independent contractor can make a profit or suffer a loss.
17. Works for more than one person or firm—An independent contractor gives his or her services to multiple unrelated persons or firms at the same time.
18. Offers services to general public—An independent contractor makes his or her services available to the general public.
19. Right to fire—An employee can be fired by an employer. An independent contractor cannot be fired so long as he or she produces a result that meets the specifications of their contract.
20. Right to quit—An employee can quit his or her job at any time without incurring liability. An independent contractor usually agrees to complete a specific job and is responsible for its satisfactory completion, or is legally obligated to make good for failure to complete the job.

The penalties for non-compliance—classifying an employee as a contract worker—are to pay all back-payments of withholding taxes, Social Security and Workman's Compensation, with interest. There could also be some legal ramnifications based upon the intent to defraud the Federal Government.

Compensation

Compensation decisions should be based on the position, the level of the employee within that position, the going rate in your area for similar positions, and the value of the total compensation package—wages plus benefits.

Once you have identified the value level for each position in your business, divide each one into three to five steps. The lowest step will be for entry level in that position—the person meets the minimum qualifications. The highest step is for the person who excels in every aspect of the job and is ready for a higher position. Then, attach a dollar range to each level. For example, an entry level operator may earn from minimum wage to $5.50 per hour. The highest range for the experienced, top performing or lead operator may be $8 to $10 per hour. To earn more, the employee must be moved to a higher paying position with additional responsibilities, such as a lead operator or production supervisor. The employee would move from the top category of the lower position to the lowest category of the higher position, assuming the minimum qualifications are met. However, if you have ranges that overlap, you cannot expect an employee receiving a promotion to take a decrease in pay. In the above example, if the low range of the supervisory position is $8 to $10 per hour, the operator who was making $10 per hour cannot be expected to start for less than that. You may start them higher or at the same rate until they have proven themselves on the job, which justifies moving them into a higher range within that job. Typically, supervisory level positions can range up to the mid $20s (at today's standards).

Such a method has two advantages: You will likely be fair in paying your employees based upon responsibility, experience and performance; and the employees will know their earning potential for their current position, as well as higher positions they may seek.

Some embroidery businesses are moving towards a bonus program in lieu of pay raises. This holds the ceiling on fixed wage expenses and rewards employees when performance merits extra pay. A bonus program can be handled individually, but usually is done on a group basis, which also promotes more teamwork. Custom Monograms by Cheri of Issaquah, Washington, has such a program. Employees must have six months on the job to be eligible, then they may earn bonuses if the number of stitches per shift per day exceeds the goal. Rejects are subtracted from the stitch count. Again, the entire shift is rewarded in order to promote teamwork rather than individual competition.

At Franklin Mills, a monthly quota is established for the number of pieces to be embroidered. The product line is very controlled; therefore, the number of pieces required is usually consistent. The quota is in line with sales objectives, which is also the basis for the annual budget. When quotas are exceeded, bonuses are paid. The bonus amount is determined, then divided equally among the operators. Those who perform the jobs of trimming, folding and bagging are also eligible for incentive bonuses.

Another concept I find interesting at Franklin Mills is the status of the embroidery machine operators. They are treated as equals among each other and treated as VIPs throughout the company. Everyone else in manufacturing is below them on the organizational chart and on the pay scale. Richard Fryer believes that a beginning operator is worth more than minimum wage. He'll start them at $5 and raise them after successful completion of their 90-day probationary period. No longer does Franklin Mills have to hire operators off the street. Competition is keen within the ranks of their own manufacturing department to be eligible for promotion to the position of operator.

"I also found that after the initial probationary period, there is merit to paying all of our operators the same rate," says Richard Fryer. "Wages aren't kept confidential among the employees no matter what you do, so if they are all treated equally, it avoids many problems of jealousy and resentment."

Employees must be made aware that any benefits you offer are also part of their compensation. The standard benefits given by most small embroidery businesses include paid holidays, paid vacation and personal or sick time. Some also offer group health insurance and a few are able to include dental coverage. Other benefits worth considering include retirement programs and educational assistance, if relevant to their work. You may also be able to find a credit union that will accept participation from several small businesses rather than exclusively from one large employer. Generally, a benefit program will add 25% to 30% to the compensation package of an employee.

Compensation for sales personnel can be handled differently. If independent sales representatives are used, they are usually paid 10%. The key here is 10% of what? Rick Songer of Sew-Cal Logo in Carson, California, says his compensation plan to independents usually works out to 10% of gross profits. However, Steve Diamond of Creative Embroidery in Bloomfield, New Jersey, pays his part-time independent representatives 10% of the sales price. His policy is that if a price change is needed to secure an order, it must be a joint decision. The sales representative does not have sole authority to change the sales price. If a lower price is agreed upon, the sales representative takes a lower commission.

Steve Diamond also employs full-time salaried people who sell for his firm. They sell to regular customers—no cold call sales. Their jobs are structured so that actual sales time accounts for only 50% to 60% of their day or work week. The rest of the time is spent in follow-through duties such as working with the art department, coordinating samples and so forth. Steve estimates the salary range for such employees at $25,000 to $30,000 annually.

Dennis Slechta of Panda Embroidery in Grapevine, Texas, employs a person whose duties combine production embroidery with outside sales. When working inside, she makes $6 per hour.

When doing outside sales, she is paid $8 per hour. Dennis provides her transportation—a van painted with the company logo!

Policies & Procedures

Basic personnel policies should be stated in writing and given to each employee. Standard policies cover such items as working hours, breaks, overtime, vacation, sick leave and other benefits, probationary periods, evaluation schedules, safety rules, disciplinary action, security precautions and any basic company philosophies that are a matter of policy for all employees. It's also nice to include a little history of your business and something about the market you serve.

A procedures manual should also be developed. Larger shops will likely need more than one. Barth & Dreyfus, for example, has a manual for all paperwork and reporting, in both the planning and operational stages. There is also a manual for its supervisors and a procedures manual for its designers.

The understanding and use of such manuals helps to keep everyone in compliance with rules and standard methods. They also help to eliminate errors and repeated instructions. Of course, the manuals need to be reviewed periodically and updated as needed. Some elements of your business most likely to require procedures manuals include:

- Preventive maintenance and care guidelines for equipment.
- Sample forms used in the business, and instructions for using them.
- Pricing methods or formulas.
- Scheduling and work flow charts.
- Petty cash rules and uses.
- Travel allowances and reporting methods.
- Shipping and receiving guidelines.
- Customer relations guidelines.
- Inventory levels to be maintained, plus a list of approved suppliers.

Training

Be sure your employees are cross-trained to handle jobs other than their own so that the flow of work will not be bottlenecked if one person's workload gets too large and overall production becomes backlogged. Cross-training can also minimize the inconvenience of absent employees. In large shops, it is a good idea to allow someone to move up to fill a slot temporarily vacated by absence. This obviously fills the vacancy, but it also enables you to evaluate the person's ability to handle the position. If a permanent opening occurs, promotion from within may then be possible.

If you have a small shop and are adding an operator to be trained internally, begin with such basics as trimming and progress to hooping different types of fabrics with various combinations of backings and toppings. This is also a good time to work on measuring and placement. The new operator should also be assigned the task of reading operator's manuals and any other publications available from your machine manufacturer. Then work with the operator on simple operations, allowing plenty of time for experimentation on remnant fabrics. Be sure your operator training includes simple maintenance, such as oiling, cleaning, changing needles and proper threading. Then proceed to tension adjustments. Provide records of previous jobs so that the trainee gets helpful information on letter heights, density settings, width adjustments and so forth. Finish with the more sophisticated features of the machine, and then start breaking the new person in on production. Closely supervise the work of the new employee until you're both satisfied. The rule for training is tell, show and watch.

I firmly believe that anyone who is put in a supervisory capacity should be trained as a supervisor. It is a very important and responsible role and can lead to costly legal problems if abused, even inadvertently. Insist on formal supervisory training to avoid problems. Find an appropriate program through an employment council or business school.

In addition to training on the machines and working with fabrics, new employees need to be taught your particular business. Again, policies and procedures manuals are very helpful. Also, introduce the new employee to repeat customers and business contacts who visit your shop often. And, for the first couple of weeks, be sure someone goes out of their way to include the new employee for lunch, provides information about the surrounding area and anything else to make the adjustment smooth.

Paperwork

When an employee is hired, have him complete a W-4 form for tax withholding information. Also, the Immigration Reform Act of 1988 requires proof of citizenship be kept on file for every employee. Acceptable proof includes a certified certificate of live birth (it must contain a raised seal in order to be certified), a Social Security card (so long as it does not state, "not for identification purposes"), a passport or a state-issued driver's license with a photo. Every employee must also complete an Employment Eligibility Verification form I-9.

A personnel file should be maintained for each employee. It should contain the person's application for employment; the resume, if one was provided; the appropriate job description; written performance evaluations; letters of commendation or reprimand; and salary history since employment with your business. Also keep a copy of the proof of citizenship or employment eligibility verification that was provided.

If other employees or supervisors have access to the personnel files, then you must be careful what else goes into those files. Photos or any information exposing race, sex and other areas open to discrimination claims should not be included. Such information could be construed as discriminatory if an employee is passed over for a promotion.

Medical information should be kept in a separate file and inaccessible to other employees and supervisors. This file would include any workmen's compensation claims, physical examination reports, medical histories needed for insurance applications and so forth.

Written performance evaluations should be handled on a regular basis—at the end of the probationary period, annually thereafter, and whenever a promotion occurs. Refer to the job description to review what was expected. Then evaluate on the basis of how well the duties were performed in the areas of quantity, quality, knowledge and cooperation. Be sure to summarize the employee's strengths and also list any areas needing further development. Sign it and have the employee sign it. The employee's signature should not necessarily denote agreement, but rather that the evaluation was read and understood. Space can be provided for employee comments.

Some firms use a numerical grading system for each category of the evaluation. I personally dislike that approach. Giving the highest grade possible in every category is usually what the employee expects, yet it leaves no room for improvement. To give less than the highest rating in even a single area invariably upsets the employee, and he will dwell on that grading even though the others may be the highest. The grade system also made me feel like a child in school again and I was tempted to send my work evaluations to my father for his signature and collect the quarters I always got for good grades. (It's probably $5 bills by today's standards!)

Paperwork is also important in disciplinary actions. Supervisors should keep reports on their assigned employees, noting any verbal warnings or discussions about correcting a problem. If a problem worsens and gets to the point where a formal written notice is prepared, then the written notice should become a record in the personnel files. Detailed documentation leading to the termination of any employee by the employer should be maintained in the personnel file. This is your protection against a suit for unlawful termination or to claims for unemployment compensation when there was just cause for termination.

When employees do leave—at their choosing or yours—they do not have the right to take with them their training materials, work created on your equipment while in your employ, customer lists, or supplies. These belong to you and you have the right to demand that all such items in their possession be returned.

Keeping Employees Happy

Your employees can and should be your most valuable asset. Keeping a good staff happy and motivated pays off in production results. John Ruskin wrote in 1851, "In order that people may be happy in their work, these three things are needed: (1) they must be fit for it; (2) they must not do too much of it; and (3) they must have a sense of success in it." The key to the first one is hiring correctly; the second one is handled by controlling the working hours and watching for signs of burnout. The third one is more complex and requires some skill in supervising and managing people.

Employees have a right to expect a safe environment in which to work. They also require adequate knowledge of what is expected and how to perform their duties. They will work best when the work is challenging—slightly beyond their experience or ability. The rest is all in how they are treated. Here are some simple, yet effective, practices to follow:

1. Praise in public; criticize in private.
2. Praise before criticizing.
3. Listen a lot—to suggestions, to problems, to personal goals, to creative ideas. (If these are not freely offered, ask for them.)
4. Know when to get out of the way.
5. Live the Golden Rule.

What all of these have in common is that they promote a feeling of appreciation and importance. These are *basic human wants*, along with health, food, sleep, money and what it will buy, life in the hereafter, sexual gratification, and the well-being of our children. I would estimate that the most frequent reason for employee turnover stems from a lack of feeling appreciated or important.

National Embroidery of Orlando, Florida, has a banner hanging on the wall in the production area as a constant reminder that 6,000 dozen caps were embroidered there in three months. The employees are proud of that, but determined to beat it next quarter. Production manager Victor Viti is a master at making his employees feel important and it's clear he believes it. His operators participate in planning and scheduling meetings. They're also free to call a meeting if they deem it necessary to work out employee problems or to make a suggestion on production. Victor also uses unplanned rewards to keep morale high. The production area has been known to close just because of beautiful weather outside (the work is made up at night or on weekends).

David Greenberg, production manager for Barth & Dreyfuss in Los Angeles, California, faced an absentee rate of more than 10% per month. He drastically reduced the absences by posting a list of those employees with perfect attendance each month. The list jumped from 15 employees to 85 in a very short time. Simply recognizing those who exemplified good attendance solved a critical problem.

Give some thought to recognition programs and incentives for your employees. They don't always have to cost a lot of money, but whatever you do for them will usually be appreciated—and the more your people feel appreciated, the more loyal they will be. Employees, like customers, are less expensive to keep than to replace. So, when you are fortunate enough to acquire good employees, take care of them. They are your business' most valuable asset.

Here are some qualities that I believe contribute to good management of people:

1. Challenging your people to *exceed* their personal expectations through goal-setting.
2. Setting an example of high standards in your own daily work habits and behavior.
3. Delegating responsibility and authority.
4. Removing obstacles or barriers so that employees can do their jobs.
5. Providing the best tools, equipment and training.
6. Acting—decisively and quickly.
7. Setting and sharing a vision (to achieve a certain rate of production or to be the best quality embroiderer in town or to sell a certain dollar amount by a certain date).
8. Respect for each individual.

Exhibit 19

SAMPLE JOB DESCRIPTION

OPERATOR

Duties

1. Responsible for complete operation and care of assigned computerized embroidery machines.
2. Responsible for production embroidery, according to work orders assigned.
3. Maintain a high level of accuracy on a weekly basis.
4. Maintain accurate logs of production and spoilages, on a daily basis.
5. Responsible for maintaining a clean working environment.
6. Participate in weekly scheduling and problem-solving meetings.

Minimum Qualifications

1. High school graduate.
2. Two years work experience in a manufacturing environment.
3. Good aptitude for and attention to details.
4. Ability to get along well as a team member.

Exhibit 20

SAMPLE JOB DESCRIPTION

PRODUCTION SUPERVISOR

Duties

1. Responsible for scheduling, assigning and supervising work of operators.
2. Responsible for proper training of operators in the operation and care of equipment, and company policies and procedures.
3. Responsible for maintaining adequate levels of embroidery supplies and spare parts.
4. Responsible for coordination of information between sales, design and production staff.
5. Responsible for seeing that all embroidery equipment is maintained in proper working condition.
6. Responsible for keeping records on production and spoilages, on a weekly basis.

Minimum Qualifications

1. Previous supervisory education and experience.
2. At least one year of production embroidery experience.
3. Good communication skills.
4. Ability to get along well with co-workers.

Exhibit 21

SAMPLE JOB DESCRIPTION

BOOKKEEPER

Duties

1. Responsible for preparing invoices on all work delivered within 48 hours of completion.

2. Responsible for collection of accounts receivable.

3. Responsible for timely payment of accounts payable.

4. Responsible for making daily deposits to bank.

5. Maintain petty cash and receipts for same of up to $200.

6. Responsible for weekly payroll.

7. Maintain the following records:
   a. Double-entry system of transactions
   b. Monthly trial balance
   c. Monthly statement of income
   d. Monthly balance sheet

Minimum Requirements

1. Graduate of accredited business college, including courses in accounting.

2. At least one year previous bookkeeping experience.

3. Ability to operate 10-key adding machine by touch, accurate typing at 60 w.p.m., and aptitude for or experience with personal computer.

4. Ability to maintain confidential information.

5. Applicant must be bondable.

6. Ability to get along well with co-workers and the general public.

Exhibit 22

APPLICATION FOR EMPLOYMENT

Name__________________________________ Social Security No.____________________

Address__________________________________ Phone: H____________ W______________

City_____________________________________ State______________ Zip______________

Position sought__________________________ Desired Salary/Wage______________

Work History (List last three employers, starting with most recent.)

Date Month/Year	Name and address of employer	Salary	Position	Reason for leaving
From				
To				
From				
To				
From				
To				

References (List three who are not relatives whom you have known at least one year.)

Name	Address	Business	Years Known
1.			
2.			
3.			

List any special skills you have or equipment you can operate:

1.__________________________________ 4.__________________________________

2.__________________________________ 5.__________________________________

3.__________________________________ 6.__________________________________

Do you have any physical limitations that preclude you from performing work for which you are applying? ___Yes ___No If yes, what special accommodations are needed?_______________

____

In case of emergency, notify:____

Name Address Phone

"I certify that the facts contained in this application are true and complete to the best of my knowledge and understand that, if employed, falsified statements on this application shall be grounds for dismissal.

Date:______________ Signature__________________________________

DO NOT WRITE BELOW THIS LINE

Interviewed by__________________________________ Date____________ Hired___Yes___No

Position:_______________________________________ Salary/Wage____________________

Date reporting for work____________________ Hours/shift__________________________

Approved by___________________________________

CHAPTER 17
EFFICIENCY

Organizing The Shop

Did you ever participate in a time study? You were clocked on everything you did, watched for the number of times you handled the same piece of paper and the number of steps you took. The point was to get you thinking of ways to minimize time-wasting motions. Apply that mode of thinking to your business.

Items used most frequently should be located in the closest proximity to where they are used: Hoops, backing and topping should be placed near the hooping table or hooping jigs, along with any other items used during the hooping process, such as spray adhesives and applique fabrics. Threads and bobbins should be located near the machine.

When one operator works on more than one machine, locate the machines so that they can be monitored easily—side by side, at right angles, across from each other, or in a U-shape. You'll be guided by the space available, size of the machines and the configuration of the room. Here are a few descriptions of floor plans from small, medium and larger embroidery businesses:

Kathy Fox Downs of Fox Fabrique in Sonoma, California, has a single-head and a four-head. They are at right angles to each other with a tape reader between for easy access to either machine. The four-head is near a window to attract the attention of passers-by. The hooping table is across from the single-head. Shelves and drawers were installed between the hooping table and the single-head to hold such items as threads, pre-cut backing, applique patterns and so forth. Rolls of backing and fabric (they manufacture many of their own garments) are mounted on the wall. A roll-around cabinet with drawers houses all tools, needles, bobbins and miscellaneous accessories.

The embroidery machines occupy about 200 square feet, but when added to the garments Kathy inventories for embroidery, about one-third of her total 18,000 square feet is embroidery-related. The rest of the space is used for manufacturing.

Freida Coonrod's shop in Cedar Rapids, Iowa, fills the house next door to her home. The well-insulated garage houses her embroidery machines: two single-heads, a two-head and a four-head, arranged in a rectangular configuration. Freida's husband, Duane, made a hoop rack consisting of a bar attached to the ceiling with large metal hooks descended to within reach. Each hook holds up to nine hoops. They are organized by hoop size on the various hooks. The remainder of the garage is for inventoried garments.

A breezeway between the garage and the house is the entrance, equipped with an old-fashioned popcorn machine. The kitchen is where finishing takes place—trimming, folding, packing and shipping. Freida's office and a chain stitch machine take up the living room. Additional chain stitch machines are located in a bedroom. The master bedroom is for chenille, and the third bedroom is used for storing records and patterns for the chenille work.

The garage is approximately 30 feet x 40 feet. The embroidery machines occupy half the space; the remaining space in the garage is used to store garments. The breezeway is approximately 16 feet x 12 feet. The house measures 26 feet x 40 feet.

Pat Somers of Somers Marketing in Englewood, Colorado, has 2500 square feet, but is quick to add, "We're really cramped here and need more space. We have three 20-heads and one 12-head. Two machines are placed side by side and across the room from the other two. Six worktables are in the center, forming aisles between the machines and the tables. On the wall behind each machine is a pegboard rack for threads. Rolls of backing also hang on the wall. Operators cut a six-foot length to take to the worktable. Individual pieces are then cut, using the hooping jig as a pattern. We're organized and efficient, but it's tight for the amount of space we have."

Digitizing equipment and single- and double-head sample machines are located in another room to maximize concentration for the designers.

Large shops with many multi-heads may do well to position two back-to-back and two front-to-front. One operator can then watch two machines at once, depending upon the operator and the workload. If you have a bridge type multi-head and want to load hoops from the back, this will be a consideration in placement of the machines also.

Here are a few other organizational ideas:

Marilyn Reichenberg uses airtight, plastic containers for storing threads. The containers are color coded and put on a shelf.

From Diane's Monograms in Houston, Texas: Hang a thread-holding pegboard on the wall behind your machine and thread directly from the peg to the thread bar guide. This is especially useful with metallic threads because it reduces knotting in the thread and enables the thread to slide off the container easily.

Discipline operators to organize supplies via tote trays or aprons with pockets for tools.

Janet Hamlin and Marian Zink of Initial Artistry in Dearborn Heights, Michigan, put trimming scissors on wrist bracelets for easy accessibility. Of course, for safety reasons, plastic protective tips are recommended. They also put work to be trimmed in a wire basket on wheels. (The basket was originally used in a supermarket display and was being thrown away.)

Marilyn also uses plastic baskets for each day's work, organized on a shelf.

Barbara Chmara suggests that when garments are received, they be organized by size and placed in colored, plastic bins—white for small, blue for medium, red for large and so forth. Another tip from Barbara: Leave garments unfastened (buttons, snaps, zippers) to indicate additional processing on the garment is needed. If it's fastened, it's ready for inspection and packing.

National Embroidery in Orlando, Florida, uses industrial laundry carts on wheels for the many hats in process. During embroidery production, a long row of hats rests on the back of the multi-head machines within easy reach of the operator who sits on a stool and pre-hoops as one run is being stitched.

Staffing The Machines

Most production embroidery shops realize the importance of keeping the machines running constantly for maximum output. To do this requires proper staffing. Several factors will determine what is a proper staffing level for your shop: number of machines, number of heads, number of needles, number of stitches in the design, hooping and trimming time, and any special handling such as applique or other types of embellishment.

Some subscribe to the theory that if one operator is able to run the machine and trim during production time, that's all you need. Others will assign 1 1/2 operators per machine, or have a floater to assist all the regular operators with their machines. Larger machines may require two operators each. There are also many shops that have a separate finishing staff so that no operator need trim their work.

It may be most efficient to have "gang changes" where everyone assists in changing threads, unloading and reloading hoops or changing needles. The person in charge of the machine reprograms while this is going on, and before starting the machine, hollars an "all clear" to be sure no fingers are near needles.

In most small and medium shops, the operators are also responsible for the care and simple maintenance of their machines. However, in larger shops, I have found that there is a dedicated crew for this. Daily and weekly routines are established for preventive maintenance, with repair work scheduled for weekends, except when an emergency occurs and a machine is down.

Businesses with employees working exceptionally long hours on a regular basis should be considering adding a second shift, even if it is only part-time to start. Adding a shift is more productive than burnout of a dedicated staff, and it is less expensive than buying more equipment.

If you operate a one-person shop, it is very important that you control your schedule and make the best use of your time. Interruptions will be your biggest obstacle. Consider using an answering machine instead of answering each individual phone call. Then set aside a certain time period for returning your calls. Try to schedule pick-ups and deliveries between certain hours so that you can better plan your uninterrupted production time on the machine.

Scheduling

The number one reason customers go somewhere else is because of missed delivery deadlines. (And you thought it was price!) This fact alone should emphasize the need for better scheduling. Good scheduling also contributes to good organization and better efficiency.

In large shops, scheduling may be a full-time job. In some shops, such as National Embroidery in Orlando, Florida, it is a team effort including the production manager, the assistant production manager and the five full-time operators. In smaller shops, the owner or a supervisor works it in with all their other duties.

Scheduling, like pricing, requires breaking a job down into tasks and estimating or knowing the time needed for each task. This will vary with each job, each operator and each shop. Consider all the possible steps, or tasks, involved:

1. Ordering garments
2. Ordering designs
3. Ordering threads or other supplies

4. Counting and sorting garments when received
5. Test-sewing the design
6. Getting design sew-out approved by customer
7. Creating work orders
8. Pulling supplies from shelf
9. Preparing garments (unpacking, removing pins and stays)
10. Hooping, measuring, marking, pattern-making
11. Changing threads, needles, bobbins
12. Programming, setting tensions, logging information
13. Sewing time
14. Unloading hoops
15. Trimming
16. Pressing or steaming
17. Folding
18. Packaging and recounting
19. Shipping
20. Invoicing

Some tasks can be done simultaneously with others, thus saving time. Others may have to be repeated. For example, if a design is put on a jacket back, and a name on the front, steps 10 through 15 are done twice.

Do some time studies on various jobs, including every task involved with those jobs. Only by knowing actual times can you intelligently guess estimated times for scheduling purposes. You will learn what garments and fabrics take longer to hoop, what fabrics, threads or designs require a slower sewing speed, which operators are faster, how many thread breaks occur, how long it takes to change your machine from accommodating flat goods to hats—many facts about your operation that will help you schedule better. Keep written records—a log—of these initial time studies, and of your shop's actual work as it progresses.

Repeat orders will be a cinch to schedule because you will have these logs to go by. Similar type jobs will also become easy to figure. Barbara Chmara knows that she can embroider 300 pieces with a 5,000-stitch design in eight hours on a 12-head machine.

You should organize your shop's schedule in chart form. This scheduling chart will be very useful in many ways. It helps keep track of what work is to be done, the status of each job, the machine or operator assignments, the priority of work and the due date.

Victor Viti, production manager for National Embroidery in

Orlando, has a large weekly chart on the wall in the production area. The majority of the shop's work is finished caps. For each job listing there are columns for describing the quantity, the style of cap, the purchase order number, the job name, the tape, the receipt of purchase order, the receipt of goods and the machine number. A checkmark under the appropriate column indicates that the tape, purchase order and goods have been received. No job is started until the information is complete.

That's a very important point. Without the organization a scheduling chart offers, garments could be hooped without the design being received or approved, or operators could be standing around not knowing what to work on next, or several employees might be spending time researching the status of a job until it's ready for production. Avoid such time wasters!

A chart should also indicate the due date or date promised. Notations can also be made as to when garments, supplies, designs are expected to arrive. However, these can be noted by the scheduler on a separate plan, and not added to the production floor's scheduling chart. Each job should be logged on the plan when the order is received. Some even find it helpful to keep a preliminary plan for jobs expected. This helps determine expected turn-around time when quoting or bidding for a job.

It is equally important to plan such things as number of machines, type of machines (cap capability, disk capability, sewing field, number of needles), number of operators and number of hoops required. Big scheduling errors can be made by overlooking such limitations.

Tracking error rates will help identify problem areas to correct and it will also help anticipate needed time for redos until the problem is eliminated. Don't forget to schedule preventive maintenance. It takes time to clean and oil machines and it should be planned, not done as an afterthought or as time allows. And, of course, you must allow for breaks, lunch, vacation, holidays and any other time-off periods for your workers.

Allow extra time in your scheduling for rush orders (if you accept them), and for unexpected down time or mistakes. By doing so, you give yourself a little room to handle the unexpected and still meet the promised date. And, if you complete jobs earlier than promised, your customers will be impressed and you'll have another reason to praise your staff!

For example, Linda Steinline of Steinline Embroidery, Lakewood, Colorado, only schedules four of her five work days. The unscheduled day is filled with any orders that were bumped or need to be redone, or with rush orders. Her scheduling rule is to plan for 16,000 stitches per hour per head. She often exceeds this rate, but prefers to build in a little extra time for unforseen needs.

When assigning jobs to machines, consider such factors as changeover from flats to hats. You may be able to schedule all hats together, eliminating the need for more than one change per week. Perhaps it makes sense for your workload to schedule by colors or needle size or type to eliminate unnecessary changes. Ira Newman of National Embroidery in Carson, California, prioritizes jobs according to the color of background fabric for emblems to avoid re-framing of the fabric. Pre-hooping is not feasible with such large pieces of fabric. Another suggestion is to schedule large stitch-count jobs early in the day to allow time to pre-hoop the smaller items. However, be sure that you don't pre-hoop more than you can embroider per day. Leaving garments hooped overnight can put permanent hoop marks on some fabrics.

For those who change needles often, it may be most efficient to batch jobs by needle type and size. It is time-consuming to change needles, especially on big machines with multi-needles.

If your schedule is too full to accept a job and meet the customer's due date, consider sub-contracting the work out to another embroiderer. This enables you to retain the customer, meet his due date and make some money on the job while you also make money on the work you are producing. Just be sure you select someone with compatible equipment and who meets your quality standards.

Paperwork

Here's one of my favorite sayings: "Make sure you're doing the right thing before you concentrate on doing the thing right!"

Ed Sheinberg of Texas Art Embroidery Company in Houston, Texas, says, "Paperwork and clarity of details is most important. The customer gives the salesperson a written order. The salesperson gives an order to the embroidery company. A purchase order is issued to the garment manufacturer and an order is given to the design center (even if you have in-house designing). A work order is created for pulling materials and for embroidery production. Packing lists and shipping information is prepared, and finally an invoice created."

If any step along the way is not complete or correct, you risk losing profits or even taking a loss. Your other scheduled work may also suffer as a result.

Cheri Schembrie of Custom Monograms in Issaqua, Washington, agrees. At her shop, an order form that contains all the customer information, as well as what the customer wants is created. Then purchase orders are issued for whatever garments and supplies are needed. No work order form is created until all materials are received and artwork approved by the customer. (Although I agree with this statement, there are exceptions. For example, if a garment shipment is one or two short, do the volume run, notify your customer and your supplier, then run those one or two on your single- or double-head machine when they arrive.)

Cheri cautions, "Be sure your work order form is simple, yet ample for all necessary information. The next step is to enforce a rule that no job is run without a fully completed work order form. Instruct operators to read, understand and follow all instructions on the form. If questions arise, they should be clarified *before* running the job. A sample run of new jobs attached to the work order is helpful for operators to see what is expected. After production is complete and goods have been inspected, trimmed, folded and counted, the final step is producing the invoice. This should be done immediately, avoiding interruptions later to check with operators about what was produced when."

A production log for each machine is helpful. This should indicate the operator, the job, the number of stitches, start and finish time and date. From this information, you can track your average production output and see if there are areas needing improvement.

Records should be kept on each job done and on each customer. Some combine these, but there is an advantage to having two separate files for cross reference. If you did a job, but don't remember who it was for, you can refer to the job file. Likewise, if a customer brings a job in that you can't recall the name of or how it was filed, you can find it in the customer's file.

The files can be actual file folders containing necessary information, copies of work orders or invoices, as well as actual sew-outs of the job. Some people use an index card file, while others use a notebook. Regardless of your system, it will be helpful for repeat orders if you keep records. A sample chart, used by Initial Artistry, is shown in Exhibit 23. Victor Viti's job spec sheet is shown in Exhibit 24, and a sample job history form appears in Exhibit 25.

Production Efficiency

Production efficiency means keeping the machines running smoothly and doing each job right the first time; total output without waste. Many important contributors to production efficiency have already been covered: having equipment that meets your needs, complete paperwork, a well-trained staff, a good design center, application techniques, a well-organized shop and careful scheduling. Maintenance will be covered in a subsequent chapter of this book. What else can you do?

Victor Viti took steps to prevent common operator errors. He printed a start-up check list on his job spec sheets (Exhibit 24). These apply to his shop's Tajima 12-head machines, but similar check-lists could easily be adapted for any machine.

Victor is rightfully proud of his shop's error rate, which is below 1 1/2%.

Susan Aldrich of Meistergram says a 2% to 5% error rate is considered acceptable. Anything over that should indicate a need for some serious problem solving.

When errors do occur on embroidered goods, don't assume it is always best to back up a multi-head machine to recover an error on one or two heads. Frank Gawronski offers this formula:

$$X = \frac{(ST/12 \text{ [or number of heads]}) + 10R\,(1/R2 - 1/R1)}{(R/R2) + 1}$$

In the above formula, X represents theoretical break-even point. ST represents total stitches in pattern. R is the running speed of machine; R1 is the initial frame backing speed (the slower speed); and R2 is the subsequent or faster backing speed of the machine.

If X = 850 stitches, this is the *total* maximum number of stitches you should back up, whether for one or more corrections; otherwise, it is more efficient to continue forward on the design. The uncorrected garments can be recovered in the next batch.

Frank also offers this time-saving tip when you have a seven-color design and a six-needle machine: Run colors one through four, then pull color seven through on needle four and change while five and six are running. Run needle four as color seven. Colors one through three are ready for the next batch because they have not been disturbed.

Begin each long running design with a full bobbin, saving partially used bobbins for short running designs.

Linda Steinline says one of her pet peeves is an operator doing nothing. She expects the machine and the embroidery to be watched, with the operator pacing the full width of a multi-head if need be. "So many little things can happen—thread slipping out somewhere in the thread path, bobbin thread running out, needles breaking and so forth. I expect the quality of the embroidery to be checked during stitching to be sure tensions are correct, columns are even and any visible signs of a problem are noticed right away before they turn into bigger problems to fix."

Production awareness is important to emphasize to your staff. Encourage little "beat the clock" games or hold a hooping or thread-changing contest periodically. Post the record and name of the person to beat next time.

Marilyn Reichenberg of Initial Stitch in Boulder, Colorado, found that she can embroider on turtlenecks without completely removing the garments from their bags. She just pulls the collar out far enough to hoop and affixes a large clothespin to hold the bag and the rest of garment out of the way during the stitching process. Marilyn says, "It really saves time. You don't have to unpackage and repackage or unfold and refold."

Barbara Chmara suggests that when doing individual names on like garments, start with the longest name. If it fits in the hoop you've selected, all the others will fit. This saves time selecting different size hoops for various names.

Any major changes you make in new techniques, methodologies, systems—indeed, anything different from the way you've done business before—can be tested on a small scale before your company commits a major amount of its time and resources. There are several reasons why you should run a pilot project before taking the plunge, so if you are thinking about major production changes, consider these reasons to proceed one step at a time:

a. If it goes wrong, it can do only minimal damage.
b. You can fine-tune it at a small cost.
c. You can get feedback from the people affected without it getting out of hand and becoming a source of companywide contention.
d. The pilot project, if it works well, serves as advance publicity for the inception of the full innovation.
e. It could create synergy, spurring other departments to update their way of doing things.

Exhibit 23

JOB FILE

NAME OF DESIGN: CUSTOMER NAME:

	1	2	3
Lettering or pattern			
Letter style or tape language			
Height			
Density			
Line or arc			
Clockwise or counter			
Radius			
Stitch width			
Horizontal spacing			
Vertical spacing			
Line spacing			
Thread color			
Placement			
Garment			

Special instructions:

Exhibit 24
JOB SPEC SHEET

Tape Information

NE tape #________________________
Tape name________________________
Mfg. tape #________________________
No. of colors________________________
Stitch count ________________________
Machine code________________________

Start-Up Check List

Throw breaker switch to "on" position
Press start button
Needle switches in off position
Turn machine on
Check bobbins - replace if necessary
Check tape in memory
Check percentage
Check needle bar sequence
Check starting point
Check brake in "on" position
Cycle machine
Wipe off back of heads
Turn needles on

Style/Color____________
Percentage____________
Frame________________
Frame material_________
RPM_________________
Color sequence:
_________ _________
_________ _________
_________ _________
_________ _________
_________ _________
_________ _________

Style/Color____________
Percentage____________
Frame________________
Frame material_________
RPM_________________
Color sequence:
_________ _________
_________ _________
_________ _________
_________ _________
_________ _________
_________ _________

Style/Color____________
Percentage____________
Frame________________
Frame material_________
RPM_________________
Color sequence:
_________ _________
_________ _________
_________ _________
_________ _________
_________ _________
_________ _________

Style/Color____________
Percentage____________
Frame________________
Frame material_________
RPM_________________
Color sequence:
_________ _________
_________ _________
_________ _________
_________ _________
_________ _________
_________ _________

Style/Color____________
Percentage____________
Frame________________
Frame material_________
RPM_________________
Color sequence:
_________ _________
_________ _________
_________ _________
_________ _________
_________ _________
_________ _________

Style/Color____________
Percentage____________
Frame________________
Frame material_________
RPM_________________
Color sequence:
_________ _________
_________ _________
_________ _________
_________ _________
_________ _________
_________ _________

SPECIAL
INSTRUCTIONS____

____

____

____

Exhibit 25

JOB HISTORY SHEET

Date	P.O. #	Style/Color	Qty.Ordered	Mis-sewn	Defects	Qty.Shipped	Date Shipped

CHAPTER 18

PROBLEM SOLVING

The best way to solve problems is to prevent them. As I have stressed throughout this book, following standard and proven procedures, being knowledgeable and communicating well are your best defenses. Still, you're faced with the human factor, and mistakes will occur. Anyone who doesn't make mistakes isn't working! Also, machines will fail, break and sometimes do unexpected little things (that's not just peculiar to embroidery machines). Whatever the reason and no matter who caused it, here are five steps to take to correct a mistake:

1. Identify the problem.
2. Fix the problem.
3. Find the source of the problem.
4. Take corrective action.
5. Evaluate and follow-up the corrective action.

For example, suppose the name "Jane" was sewn and it should have been "Jan." The customer will certainly identify the problem for you. You'll fix the problem by ripping out the embroidery and restitching it or replacing the garment. But don't stop there. Find the source of the problem. That doesn't necessarily mean speak to the operator who read it wrong. How did it pass inspection? Perhaps the order was illegible, and you need to adopt a policy of printed or typed orders. Or perhaps the order was clearly marked "Jane," yet no one had the customer approve and sign the order.

Whatever the reason for the problem, get to its root and take corrective action. Monitor the area or phase in production where the mistake took place to see that it is not repeated after corrective action has been taken. If it is repeated, start the process all over again.

Fixing Garments

Some garments may not be worth the time it will take to fix them. If ripping out appears to be time-consuming or difficult and the garment is inexpensive, it may be better to use it for future test sewing. If the mistake is because the garment doesn't meet the customer's requirements, perhaps it could be sold to someone else. For instance, a generic design (never a customer's exclusive design) that was done in the wrong color, may be just the color someone else prefers. Or a design placed on the left, when it should have been on the right, side of the garment could be sold to someone else. Also, selling slightly flawed items at a reduced price as "seconds" is a common practice.

When a fix is in order, most often you will rip out and resew. When there is need to remove embroidery, the sooner you can do it, the better. The longer embroidery stays in the garment, the more noticeable the needle holes. When this occurs, try using sizing and ironing the garment to help disguise needle holes.

The way to rip out is to cut the bobbin thread first and pull the threads out from the top stitching. Be careful not to cut the garment. Allowing the garment to hang loosely while ripping will make it easier to avoid cutting the garment. The backing helps separate the stitching from the garment (a good reason to use backing even when a fabric is stable enough without it). Curved, sharp scissors or a seam ripper should be used. The latest gadget out is a razor tool called a Stitch Eraser®, which is available from Madeira. Those who use the Stitch Eraser recommend practicing on remnant fabrics first until you are able to control the amount of pressure to apply. Gentle strokes across the bobbin thread literally shave them away. There are also those who use an ordinary safety razor. Again, pull threads out from the front. On fills, cut the bobbin thread cross-grained and pull from the front.

A flaw in the fabric or a damaged garment can sometimes be fixed by sewing a design over it or covering it with an applique.

Susan Aldrich of Meistergram offers a few other helpful hints:

> Some garments, such as sweatshirts, can be fixed by adding a decorative band of fabric across the shirt body and covering the flaw. It will look like the shirt was designed with it.
>
> Hand-painted shirts are very popular right now, so try splashing a little paint over a flaw and working it into a design.
>
> Use a magnifying glass when ripping out small stitching.

On volume orders or fabrics you've not worked with before, ask the customer to provide a couple of extra garments for sampling purposes. Then test sew.

Know when to say "no."

To elaborate on Susan's last recommendation, here's a list of OK's for inexperienced or timid embroidery entrepreneurs:

It's OK to refuse work to protect your reputation.

It's OK to refuse sub-standard garments.

It's OK to reject a design.

It's OK to discipline employees for consistently poor work.

It's OK to admit mistakes and correct them.

Occasionally a sense of humor can salvage a garment. Rich Hirsch of ARC embroidered a shark on the breast pocket of a golf knit shirt. After he was finished, he discovered he had sewn the front of the shirt collar into the design. He also noticed that the collar was stitched right at the mouth of the shark. Rich clipped the corner of the collar with pinking shears, causing the cut to resemble tooth marks. He then sewed "Shark Attack!" on the remains of the collar.

I once cut a small hole in my husband's jacket while trimming a design. It was just underneath a letter. Using a plain block style alphabet (no serifs), I swapped the image and sewed the capital letter "I" on its side. It underlined the letters and covered the hole. He never knew about the hole. (Wonder if he'll read this book!)

Linda Steinline of Steinline Embroidery in Lakewood, Colorado, suggests using heavy cut-away backing when stitching over a hole. Don't trim the backing around the hole, either. This will protect the hole from enlarging on the backside.

Small areas that need to be filled in from skipped stitches, thread breaks or design flaws can be handled several ways. Some machines allow you to back up in the design to the point desired, and restitch a section. Others enable backing up to the beginning and fast forwarding to the desired point. So long as the garment remains in the hoop, you can usually recover a mistake using your embroidery machine, and the same sewing head. Changing to a different sewing head to finish a design could cause registration problems. The backing-up method also works for large areas missing stitches, such as when the bobbin thread ran out and wasn't caught right away. If your machine doesn't have these capabilities, you can always repeat the design over the same area, removing the needle and thread until it reaches the point for correction. If the problem is more towards the end of the design, finish the design and then go back. If the error occurred closer to the start, go back to the beginning before finishing the design.

Home sewing machines with zig-zag capability, manual industrial machines or hand-sewing may be less time-consuming fixes for some of those small boo-boos. For example, Linda Steinline uses a Singer mending machine for quick fixes. Embroiderers have also been known to use permanent, colorfast, colored markers to fill in a missed stitch or cover a little bobbin thread.

When a garment pops out of a hoop before the embroidery is completed, it is difficult to recover, but not always impossible. If hoop impressions are left in the garment, it may be possible to realign the hoops, but you really need a good eye to do it. Once the garment is rehooped, finding the correct place for needle penetration is not difficult, but you may need to do some jogging around to find it.

When a loop needs to be cut or a lockstitch is inadvertently clipped or missing, Fray Check® liquid can be applied to the front or back of the design, depending upon which side requires sealing, to prevent the rest of the stitches from unraveling. Fray Check can also be useful in sealing wide column stitching to help prevent snags.

Solving Poor Sewing Quality

Here are the symptoms of the most common sewing problems, and some probable solutions:

<u>Puckering</u> - Check hooping. Garment must be flat; hoop must be flat on tabletop of machine; garment could be too tight or too loose in hoop.
Loosen tension.
Reduce density.
Add backing.

Looping -	Tighten tension. Lower needle depth to catch loop underneath. Adjust hook to ensure proper catch of loop underneath. Check thread and needle compatibility. Try a larger needle.
Uneven stitching -	Adjust tension. Check needle type (ball vs. sharp) and check for dullness. Reduce sewing speed. Remove stays or other obstructions.
Poor registration -	Check slack in hoop. Tighten hoop. Increase backing or use spray adhesive with backing. Adjust tension. Heads may be out of synchronization. Consult technician.
Missed stitches -	Consult technician. Electronics and mechanics may not be timed together.

Flagging is another common problem. This occurs when the inside hoop is not all the way in, thus causing the material to not lay flat on the table. Flagging causes bobbin thread to show on top of the design. It also causes the fabric to move and the needle to drag the fabric prematurely. That premature dragging can bend the needle, causing it to hit the needle plate and break. Flagging also causes narrower columns.

Too wide a column can occur when material is too loose in the hoop or when there is too much slack in the frame.

Reducing the sewing speed may also solve any of these problems. Conversely, Melco's trainer Sandy Behr discovered that increasing the sewing speed eliminated thread breaks on Rip Stop nylon (the light weight nylon with visible 1/8-inch squares). Other than a deadline crunch, that's the only example I've ever heard where faster sewing solved a problem. To determine if a quality problem is in the design, as opposed to your machine's mechanics or your sewing technique, follow this procedure: Sew the design again at a 90-degree angle (swap it on its side) and rehoop accordingly. Make one run. If the problem is the same, it's probably the design, unless you hooped improperly both times. If the problem goes away, it's definitely not in the design.

Linda Burney of Gunold + Stickma cautions us to be sure all the needles are turned the same way in a multi-needle or multi-head machine.

Thread Breaks

Thread breaks are a terrible nuisance and waste of time, particularly on multi-head machines. Here's a prime example of the importance of determining the cause of a problem. Just rethreading a machine isn't enough because chances are good you will continue to break threads until you figure out what's causing the problem and solve it.

Basic thread-break prevention involves using only high quality embroidery threads, storing thread to avoid exposure to air and dust for extended periods, and storing it for no more than two years. Avoid taping loose thread ends to the spools (use a slip knot) because the adhesive on the tape can weaken or damage the thread fibers. You may also wish to consider polyester thread, which is stronger than rayon or cotton.

Here is a list of simple ways to handle thread breaks. The list is presented in a declining order, the first suggestion being the one that will most frequently solve this problem, and so on. It should be posted near every embroidery machine, with instructions to the operator to proceed through the list until the problem is solved.

a. Check thread path from spool to needle.
b. Check tensions.
c. Check needle insertion and quality of needle (even a new needle may contain burrs).
d. Clean hook assembly.
e. Check design for too much density or stitches being sewn over a previously sewn area.
f. Check thread itself. Try pulling off several yards in case there is a bad spot in the spool.
g. Change to a different spool.
h. Check to see if bobbin is wound evenly.
i. Check to see that needle is not rubbing against presser foot.
j. Check for burrs on presser foot.

More troubleshooting ideas will be included in the following chapter on maintenance.

CHAPTER 19

MAINTENANCE

Preventive

The two most important preventive measures you can take in the care of your computerized embroidery machine are to oil it and clean it. I can't emphasize these precautions enough. Every owner, manager and supervisor should absolutely insist upon these tasks being done on a regular basis, so be sure time is scheduled for these procedures.

Proper lubrication of your embroidery machine is vital to its operation and longevity. Failure to oil the machine regularly can cause bearing failures in the sewing head, poor sewing quality, or component failures requiring replacement parts and/or service calls that could otherwise be avoided. Over-lubrication of the machine is also undesirable. Continuous over-lubrication will saturate the oil distribution network within the head. This causes the oil to pool at various unwanted areas, contributing to soiled garments. It's a good idea to test-sew a small design or some lettering if you suspect you may have oiled the machine too heavily.

Always use a high quality sewing machine oil. Sewing machine oil is specially formulated for use in sewing heads. Never use motor oil, castor oil, light machine oil or any other oil not specifically made for use in sewing heads. The results will be disastrous and expensive to repair.

The hook is the area needing oil most frequently. It should be oiled after every four hours of sewing time. Use one drop of sewing machine oil in the track where the hook rotates around the bobbin case holder. For head bearings, use two drops in each oil port after every 40 hours of operation. Even if not all heads of a multi-head machine have been used, you must lubricate each head and hook. For other lubricating procedures, it's best to follow your machine manufacturer's guidelines as outlined in the operator's manual. You will find there are some places in your machine where a different kind of oil is required. Sewing machine oil should not be used in those areas.

The hook and bobbin areas are the most critical places to clean the machine. A build-up of lint and loose threads in these areas can play havoc with your machine. Lint brushes, small vacuums and canned air are excellent tools. Some embroiderers use air compressors and air hoses, which also work well. However, **do not** use compressed air or canned air for cleaning circuit boards. It generates static electricity, which could damage the boards.

The spring in the bobbin case should be cleaned with canned air or a piece of thread used as floss. Do not use needles or other objects to clean the spring. If the spring is damaged, replace the bobbin case; otherwise, you may experience intermittent tension problems.

Cleaning up at the end of the day or eight-hour shift should suffice. However, the use of cotton threads, excessive trimming at the machine or any other lint-causing operations will require more frequent cleaning. In addition to removing dust and lint from all the little nooks and crannies—even the tension disks—dust off the machine's tabletop whenever lint or threads appear and vacuum or sweep the floor daily. Covers or tarps are recommended when the machine is not in use for hours at a time or when vacuuming.

At Barth & Dreyfuss, the motors and filters of the machines are cleaned once a week. Bob Bell of Tex-Ace in San Antonio, Texas, also suggests wiping down the machine body, including the legs at least every two weeks.

Disk drives may need to be cleaned occasionally. Disk drive cleaning kits are readily available at computer supply stores. The wet type of cleaning kit is preferred. Do not clean disk drives more than twice a year, unless the machine's performance indicates a problem.

Papertape readers need to have the read heads cleaned once a day with a brush designed for this purpose. Technicians tell me that the majority of tape readers sent in for repair only need to be cleaned, so here's a good way to save a repair bill with just common daily preventive maintenance. If a problem occurs in the tape, examine it for a defect. It could be that a hole is not completely open. If you cannot see a defect, mark the place on the tape where the problem occurred and run it again. This will help you identify the actual place and be able to splice a new piece of tape to correct the problem. Be sure you use only splicing tape for splicing purposes. Never use transparent tape. It is also advisable to have a duplicate copy of your tape so that you can solve such problems without having to order a new tape from your design center.

Let common sense prevail. Keep food and beverages, straight pins, scissors and all objects away from your embroidery machines and all related equipment. It just isn't worth the risk of parts damaged by a careless accident. Prohibit smoking near the machines, particularly disks and disk drives, but also to prevent accidental burns in garments.

If you travel with your machine, expect excess dirt and take reasonable precautions. Don't set the machine in a barnyard full of hay or whatever, or in a booth next to the chainsaw being demonstrated on logs! Line voltage regulators are a must when using your machine at a show, fair or anywhere power is likely to be less than the constant amount of proper voltage. Also, people who travel with their machines experience higher maintenance and repair costs, so be sure to allow extra dollars in your budget if you anticipate such travel.

Static electricity is another problem common to computers. There are anti-static floor mats and sprays for the area around computers and for people's clothing. Static is more prevalent in cold, dry areas. It also occurs more frequently on carpeted floors than on wood or vinyl floors.

Be sure your electrical outlet is properly grounded. As stated above, voltage regulators are mandatory when operating your equipment at shows or fairs. Voltage regulators and line surge protectors are also very highly recommended for all embroidery machines, regardless of location. Nothing is more frustrating than to lose a program or a design being sewn because of irregular voltage or power surges. There are also radio frequency interference (RFI) protectors available if radio or television signals interfere with your machine.

If you're using disks, there are preventive precautions for them. First, **always have a back-up!** When you're in the middle of a job or have one due tomorrow and the disk suddenly goes to magnetic heaven, you'll be glad for that back-up. Next, protect your disks by storing them in a proper disk container. This also applies when shipping disks. There are special bags, boxes or other storage devices available that protect them in transit. Don't set a disk on top of the disk drive, a computer or anything with an electric motor, because of the magnetic properties of the disk. Finally, never turn the power of your equipment on or off while a disk is inserted in the disk drive. It will probably damage the disk.

Never unplug your equipment when the power switch is on. Turn the switch off, then unplug the cord. Always turn the machine off and unplug it during an electrical storm. Damage can occur even when the machine is off.

Troubleshooting

Whoever is in charge of simple maintenance should be able to set the hook timing on the machine, following the manufacturer's guidelines. Yet, the timing doesn't need to be set all that often. Far too often, people time their machines when it's not really necessary. It should be viewed as a last resort when you've tried all other recommendations to solve poor sewing quality or thread breaks. After a hoop has been hit by a needle bar, it may or may not cause a timing problem. But, when a timing problem *does* exist, it is usually as a result of the needle bar hitting the hoop. When the needle bar and hoop do collide, chances are good that you will have to reset the needle bar depth. Your manufacturer may have a gauge to help with this adjustment on your machine. However, such gauges are usually for use only with a specific brand of needle.

When a sewing quality problem is encountered, hook timing should only be *suspected* as one of the possible causes. Other items to check when trouble occurs include:

- Is the thread tension set properly?
- Is the needle bar height adjusted properly?
- Is the presser foot bent?
- Are there nicks or burrs on the hook, needle plate or presser foot?
- Are there foreign objects, such as broken needle pieces?
- Is the bobbin thread tail too long? (2 inches to 3 inches is maximum desired length.)
- Do belts need replacing?
- Is the head lubricated properly?

Pantograph problems usually indicate trouble with the motor drive system of the machine.

If none of the above seem to be the problem, and assuming there is no problem with hooping, backing, needles and threads, the next step should be to call your service technician. Major manufacturers are now able to successfully telephone diagnose in approximately 80% to 95% of the calls they receive. Replacement parts can be shipped and, with their telephone assistance, be installed by you.

Some parts will be shipped with instructions. Others are not, and require step-by-step instructions from your technician over the phone while you perform the repair. If you receive a part with instructions to call your technician when you receive it, do it!

Don't assume you know what to do—you could overlook an important step and cause more damage.

When returning parts to your manufacturer or distributor, be sure to follow their returned goods policy. I know first-hand from when I was customer services manager at Melco, that items received without proper authorization or return labels can get lost in the shuffle. When systems and procedures are established to expedite such processes, it is in your best interest to follow them.

In order to assure the greatest probability for telephone diagnosis, you need to provide sufficient information:

Your name and the name of your business
Machine model
Serial number
Description of the symptoms as detailed as possible
Any messages of warning signaled by the readout display
Frequency of the symptoms
Any troubleshooting measures you have tried

It's helpful for the service technician to know, for example, if the problem occurred when you turned the machine on or just when you're sewing a certain design. Perhaps the problem only occurs during the second shift. This could be a signal that the operator on that shift is doing something to cause the problem.

Keep a service log or diary. It need not be elaborate—just a listing of the date, description of the problem, the solution, parts replaced and cost. This could be very useful in future diagnosis of the problems, especially repeat problems. It will also help you budget for service in the future.

Should telephone diagnosis fail, you will need to schedule a service call or arrange an appointment to take your machine to the service site. Again, the more detailed information you can provide, the better your chances of proper diagnosis and expeditious repair.

Be honest when providing information to your service technician. He is only interested in doing his job and getting your machine up and running as quickly as possible. He is not there to pass judgement on you if you made a mistake. Knowing exactly what happened will help him accurately diagnose the problem and recommend a solution more quickly than if he has to guess all the possibilities. Another tip for working with your technician is to stay calm. Yes, it's very frustrating to have a machine down, but again, the sooner you state the facts rather than curse the machine or the manufacturer, the sooner you'll be up and running. Stop, take a break to calm down, and think through what is happening. Make some notes. Perhaps an obvious solution will come to mind, but if not, at least you'll be able to be more helpful when requesting assistance.

Freida Coonrod of Cedar Rapids, Iowa, practices this approach regularly. Whether a sewing-related problem or a machine-related problem, she always walks away from it before getting too frustrated. By rationally thinking through the situation, more often than not, she can go back and resolve it herself.

Many people have learned to perform a variety of repairs on their own machines. While there are no customer training programs for this, Melco's Epicor system does provide a video with service instructions for do-it-yourself repairs. A service manual is provided for Epicor system embroidery machines. (Hopefully, we will see more of this in the industry to help defray the costs of service.) A lot can be learned from reading your manuals, talking by telephone with your technician, and observing and asking questions when a technician makes a service call to your site. However, not all problems can be fixed in the field. There are some failures that require the machine to be shipped to the manufacturer for repair because specific or elaborate test equipment is needed.

Most importantly, do not attempt to fix something unless you know what you're doing. All too often this will cause bigger problems, which could also mean bigger repair bills and a longer wait before the machine is repaired. As a precaution, always turn the machine off before working on it, and if you're working on an electrical source, unplug the machine.

When a service technician repairs your machine at your site, he will ask you to sign a work order when he is finished. Be sure you read it before signing to be sure it accurately lists the work done. Your signature on the work order denotes agreement. It will do no good to disagree with it after you've signed it. If you have any questions or concerns about the work performed, the parts installed, the time or travel charges, ask before you sign.

CHAPTER 20

RECORDS

Bookkeeping

The double-entry bookkeeping system is the most widely used. Its basis is that for every debit, there is a credit, so that when both parts of a transaction are recorded, the books are in balance. Various accounts are used and arranged so that appropriate statements and financial documents can be easily derived for accounting and management purposes. Single-entry day books or the use of a checkbook only will not provide these benefits.

The key factors in any recordkeeping system are simplicity, understandability, reliability, accuracy, consistency and timeliness. There are many computer software programs available today that are designed with these factors in mind. Be sure whoever is responsible for keeping your books has input in selecting the program, if you're considering such a purchase. If you already have one, thorough training and understanding of the system will help the bookkeeper be consistent, reliable and timely. A computerized system is not necessary, particularly if your business is small. But, it is very helpful and becomes more necessary as your business grows. If you can afford to start out with a computerized system, it will save time and confusion later when making the conversion.

Your embroidery system may already include a computer suitable for business applications. If so, all you need is compatible software for the business programs you want. The Epicor system enables you to program up to 16 jobs for each peripheral, thereby enabling the computer to be used for other functions while the machines are embroidering.

Before you can even begin your bookkeeping system, you must have complete records. First, a record of all sales and cash receipts must be kept. These may be your sales orders, your customers' purchase orders, cash register tapes, or other cash receipts. Without a cash register, cash receipts can be recorded in a journal showing the necessary information, including an invoice number, if appropriate. Even if you accept a telephone order or other verbal order, document it with a written order. Even if a sale is made with an agreement for payment at a later date, the transaction is recorded as a sale at the time of the sale.

For inventory purposes, the sales record or cash journal should show the quantity and description of any garments or goods sold. In addition, the sales record should show the price of the goods and a separate line item for the price of the embroidery, unless the embroidery was included in the price of the goods. Separate the amount of tax from the sales price. The date of the sale should be reflected on the sales order.

You must also maintain records on all disbursements. When writing a check, use an invoice or bill to support the check. In the checkbook, record the purpose of the check, the date, name, check number, and the amount of the check. Bank charges should be recorded in the same manner as a check except, of course, they would not have a check number.

A petty cash fund should be used for small items. Here again, record all transactions on a petty cash journal.

Another important set of records is accounts receivable. Whenever you extend credit, or for whatever reason monies owed are not paid, record it in accounts receivable. At the end of the month, accounts should be aged. Aging means listing all accounts unpaid for 30 days, 60 days, and over 60 days. This record is not only necessary for accounting, but is also helpful for collection purposes.

From these various sources—sales orders, cash receipts, check stubs, deposit slips, petty cash—books of original entry, or journals, are created. The data in the journals are summarized daily, weekly, or monthly, and then posted to a general ledger. A general ledger is a compilation of account classifications that describe your business' financial activities. The journal is the detail—the general ledger is the summary of the journals.

In order to compile a general ledger, accounts must be classified. Following is a sample listing of account numbers, account names and a description of the accounts:

Account Number	Account Name	Description
Assets		
100	Cash in banks	List checking and savings account numbers and name of banks.
101	Petty cash	Cash on hand for minor expenses.
102	Accounts receivable	Balances owed, but not paid, to your business.
103	Inventory	Listing of all goods purchased for sale.
105	Materials and supplies	Purchases of threads, bobbins and so forth.
107	Deposits	List deposits to all bank accounts.
120	Equipment	Record purchases of embroidery machines and all office equipment.
121	Accumulated depreciation	List reduction in value of all equipment.
Liabilities		
200	Accounts payable	Money owed on account.
201	Notes payable	Short-term debts due within one year or less.
205	Sales taxes payable	Amounts collected and owed to the state.
206	FICA taxes payable	Amount withheld from employees and owed to Social Security.
207	Federal withholding	Amount withheld from employees and owed to IRS for taxes.
208	State withholding	Amount withheld from employees and owed to state for taxes.
209	Unemployment taxes	Amount owed for unemployment compensation.

220	Long-term debt	Loans with maturity of more than one year.

Capital Accounts

300	Proprietorship account or common capital stock	Amount invested if proprietorship or amount of stock, if corporation.
301	Preferred capital stock	If corporation.
	Proprietor's withdrawals	If proprietorship.

Sales

400	Retail sales	Goods sold to retail accounts.
401	Wholesale sales	Goods sold to wholesale accounts.
402	Retail services	Embroidery sold to retail accounts.
403	Wholesale services	Embroidery sold to wholesale accounts.

Expenses

500	Salaries and wages	Record amounts paid to employees.
501	Contract labor	Amount paid for services of contract workers.
502	Commissions	Amount paid to sales representatives in commissions.
503	Payroll taxes	Employer portion of taxes paid.
504	Utilities	Gas, electricity, water, sewer, trash service.
505	Telephone	Telephone service and long distance.
506	Rent	Amount paid for shop space.
507	Office supplies	From business forms to paperclips.
508	Shipping and postage	All charges for sending mail and packages.
509	Maintenance expense	Service and replacement parts for machines.
510	Insurance	All business insurance.

511	Interest	All interest and finance charges paid.
512	Travel expense	All business-related expenses for travel.
513	Entertainment	Expenses incurred while entertaining for business reasons.
514	Advertising	All promotional expenses.
515	Dues and subscriptions	Professional organization memberships and fees for business-related publications.
520	Miscellaneous expenses	To record infrequent transactions or to adjust accounts for reconciliation purposes.

In developing your General Ledger, each account should have a separate page, but you should use the same format for each page. Here is a sample general ledger page:

#100 - Cash In Banks

Date	Reference	Debit	(Credit)	Balance
11/30/89	Balance in FNB Checking Account			$1,780.45
Dec. '89	Journal Entry #1 - Sales	1,514.00		
	Journal Entry #2 - Cash receipts	265.00		
	Journal Entry #3 - Cash disbursements		537.26	
	Journal Entry #4 - Payroll		1,000.00	
12/31/89	Balance			$2,022.19

At the end of each section—Assets, Liabilities, Capital Accounts, Sales Accounts and Expenses—enter the total for each account in that section and calculate a total for the entire section.

Here is an example of the total assets:

Account #	Amount
100	$ 2,022.19
101	37.63
102	578.00
103	797.35
105	(129.26)
107	1,779.00
120	19,500.00
121	(3,775.00)
Total	$20,809.91

From the General Ledger, the financial documents recommended in Chapter 7 can be prepared using actual numbers. Other information which should be monitored regularly can be easily determined by maintaining the receipts, journals and general ledger. Here's a listing of the information you should have on a daily, weekly, monthly and quarterly basis:

Daily .... Cash on hand
Bank balance
Daily summary of sales and cash receipts
Record of all money paid out by cash or check

Weekly .... Accounts receivable
Accounts payable
Payroll
Taxes and reports to all government agencies

Monthly .... Journal entries made
General Ledger posted
Profit and loss statement
Balance sheet
Bank statement reconciled
Petty cash balanced
Tax deposits made
Accounts receivable aging
Inventory report

Quarterly.................... Form 941 Tax Withholding forms and reports

Embroiderer Janet Hamlin's husband, Ed, prepares an additional account analysis on a monthly basis for Initial Artistry. The analysis lists the account name, address, phone number and contact person. It also lists the amount owed by that account, number of days past due, high balance and the total year-to-date charges. Another helpful report he prepares is a profit and loss statement on tape designs. For the accounts receivable aging, he shows the percentage owed in each category—0 to 30 days old, 31 to 60, 61 to 90, and over 90 days. Ed says, "I treat the general accounting, the accounts receivable and the inventory of designs as separate departments. I do this for anything I want closely tracked. I prepare an income statement and balance sheet for each of them on a monthly basis, and they are audited monthly."

Ed uses an IBM®-compatible personal computer. He purchased the ACCPAC™ software from Computer Associates. "The system is planned for growth," according to Ed. "Even if the business grows to five times its present size, our existing accounting system can handle it."

While you don't want to be overburdened with unnecessary paperwork, you can add to or detract from the system as you see fit for your business. However, it has been my observation that insufficient recordkeeping is prevalent among small embroidery businesses. Better to have a little more than necessary than to eliminate important recordkeeping, until you've been in business long enough and have worked with your accountant enough to know what is truly important for sound management and planning.

Purchasing

In the beginning of your business and while it is very small, purchasing and inventory control may be your responsibility alone. As your business grows, your time will be spread too thin and unless you delegate this job, inefficiencies will increase. The goals are to have on hand or be able to quickly acquire the right quantities of the right goods at the right time and at the lowest cost. Achieving these goals is critical to meeting your customer's timelines and to assure your profits are not jeopardized by having to pay premium prices because you did not plan ahead.

You must set guidelines such as:

- Who has the authority to buy?
- Which vendors or suppliers are acceptable?
- What terms of price and delivery are acceptable?
- What type of information should your employees consider confidential?

- Where does the company stand with regard to giving and taking of gifts and business entertainment?

If employees who are not authorized to make purchases need certain supplies or goods, they should be required to complete a recquisition form. A typical recquisition form includes such information as quantity of item requested, part or catalog number, description of the item, date required, unit price and total price. The recquisition should bear an authorized signature before being submitted to the purchaser.

Everything purchased (except through petty cash) should be documented with a purchase order (see Exhibit 26). It clarifies the quantities, type of product, price, delivery and any other terms of agreement. Even if ordering via phone, a follow-up purchase order provides evidence of a contract. It also enables you to eliminate unauthorized purchases, plan cash flow, check on how suppliers are meeting schedules and establish an effective inventory control and accounts payable system.

The original copy of the purchase order is sent to the vendor, with a copy retained in the file, and a third given to the bookkeeper or accounting department. When the goods are received, they should be inspected and counted. Check to see that what was received matches the information on the purchase order and on the packing list. Initial the packing list if everything is OK. This should be done within 24 hours of receipt or as soon as possible so that discrepancies or damaged shipments can be reported and corrected quickly.

Ordering additional quantities as a safety stock may save an order when shipments are received late, not filled completely or contain a few items that are not up to your quality standards.

When the invoice is received for payment, note the check number on the invoice before filing it. This is a good habit to form because it saves hours of search time in the event of a discrepancy or dispute over payment.

It's usually a good idea to take advantage of some trade discounts and to buy direct from manufacturers whenever possible. However, whatever discount you receive for large quantity buying will not compensate for the problems that may result from overbuying. Do not deplete your working capital to finance excessive inventory. Average inventory carrying costs are about 24% of inventory value. Expenses include storage and handling, taxes, insurance, interest lost on capital, labor, paperwork and spoilage.

In addition to quantity discounts, your supplier may offer seasonal discounts. Use caution to avoid buying out-of-style garments or obsolete technical items.

Cash discounts are often offered for timely payments. Typical terms are 2/10, net 30. This means if you pay within 10 days of the invoice date, you can deduct two percent from the price. However, you must pay the full invoiced amount within 30 days of the invoiced date. Always try to capitalize on cash discounts. Many times it even pays you to borrow at local bank rates in order to take advantage of such discounts. It can cost you not to use them, as the following listing illustrates:

Credit terms	Annualized cost if cash discount is not taken
1/10, net 20	36.36%
1/10, net 30	18.18%
2/10, net 20	73.44%
2/10, net 30	36.72%

Inventory

Begin an inventory system by listing all the items you now have in stock and those you intend to carry in the near future. Have someone edit the list to be sure that all item descriptions are complete. Each employee should have a copy of the list so that they may use it for reference when making requisitions. Your accountant may want to observe the inventory count to make a financial adjustment to your books. Then physically take an inventory count of each item in stock.

How often you take an inventory count depends upon your particular business. A one- or two-person shop can usually manage a visual control system once a week. In such small shops, usually a big order that depletes stock of an item will be known and a purchase order can be generated immediately. If your business has a fairly steady usage of items, then regular ordering, and the practice of keeping a safety stock on hand, may be effective. In such cases, try the bin tag control system whereby the bulk of the stock is kept in a main storage bin or area. The back-up or safety stock is retained separately. Dipping into the back-up stock automatically signals that it is time to reorder. Of course, this requires that your back-up stock be sufficient to last until a new shipment can be ordered and received.

Those businesses that handle a wide variety or a large volume of inventory should consider a stock balance card system or a computerized system. As items are received or issued from stock, each entry is made. References to purchase order numbers are made and each order received from a customer is checked against the inventory control data before commitments are made for delivery time.

Physical inventory counts should be taken on businesses using this system monthly, quarterly, or semi-annually, depending upon how accurate your systems are or if you are experiencing any mysterious disappearance of stock.

Inventory management experts recommend that businesses have a turnover ratio of four to six times per year. To calculate the turnover ratio, divide the cost of the goods sold during a fiscal period by the average of the opening and closing inventories. For example, if the cost of goods sold was $75,000 and the average of the initial and ending inventories was $15,000, the merchandise-inventory-turnover ratio would be five ($75,000 divided by $15,000). This does not mean that every part of the stock has been sold and new stock purchased five separate times during the fiscal year. It means that the equivalent of this has been accomplished in terms of the total goods handled during a 12-month period. Some items will have turned more and some less.

Watch for items that are particularly slow moving so that they can be marketed more aggressively or discounted to take your losses and replace the stock with items that move.

In general, embroidery businesses that stock their best-selling garments fare better than those who offer no garments. Your customers usually appreciate the one-stop shopping concept and will buy more readily than if they have to go elsewhere to purchase the jacket or cap or whatever, then return to your shop for the embroidery. You also make a profit from the sale of the garment as well as for the service of embroidering it.

Give your customers what they want and you'll make more entries in your sales journal!

Exhibit 26

PURCHASE ORDER

THIS NUMBER MUST APPEAR ON ALL INVOICES AND PACKAGES. ORDER NO.

TO	
ADDRESS	DATE
SHIP TO	REQ. NO. OR DEPT.
ADDRESS	FOR

PLEASE NOTIFY US IMMEDIATELY IF YOU ARE UNABLE TO SHIP COMPLETE ORDER BY DATE SPECIFIED.

	QUANTITY	PLEASE SUPPLY ITEMS LISTED BELOW	PRICE		
1.					
2.					
3.					
4.					
5.					
6.					
7.					
8.					
9.					
10.					
11.					
12.					

DATE REQUIRED	HOW SHIP	PLEASE SEND COPIES OF YOUR INVOICE
TERMS		PURCHASING AGENT

CHAPTER 21

WHO'S THE BOSS?

That's a question that could be put to thousands of working people and few would answer correctly. There is only one boss, and whether you're an entrepreneur or an embroidery machine operator or a receptionist or a part-time trimmer, the boss remains the same. **The real boss is the customer.** He is the person who pays everyone's salary. He decides whether a business is going to succeed or fail. And he doesn't care if a business has been around for years. The minute it starts treating him badly, he'll put it out of business. He buys your clothes, your home, your car, pays for your children's education and your vacations. He pays your bills, and he pays them in exact proportion to the way you treat him.

This is not to say that the customer is always right. I do not believe that common slogan. We all know that sometimes the customer is wrong. Sometimes he is also rude, argumentative, or even yells loudly and acts out of control. Still, the customer is the boss, and therefore is deserving of your respect, courtesy and professionalism, regardless of who's right and who's wrong.

The best way to avoid customer problems (or any problems, for that matter) again, is to prevent them. If you take pride in your work, meet your deadlines, adhere to good policies and procedures and have a positive attitude toward the boss, you'll certainly minimize the chances for problems. To do this, the owner or manager must establish the guidelines and set a good example. It is unrealistic to expect employees to treat customers well if the manager is abusive. Adopt a written code of ethics pertaining to customers. Hang it on the wall in a place that is visible to both employees and customers. Avoid insolent signs. Customers are the brunt of many such signs which are intended to be humorous, but they're not worth the risk of losing even a single customer who may be offended. An example customer code of ethics is shown in Exhibit 27.

Policies and procedures are often overlooked in small businesses, unfortunately. How much easier it would be on employees, new trainees and customers if everyone were playing by the same rules. Ignorance may be no excuse of the law, but ignorance about a company policy that wasn't communicated gives employees and customers alike grounds for legitimate complaints.

Many shops develop policies as they go along, usually after they've been burned. For example, failure to pay for work may instigate a policy of 50% down or C.O.D. terms. Items returned months after the work was performed may lead to a 30-day limit on returns. Disputes over the number of garments received may cause an inventory check-in/check-out policy. Objections to a particular style of letter in a word may prompt a policy of showing customers a sample sew-out of the letters prior to performing the work. A few hours invested in typing a set of policies will save many hours of frustration later and may even save a few customers.

The more knowledgeable you are, the better you can serve your customers. Knowledge of embroidery is essential. Knowledge of garments and fabrics will help avoid problems. Knowledge of your customers is also very important. Harvey MacKay says that knowing something about your customer is just as important as knowing everything about your product. He developed a 66-question customer profile. It includes information about the customer himself, his education, military background, family, business background, special interests, lifestyle and relationship with your business. I doubt if Harvey MacKay had the embroidery industry in mind when he developed these areas for a customer profile, but just think of how each category can increase your chances of selling more personalized goods or establishing better rapport or providing an idea for a gift. You might also consider a card file on customers, listing each one's favorite type of thread, style of lettering, brand of shirts, placement preferences and taste in color coordination. It would also be helpful to include method of delivery, such as pick-up, UPS, rush service or any standard the customer expects.

Always make the customer feel important and appreciated. The routine, monotone "thank you" is certainly better than nothing, but think how much more could be gained if the customer heard an enthusiastic, "We really enjoy working with you!"

When customer problems do arise, you must give them your full attention until they are resolved. Nothing frustrates customers more than the feeling that no one cares or intends to do anything about their problem. However, customers will forgive mistakes if they are corrected fairly, quickly and courteously. Studies indicate that 70% of customers who have experienced a problem remain loyal if mistakes don't occur repeatedly; 13% of dissatisfied customers will tell 20 people about their bad experiences.

Studies have also shown that only 4 out of 100 dissatisfied customers will complain. Therefore, don't assume that all is well just because a complaint was not received. Follow-up with your customers and ask them if their last order was satisfactory. (If all is well, use the opportunity to thank them again for their business and to suggest new ideas that might interest them for future orders.)

If the customer is wrong, be firm, but gentle. Express empathy, not sympathy. Don't be obvious in laying blame on them—toss if off to a misunderstanding. Most importantly, stress what you *can* do about it, rather than what you can't. And, don't argue. There is such a thing as being dead right—it's like the person who ran across the street without looking at traffic. He may have had the green light, been in the crosswalk and perfectly in the right, but what good is it to be right when you're dead? Winning an argument and losing a customer makes about as much sense.

Handling the truly irate customer takes patience and skill. First, try speaking calmly and lowering your voice. This may prompt the customer to do likewise. Another method is to take out a pencil and paper and tell the customer you want to make notes about the problem so that you can accurately understand and resolve it. This forces the customer to speak more slowly and present the facts of the situation rather than his emotional responses to that situation. If possible, take the customer to a private office or area away from other customers and employees. If you can offer him a chair and a cup of coffee (decaf?), this too will have a calming effect.

If the customer is blatantly offensive and all calming efforts fail, you have a choice: Allow him to rant and rave to get it out of his system, or ask him to leave. Fortunately, these situations don't occur very often, and this is a last-resort method for those customers who show no signs of reasonableness.

Most embroiderers guarantee their work. Some will limit their guarantee to problems they caused. Retail embroiderers, when faced with an unhappy customer involving one or a few garments will guarantee no matter what the circumstances. Large volume, production embroiderers can ill afford to guarantee a big order just because the customer changed his mind.

Everyone agrees, in principle, that good customer service is important, but few businesses today really practice going that extra mile to establish and maintain excellence in customer relations. Very few practice the strategies outlined in such books as, "In Search of Excellence," or the latest best seller, "How to Swim With the Sharks Without Being Eaten Alive," or the old standby, "How to Win Friends and Influence People." The few who do practice such proven strategies will be amply rewarded in terms of selling more per customer, gaining repeat business from customers, gaining referrals, receiving advertising of the best kind (word of mouth), making friends, having favors returned and having a successful business. It takes commitment from the top down. It takes practice and it takes constant monitoring. Just remember who's the boss!

Exhibit 27

"THE CUSTOMER"

1. The customer is the most important person in any business.
2. The customer is not dependent on us; we are dependent on the customer.
3. The customer is not an interruption of our work, but is the purpose of it.
4. The customer does us a favor by calling; we are not doing the customer a favor by responding.
5. The customer is not to argue or match wits with.
6. The customer is the person who brings us a list of wants; it is our job to fill those wants.
7. The customer is part of our business, not an outsider.
8. The customer is not a cold statistic.
9. The customer is deserving of the most courteous and attentive treatment we can give.
10. The customer is the person who makes it possible to pay your salary.
11. The customer is the lifeblood of our company.
12. The customer is the boss.

CHAPTER 22

STATE OF THE INDUSTRY

During the 1980's, we saw a transition from Schiffli (large, industrial machines) and manual embroidery machines to computerized machines. The others are still around and still in use, but the industry expansion has certainly kept pace with the computer age. We also saw an influx into embroidery of screenprinters, engravers and people who work with chenille. As we progressed through the '80s, monogramming, although still a viable market, took a back seat to business logo and sports identity markets. Sales of disk drives outnumbered sales of papertape readers. Embroiderers proved their preference for creating their own custom designs. Now they have the experience, knowledge and confidence to take on more—more volume of work, more sophisticated computers, more product lines and more types of personalization.

Sundel Research Inc. of Denver, Colorado, prepared a study of the U.S. computerized embroidery machine market in June 1989. A total of 250 businesses, each having at least one machine with four or fewer heads, were interviewed. The following are some interesting statistics about our industry as of that date:

- The business' average number of years in the embroidery industry is 7.46.

- The average amount of wholesale embroidery sales for a business is 46.2%; retail embroidery sales total 53.7%.

- 40.4% of the embroidery companies are located in communities with a population of fewer than 25,000; 14% are in communities of 25,000 to 50,000; 11.6% are in areas with a population of 50,000 to 100,000; and 34% are in cities of more than 100,000 people.

- 4,872 companies were listed in the Yellow Pages under the headings of monograms, embroidery and emblems.

- When respondents were asked to describe the biggest problem they face in their business, the top five answers given were:

- A lack of qualified employees.
- Meeting deadlines or workloads that are too heavy.
- Pleasing customers and helping customers make decisions.
- Marketing and advertising.
- Setting prices.

o 82.8% of the respondents think the embroidery business will expand in the short term, through December 1990. 75.6% think it will also expand in the long term, three to five years. Here are some of their reasons:

- Sales are stable or increasing.
- Embroidery is popular and becoming more known to the consumer.
- The industry is on an upward growth trend.
- There is a trend toward better quality in personalization.
- Product innovation.
- There is a general economic upturn.
- Commercial advertising of shirts and jackets.
- Personal research and reading indicates expansion.
- More companies are entering the market.
- Multihead technology increases production.
- Product prices are reasonable for their quality.

o Nearly 9 in 10 of the respondents also think their embroidery sales will increase in the next three to five years.

o For 55.6% of the respondents, embroidery is their principal business, representing half or more of their total revenue. Considering all forms, 64.8% indicated that their principle business is personalization. Only 20.4% have embroidery as their exclusive business activity.

o 32.4% of the respondents also do screenprinting; 13.6% do engraving; 10% do chenille; 8.4% do iron-ons and/or heat transfer; and 8% do tackle twill.

o 21.2% have plans to offer other forms of personalization in the next two years.

New markets are constantly being introduced for or by embroiderers. A trend just beginning, but certain to grow, is the use of computerized embroidery in fashion. In women's fashions, we're seeing blouses or tops coordinated with skirts, each featuring an elegant or trendy matching design. Colorful, scroll-like embroidery is becoming more popular on the front placket of women's blouses and men's shirts. Crests are being added to sportswear, such as sweats and socks, and are coming back in style for blazers and sport coats. For children and infants, the trend is large, playful designs and characters combining embroidery, applique, ribbons, buttons, yarns and other embellishments.

Other forms of embellishment are also combined with embroidery for high-fashion looks. Chenille, cording, sequins, beading and the addition of decorative stones in different shapes, sizes and colors are popular for casual wear, office attire and formal evening wear.

Fashion for the home is a growing business, as well. No longer confined to monograms on linens, elegant embroidered designs or trendy motifs can accentuate and coordinate with virtually every fabric used in home furnishings and decoration.

According to Neil Macpherson, CEO of Macpherson Inc. of Greensboro, North Carolina, "Monogramming and embroidery offer the very exciting dynamics of growth and expansion. One important reason is that the garments can be made anywhere in the world. People here are demanding more items made in the U.S.A., but for embroiderers, the source doesn't matter. They can embroider goods made here or imported from anywhere in the world."

Paul Levine, vice president of Hirsch International in Hauppauge, New York, says, "We haven't even scratched the surface for growth, use, application and different markets. The competent businesses in this industry will grow—some will vary their personalization and most will just grow bigger. The ability to *deliver* will become a determining factor, especially for premium and advertising specialty items."

I agree. Embroiderers are faced with a demand for more rapid service. Their customers want it *now*. They also seem to want more one-stop shopping for all their personalization needs. Just as screenprinters have added embroidery to keep pace with the market demand, more embroiderers are destined to vary their services. The embroidery machine manufacturers recognize this. Look at the diversity of machines now offered:

Meistergram offers the Etchmaster, available in two models. Both handle curved or flat glass, ceramics, plastic and metal. Model 2000 is a portable machine for surface etching (the frosted look on glass). Model 3000 is more powerful and uses a compressor for deeper penetration. Pressure sensitive, adhesive backed dyes are available for alphabet styles, first names and designs and sayings. Custom designs are also available.

Melco offers LE1, a laser engraving peripheral for the Epicor. It engraves flat surfaces up to two inches thick, including wood, glass, acrylic, slate and engraver's marble. It also removes coatings on many metals. It is compatible with many alphabets and stock designs available from Melco and ARC. An optional scanner enables custom designs without the need to digitize.

Barudan, Tajima and ZSK are also offering machines or machine options to do sequins, cording, boring and braiding—the processes that, with embroidery, are gaining popularity in the fashion world.

From trophies to wall decorations to glass, consider the possibilities for personalized goods! One of the fastest growing markets is the field of recognition. Engraved awards are given for recognition of employees, volunteers, community leaders, supporters and advisors of organizations and fund raisers, to name a few. Also, consider that the potential for multiple sales to a single customer is greatly increased when you have the capability to put the same design on a cap and trophy, a towel set and bathroom mirror, a ballpoint pen and a tie, monogrammed glassware to match monogrammed placemats, and on and on.

The observance of what manufacturers are developing and what is displayed in the windows of fashionable stores is very enlightening about the future of embellishments and personalization. Another way to predict the future of this industry is to talk with those who are driving it. Here are comments from a few:

Henry Arnberg
President, Hirsch International
Hauppauge, New York

"I believe we will see more automation and higher productivity. However, the individual and creative artistry will never be eliminated. There is a difference between an artistic owner and an entrepreneur owner. Both can create for the public. Those who will be successful in the future will use the advanced automation to put their own versions of creativity into embroidery, with an emphasis on quality.

"The technology for producing good-looking embroidery is available to both large and small shops. Small shops have started growing into multi-head businesses. I think this trend will continue, but those who remain small must manage their businesses better if they are to *stay* in business and make money.

"Looking further into the future, I think embroidery technology will be used by manufacturers in the garment industry for assembly. It will have uses for such operations as affixing collars to shirts, pockets in pants, attaching two-piece industrial type gloves and many other applications. Already manufacturers, such as Tajima, have large quilting machines that stitch through several layers of fabric. We'll see many more uses for the technology already developed in the embroidery industry."

Dave Davidson
National Sales Manager for Barudan Multi-heads
Macpherson Inc.
Greensboro, North Carolina

"We are seeing a large growth in embroidery on fleecewear. Also, the sweater manufacturers are coming back to embroidery after being out of it for a couple of years. The children's wear market has always been strong, but is growing at an even more rapid pace now than previously. The sporting goods industry and the screenprinters are still interested in embroidery. Their needs are for the two-, four- and six-head machines, rather than the bigger production machines. We sell a lot of cap machines, so there is every indication that the cap market will continue strong.

"The composite industry—people sewing on different types of materials and using the machines for stitching rather than embroidery—is very small right now, but I believe it could grow. This is true for the fashion industry also. The market for sequin and chenille machines is fair, but growing in Europe, so it could gain momentum here as a result. The problem with the fashion industry now is that there's very little payback. The sequin and chenille machines are only available with six or more heads. Until the industry grows, the demand is not there to keep that many heads busy.

"As far as the machines themselves are concerned, I don't look for speed to be a big factor in embroidery. The manufacturers just need to be quality-conscious to provide equipment that will sew continuously, two shifts per day."

Ron Krasnitz
Chairman of the Board
Sewing Machine Exchange
Chicago, Illinois

Marty Krasnitz
President
Sewing Machine Exchange
Chicago, Illinois

"We will see a merger of technology between the industrial machines used in the garment industry and the embroidery machines used commercially. The garment industry will gain the programmability, design, editing and scanning features that already exist and are constantly being developed. The embroidery industry will gain the high-speed technology already developed in the garment industry. Machines may eventually sew up to 2,000 stitches per minute, without sacrificing the satin stitch or the quality. More development for hooping and clamping devices for embroiderers should also result from this merger of technology. Laser technology will be expanded. For example, die cutters used now in sign making and for cutting tackle twill letters will be replaced by lasers.

"The price of equipment will come down as more people enter the field of embroidery. Yet, the demand for embroidery by consumers will maintain the prices of the finished embroidered products. Speaking of pricing, we will see better methods of pricing goods. At Sewing Machine Exchange, we have developed and sell a hand-held pricing calculator for $275. There are also computer software programs coming on the market to help price individual orders. Eventually, we may see bar coding to program such things as pricing, or all the parameters of a job."

Bill Fenimore
Sales Manager, Monogram Division
Macpherson Monogram
Greensboro, North Carolina

"When I entered this industry in 1982, someone from the Schiffli industry told me that with the advent of computerized embroidery, we'd soon see one on every street corner in America. It's happening. More people are getting into embroidery every year. I expect that to continue because embroidery is a localized, rather than nationalized, market.

"Our customers want the computer technology of other industries incorporated into the embroidery machines. Therefore, we will see the most dramatic changes in the design systems and in specialized software developed to help manage an embroidery business.

"The mechanics of the machines have remained the same, but we will probably see faster framing techniques develop. This will enable quicker loading and unloading of jobs. Also, more people are specializing in niche markets, and this will lead to more specialized apparatus for the machines."

Larry Pearson
Vice President of Sales and Marketing
Melco Industries Inc.
Denver, Colorado

"The market is demanding more features. Our customers want all the bells and whistles on their equipment. Yet, the machines must become more user-friendly. The operation of the equipment needs to be simplified so that owners don't have to rely on highly skilled operators. The technology has come a long way in terms of sophistication—now we need to simplify how we use it and we need to put the language into laymen's terminology. We're a long way from that as an industry. I compare it to the printing industry, whose equipment progressed like this:

1. Wooden
2. Metal
3. Negatives
4. Digitizing
5. Desktop publishing via computers

"The embroidery industry is about at Step 2 in the process of development. So, the future looks good, but because of the rapid advancement we're experiencing, embroiderers can expect to continue upgrading about every four years or so if they want to maintain state-of-the-art equipment.

"As the technology advances, I believe we will see more garment manufacturers adding embroidery capability. Again, as the need for skilled labor decreases, the number of firms entering the industry will increase.

"Another area demanding more automation is the design process. Users are tired of waiting so long for artists and designers to create their custom work. A simpler method of taking artwork to embroidery media is needed. Thus, scanners will soon become the buzzword of the industry, and the need for artists to create, enlarge and adjust all those cartoons will diminish.

"Prices of the equipment and components will come down, but this will be offset by increased prices for software, which will become a greater portion of the price.

"In conclusion, we're not even close to any saturation points in this industry. The future looks to be very exciting and the innovations will continue for those who have found or are yet to find their niche in embroidery."

William R. Childs
Chairman of the Board
Melco Industries Inc.
Denver, Colorado

"The future for embroidery machines is bright for several reasons:

1. Personalization is a growth area. Buyers in the future are going to demand more customization, and the easiest way to customize clothing is with embroidery.
2. Entrepreneurship is growing, and starting an embroidery business is relatively inexpensive, compared to other types of small businesses.
3. As equipment becomes less expensive and less labor intensive, more individual machine owners will be able to easily create their own designs. Thus, costly embroidery designs which were previously feasible only for high production runs will be available for the small shop. As a result, this will have greater appeal to consumers, which means increased sales of embroidered goods.

"Many more software features will become available to simplify machine use and to enhance the quality of the finished embroidery product. Although the most intricate designs will continue to require skilled embroidery designers, the process of creating custom designs will gradually evolve into an automatic process with the elimination of hand artwork. Also, the conversion of computerized artwork to finished embroidery will be accomplished with a minimum of interaction between the designer and the machine operator. The embroidery machine operator of the future will generate more of his custom designs himself and not have to order them from a design center.

"I also foresee that a more cost effective and easier to use single-head embroidery machine may become standard equipment in clothing departments of stores in the future. Personalized embroidery on shirts is the biggest potential growth area, whether in the form of a monogram, a company or personal logo, or a name for the purpose of identification—that is, not visible when worn.

Although many golf shirts, sweaters and hats are personalized today, it is still not the standard. Our industry will benefit greatly when these *are* embroidered as a standard."

Randall Melton
President
Melco Industries Inc.
Denver, Colorado

"At the turn of the last century, punching centers, such as Gunold, were big in Europe. After World War II, Japan entered the industry and everyone wanted their own punching centers. In this country as well as in Europe, the art of punching was kept secret, passed down from generation to generation within a family. Now, our customers are doing their own designing, even with a single-head embroidery machine. Ten years ago this was unheard of, and now 50% of them are digitizing. In Europe today, embroiderers are editing and revising designs themselves, without being a punching center. This changes the worldwide approach of the embroidery industry.

"Embroiderers want to be self-supporting. They want to create their own designs, sell garments as well as embroidery, and now they are spending more on equipment to become more versatile, wanting different types of machines mixed together.

"I personally don't see the market ever reaching a point of saturation. There is such a wide selection of equipment available today with prices ranging from $6,000 or less on up. It's very affordable.

"The industry may level off to a few manufacturers. Probably less than six will provide 95% of the world's embroidery equipment in the future. Those that survive must provide more versatility in personalization. They also must offer excellence in quality and keep up with technology. I also believe we'll see more communication between manufacturers.

"A leveling off may also occur with regard to stock designs. There is some trading going on and this will lead to fewer, but vast, libraries of designs.

"Embroidery is becoming more commercial and less industrial. Individual creativity combined with machines that are fairly easy to use will enable embroiderers to offer a 30-minute, while-you-wait service. What they embroider is changing, too. No longer are people satisfied with just a name or lettering. Personalization today means sewing a design of the San Francisco Bridge to identify where the customer has been.

"We'll also see the major garment manufacturers entering the industry as the fashions coming out of Paris, Milan and other couture capitals in the world, feature more embroidery. After all, **embroidery is the ultimate decoration of fabric**."

SUGGESTED SUPPLEMENTAL

READING LIST

1. *Ogilvy On Advertising*, by David Ogilvy. Publisher: Vintage Books, Division of Random House.

2. *Tested Advertising Methods*, by John Caples. Publisher: Reward Books, Prentice Hall Inc., Englewood Cliffs, New Jersey.

3. *How To Get Free Press*, by Toni Delacorte, Judy Kimsey and Susan Halas. Publisher: Avon Books, New York, New York.

4. *How To Win Friends and Influence People*, by Dale Carnegie. Publisher: Simon and Schuster, New York.

5. *Swim With The Sharks Without Being Eaten Alive*, by Harvey Mackay. Publisher: Ivy Books, New York.

6. *Guerrilla Marketing*, by Jay Conrad Levinson. Publisher: Houghton Mifflin Company, Boston.

7. *Guerrilla Marketing Attack*, by Jay Conrad Levinson. Publisher: Houghton Mifflin Company, Boston.

8. *How To Run A Small Business*, by J. K. Lasser Tax Institute. Publisher: McGraw-Hill Book Company.

9. *Shut Up And Sell!* by Don Sheehan. Publisher: AMACOM, A Division of American Management Associations.

10. *13 Fatal Errors Managers Make And How You Can Avoid Them*, by W. Steven Brown. Publisher: The Berkley Publishing Group, New York.

11. *What They Don't Teach You At Harvard Business School*, by Mark H. McCormack. Publisher: Bantam Books.

12. *The Sky Is The Limit*, by Dr. Wayne Dyer.

13. *Mary Kay On People Management*, by Mary Kay Ash.

14. *See You At The Top*, by Zig Zigler.

Freestanding floral design by Balboa Threadworks Inc., Balboa, California.

Left: Dave Kozoh - Right: Tim Beedle, both wearing knit golf shirts embroidered by Macpherson Monogram Inc.

Left to right: Dawn Semmen wears a turquoise shirt embroidered and appliqued in metallics, by Balboa Threadworks Inc., Balboa, California. Karen Fox wears a sweater embellished with embroidery, cording and stones, courtesy of Barbara J. Behm. Mary Henry models a Southwest Indian sweater designed by Carol Burns, Olde Red Shirt House, Georgetown, Colorado, courtesy of artist Harry Jay.

Kim Alphin wears a flamingo design by ARC. Dave Kozoh's sweater embroidered by Macpherson Monogram Inc.

Dave Kozoh in a fireman's jacket by Initial Artistry of Dearborn Heights, Michigan. Tim Beedle models a jacket by Ellison Designs, Franklin, Texas.

Jamie Allison Davis wearing an appliqued rabbit design on a pullover done by Monogramit, Vidor, Texas, courtesy of Stitches Magazine. School bag by Macpherson Monogram Inc.

Embroidered baby blanket, overalls and swim trunks by Macpherson Monogram Inc.

Lingerie bags embroidered by Personal Touch Monogramming & Embroidery, Scotia, New York; towel embellished with ribbon and ivy design by Wings & Things Monogramming, Pensacola, Florida, both courtesy of Stitches Magazine. Socks embroidered by Initial Stitch of Boulder, Colorado; seashell and floral towels and monogrammed pillowcase by ARC.

Monogrammed shirt and sweater by ARC; tie by Macpherson Monogram Inc.

Left: Diana of Kristi's, Denver, Colorado, wears a fringed zebra applique design by Korinos Village Embroidery, Roselle Park, New Jersey.
Center: JoAnn Rose wears a design combining screenprinting and embroidery by Patricia Davis of Harrington's Sportswear, Augusta, Georgia.
Right: Karen Huff's shirt features a contemporary lotus design combining embroidery and chenille, by Jay Fishman of The Wicked Stitch Of The East, Beachwood, Ohio.
All courtesy of Stitches Magazine.

Dawn Semmen models aqua dress with embroidered bow by The Embroidery Studio, Greensboro, North Carolina; Mary Henry's shirt features appliqued hearts to match belt buckle, done by Initial Stitch of Boulder, Colorado. Both garments courtesy of Stitches Magazine.

Close-up of Indian weaver design by Carol Burns of Olde Red Shirt House, Georgetown, Colorado. Courtesy of artist Harry Jay.

Leather belt, earrings and bolero tie designed and embroidered by Heart to Heart of Edmond, Oklahoma.

Diana of Kristi's, Denver, Colorado, as Marilyn Monroe. Dress designed by Ken Parsons of Hirsch International, Hauppauge, New York.

Diana of Kristi's, Denver, Colorado, models an evening dress featuring embroidery and silk flowers. Dress designed by Ken Parsons of Hirsch International, Hauppauge, New York.

Ski design by Roffe Inc. of Seattle, Washington; snowflake sweater by ARC; bowling shirt by Melco; tennis racquet cover by Initial Stitch of Boulder, Colorado; jacket and cap embroidered by Freida Coonrod Embroidery, Cedar Rapids, Iowa.

Audrey Gedminas models restaurant uniform embroidered by Initial Stitch, Boulder, Colorado.

Left: Steve Garnier wears a hat embroidered by ARC.
Center: Kim Alphin models cap by Tajima West of Los Angeles, California.
Right: Glen McCarthy's fishing cap by ARC.

Liturgical embroidery by Walter Floriani, Jr., Floriani Embroidery Ent., Tehachapi, California.

Left: JoAnn Rose wears a Christmas goose appliqued in satin on a sweatshirt.
Center: Karen Huff models an embroidered holiday greeting.
Right: Karen Fox's shirt features a detailed, decorated Christmas tree embroidered on the front and Legende Script lettering on the sleeve. All designed by ARC.

Holiday monogrammed towels by Macpherson Monogram Inc.; decorated apron and shirt with bells by Initial Stitch, Boulder, Colorado; stocking by Personal Touch Monogramming & Embroidery, Scotia, New York, courtesy of Stitches Magazine; appliqued candle towel, embroidered napkins, placemat and ornaments by ARC.

Dining elegance features tablecloth and napkins embroidered to match china. Designed by ARC and embroidered by Barbara J. Behm. Floral centerpiece by Westminster Floral & Gifts, Westminster, Colorado.
All embroidery photographs by Michael Peck Photography, Denver, Colorado.

INDEX